MUSLIM WOMEN RECLAIM *their* GENDER LEGACY

MOIN QAZI

INDIA · SINGAPORE · MALAYSIA

Copyright © Moin Qazi 2024
All Rights Reserved.

ISBN 979-8-89446-351-3

This book has been published with all efforts taken to make the material error-free after the consent of the author. However, the author and the publisher do not assume and hereby disclaim any liability to any party for any loss, damage, or disruption caused by errors or omissions, whether such errors or omissions result from negligence, accident, or any other cause.

While every effort has been made to avoid any mistake or omission, this publication is being sold on the condition and understanding that neither the author nor the publishers or printers would be liable in any manner to any person by reason of any mistake or omission in this publication or for any action taken or omitted to be taken or advice rendered or accepted on the basis of this work. For any defect in printing or binding the publishers will be liable only to replace the defective copy by another copy of this work then available.

For

my mother

Khaleda Sultana

CONTENTS

1. INTRODUCTION

Believing men and believing women,
obedient men and obedient women,
truthful men and truthful women,
enduring men and enduring women,
humble men and humble women,
men and women who give in charity,
men who fast and women who fast,
men and who guard their private parts,
men and women who remember God oft –
for them, God has prepared forgiveness and a mighty wage.
(Qur'an 33:35)

A man is a shepherd over his family, and he is accountable
for their welfare. A woman is a shepherdess over her husband's
household and children, and she is responsible for their
welfare. A man's servant is a shepherd over his master's property
and he is responsible for it. Be careful! All of you are shepherds
and shall be accountable for your flocks.
(Sahih Bukhari 6719, Sahih Muslim 1829)

In this book, the author, Moin Qazi, delineates the trajectory of Islamic feminism, which scholars are now actively researching on account of the transformative advances by Muslim women. These women have escaped the subjugation and oppression they endured for centuries. Women have always carried visions of a debased world in which vengeance is a synonym for justice. The lives of women of the pre-Islamic period are a vivid metaphor for the oppression of their predecessors that continue to linger in the minds of several women. The continuing grim portrayals of these women hit the author's nerve. He believed it was imperative to highlight modern Muslim women's true breadth of experience.

The Islamic feminist landscape is already undergoing a profound transformation. Historically, Islam was incredibly advanced in providing revolutionary rights for women and uplifting their status in the seventh century. Scholarship on Islamic women has expanded exponentially over the past few decades, and there has been cross-pollination between other fields and disciplines. Islamic doctrine has enabled women to participate in battlefields, independently carry on trade and business, and, when circumstances demand it. The most outstanding accomplishment of early Islam concerning women was its strict prohibition of female infanticide. A preference for male babies was evidence of deep-seated and hidebound bias against girls.

Many of the revelations in the Qur'an were by nature reform-oriented, transforming critical aspects of pre-Islamic customary laws and practices in progressive ways and eliminating injustice for women. The book is a prism from which to view the Muslim feminist revolution. The author analyses how the patriarchal-oriented rulers and clerics have obliquely tried to roll back these reforms and started scripting flawed narratives which have cruelty as their epicenter. The ruling of the clerics has its roots in flawed and absurd assumptions. But of late, women have finally been able to morph from their pathetic condition and redefine the contours of their gender space. The approach of clerics count resonates with the society.

2. WOMEN DOWN THE AGES

In the past several decades, there has been an explosion of research and an effort to present the experiences and contributions of women not only in the Western world but across the globe. Scholars have investigated women's daily lives in virtually every area and researched the leadership roles women have filled across times and regions.

From earliest recorded history, human society has been patriarchal, with women confined mainly to the home and the nearby fields, treated as the property of their husbands, and generally forbidden the society of men outside their families. In the societies of the Eastern Mediterranean, which formed the roots of Western culture, the patriarchal tradition also persisted. The nomadic Hebrew was strongly patriarchal. In Athens, the "freewoman" took no part in public life and was perpetually under the guardianship of her father or husband. The attitude of writers and theologians of the early Christian church was often inspired rather literally by the tradition of Eve created from Adam and a paradise lost. The epistles of St. Paul, who shaped the new faith, and masses of early church writings fairly breathe misogyny: a woman is applicable solely for procreation; outside that, she functions only as a temptation to sin and had best stay at home when she is not going to church.

In Hindu scriptures, a good wife is "a woman whose mind, speech and body remain in subjection acquires high renown in this world, and, in the next, the same abode with her husband." In Athens, women were not better off than the Indian or Roman women. Athenian women were always minors, subject to some male - to their father, brother, or male kin. Her consent in marriage was not considered necessary, and she was obliged to submit to her parent's wishes and receive her husband and her lord from them, even though he was a stranger to her.

According to the English Common Law:" All real property that a wife held at the time of marriage became a possession of her husband". He was entitled to rent from the land and any profit that might accrue from operating the estate during the joint life of the spouses. As time passed, the English courts devised means to forbid a husband from transferring real property without the consent of his wife, but he still retained the right to manage it and to receive the money it produced. The husband's power was complete as to a wife's personal property. He had the right to spend it as he saw fit".

It was only by the late nineteenth century that the situation started to improve. Through a series of acts, starting with the Married Women's Property Act in 1870, amended in 1882 and 1887, married women achieved the right to own property to enter contracts on a par with spinsters, widows, and divorcees. As late as the nineteenth century, an authority in ancient law. Sir Henry Maine wrote: "No society which preserves any tincture of Christian institutions is likely to restore to married women the personal liberty conferred on them by the Middle Roman Law."

Jahiliyyah- age of ignorance

Religions often articulate worldviews that sharply contrast a morally corrupt social order with a purer, if utopian, counterpart. In the Abrahamic tradition, the time of corruption is contrasted with when an agent of God, or prophet, arrived (or will arrive) to lead the people into a new era of righteousness or guidance. For instance, in Christianity, the world was corrupted by the primordial parents of humanity, Adam and Eve, who sinned in the blissful Garden of Eden and corrupted the world and their countless human descendants (i.e., Original Sin). This world of imperfection and sin will one day be set into perfection when Jesus Christ, who underwent sacrifice to redeem humanity from Original Sin, returns to the world and ushers in the eternal Kingdom of Heaven.

The portrayal of Muslim women that we have glimpsed in the media about several societies is grim and sombre. The public perception of them is one of the stubborn stereotypes: supposedly powerless and traumatised, behind walls and veils, demure, voiceless and silent figures, discriminated against and bereft of even fundamental rights. This picture keeps reinforcing itself, mainly because this is how the Western media caricatures women in Islam. Recurring images beamed into our homes and phones keep strengthening the belief that Muslim women are being denied access to education, social space, privacy and educational and development programmes for their socio-economic uplift. The prejudicial media keeps using selective stories to reinforce its notions. Because of these projections, the general public's views remain skewed. Inequalities exist in many Muslim societies, but it is also true that gender inequalities exist in many offensive non-Muslim societies as well.

Jahiliyyah is a polemical Islamic and Arabic term that refers to the period and state of affairs in pre-Islamic Arabia before the advent of Islam in 609. It usually refers to the Age of Ignorance. The society had already descended into a darker era. *Jahiliyyah* may originate in the verbal root jahala, which means ignorant or stupid or to act stupidly. Alternatively, it is an abstract noun derived from jāhil, referring to barbarism. Islamic historians state that female infanticide was common in seventh-century Arabia. However, the information in the sources may have been greatly exaggerated to criticize the Age of Ignorance, both for religious concerns and other reasons. The time of Fatrah and *Jahiliyyah* are somewhat similar concepts in Islam, although there are some minor differences. Generally speaking, Fatrah refers to those to whom the message of God was not or could not be transmitted, typically due to time or location. This book explores and helps in decoding this horrific practice. It transpires that it was a powerful tool in the hands of men for subjugating and humiliating women.

Meanwhile, *Jahiliyyah* refers to those who might have had the option of following monotheism (Hanif) as per their knowledge but chose not due to ignorance, pride, or similar reasons. It transpires that it was a powerful tool in the hands of men for subjugating and humiliating women. Before the Islamic conversion, some Arab tribes were nomadic, with a strong community spirit and some specific societal rules. Their culture was patriarchal, and the toxic effects of this phenomenon contaminated the society with rudimentary religious beliefs. Although there were some traces of monotheism in the "hanifs" figures, their religious beliefs were not coherent. They were primarily based on idol adorations and social congregations around the Ka'bah for trading and exchanges once a year. Since the term is, in its profound sense, used as a condition and not as a historical period, the *Jahiliyya* is used to describe the period of ignorance and darkness that pre-dated the arrival of Islam. It refers to the general condition of those who didn't accept the Muslim faith and continued to practice their original religion. The practice of *Jahiliyyah* manifested in cruelty and oppression of women.

Although sometimes used synonymously, the phrase "pre-Islamic Arabia" and the Arabic *al-Jahiliyya* have different connotations. The English phrase implies only a temporal relationship to Islam. On the other hand, the Arabic expression (meaning literally "the age or condition of ignorance") indicates an evaluation of selected parts of earlier Arabian history from a strongly Islamic perspective. The idea of the *Jahiliyya* is a construct of Islamic thinkers, developed for particular purposes. It ignores much interest in modern scholarship on the Arabs and Arabia. It focuses on the immediate background of Islam and the life of the Arabs of western central Arabia (the Hijaz) in the century or so up to and including the early career of the Prophet Muhammad.

Pre-Islamic Arabia

The essential reference work for all aspects of the study of Islam, including pre-Islamic Arabia and the *Jahiliyya*, is the second edition of the *Encyclopaedia of Islam*. Following Islamic historical tradition, most works on Islamic history begin with a discussion of the *Jahiliyya*, although they often go beyond the Islamic treatment of it. These are frequently pleasing entryways into the subject for the beginner. While still treating pre-Islamic Arabia, reflecting an understanding that the rise of Islam needs a broader historical and geographical context. Many works are devoted entirely to discussions of the history of the Arabs and Arabia before Islam, ranging much more widely than the traditional understanding of the *Jahiliyya*.

A notable usage of this practice during the Islamic Golden Age is from the 13th-century theologian Ibn Taymiyyah (d.1328), who pronounced Takfir (excommunication) upon the Mongol monarchs who had publicly professed themselves as Muslims yet implemented a legal system which originated in Yassa replacing *sharī'ah* (Islamic law). According to Ibn Taymiyyah, who claims to be Muslim but codifies artificial laws for governance, is guilty of the pagan idolatry of *Jahiliyya* despite his declaration of the shahada (Islamic testimony of faith) or regular observance of salad (prayers), swam (fasting) and other outward expressions of religiosity. *Sharī'ah* is an Islamic canonical law based on the Qur'an's teachings and the Prophet's traditions. It has customarily been executed following legislation adapted to the day's conditions. However, its application in modern states has given rise to disputes between Islamic fundamentalists and modernists.

The religious law of Islam is seen as the expression of God's command for Muslims and, in application, constitutes a system of duties that are incumbent upon all Muslims under their religious belief. It is the sharī'ah (the path leading to the watering place). The law represents a divinely ordained path of conduct that guides Muslims toward a practical expression of religious conviction in this world and the goal of divine favour in the world to come.

Women suffered a great spectre of injustices and diverse kinds of humiliation in the pagan Arab society before the advent of Islam—the patriarchal approach curtailed the rights of women. The vitiated social environment made them vulnerable to oppression by men. Slavery, debauchery, drunkenness, sexual abuse, and duplicity were rife when destitute women could be humiliated without redress, and wealthy women could live totally without morals if they wished, without much criticism. Women were not entitled to inherit from their parents or husbands. Arabs believed inheritance should be granted only to those with martial abilities, like being able to ride a horse, fight a battle, gain war booties and help defend and protect the territory of the tribe and clan. Since women did not generally have martial qualities, they became a moveable commodity after the death of an indebted husband.

Husbands kept the women in bondage; they could keep or divorce them at their will and pleasure. Women were an embodiment of sin, misfortune, disgrace and shame. If the deceased husband had adult sons from other marriages, the oldest son amongst them had the right to add her to his household, just as a son inherits other chattels of his deceased father. She was unable to leave the house of her stepson unless she paid a ransom. Generally, men could acquire as many wives as they desired without limits.

The birth of the daughter was embarrassing for the father, who considered it a disgrace and a matter of shame. Therefore, the Arabs of that time practiced 'female infanticide': burying their female child alive. Arabs of al *Jahiliyyah* used to think of different ways to kill their daughters. Some would ask their mothers to dress their daughters in their best clothes and decorate them with jewellery as if the father were taking them out for a visit. Instead, he would locate a well in the desert, throw his daughter alive and then dump the well with garbage.

This book explores and helps in decoding this abominable concept. It transpires that it was a powerful tool in the hands of men for subjugating and humiliating women. It manifested in extreme cruelty to women.

Women's inferior position in pre-Islamic Arabia was reflected, amongst other things, in the predominant marriage contracts, which closely resembled a sale through which a woman became her husband's property. Having no say in initiating or terminating her marriage, a woman followed her husband to his tribe and bore children. Since she left her tribe, a woman received no inheritance from her family (notably if the inheritance consisted of fixed property, such as land). She was subject to and dependent upon her husband and his family as a wife. Against such a background, the women must clearly understand the Qur'anic prescriptions relating to family law.

Resistance to all this was, of course, compelling. Islam triumphed only in certain limited spheres of social and family life. Most political and public matters were overwhelmed by the more ancient traditions of the regions, which survived in an Islamic disguise, notably in the persistence of the autocratic, monarchical form of government. So we find through the centuries a recurring theme of revolt: a feeling that history had somehow taken a wrong turn, that Islam was distorted, that the Islamic community was being ruled by non-Muslims, by bad Muslims, by renegade Muslims, by those who had betrayed the heritage of the Prophet and were leading the community as a whole into sin.

The Qur'an describes the mentality of ignorance underlying such practices: "When the news of the birth of a female would come, their face becomes dark, and he feels inward grief! He hides himself from the people because of the evil (and shame) of that which he has been made aware of. Shall he keep her with dishonour or bury her in the dirt? Certainly, evil is their decision." (Q16:59)

There is a powerful scene in the Qur'an depicting the Day of Judgment where the souls of all slain girls would rise and confront their fathers, asking the men: "For what crime did you kill me?"(Q81.8-9) and then their fathers would be flung into Hell. It is a vivid image meant to teach the true horror of such crimes in the minds of Arabs accustomed to centuries of brutal child infanticide.

The demeaning treatment of women

We don't have to personally visit places to see the face of the demeaning levels of poverty and deprivation women suffer in so many countries. Newspapers and media are blaring day in and day out the plight of these women. We have legions of stories of woman in Somalia who have been walking for miles to reach a fetch of firewood and water; successive droughts have ravaged their land, their body, and their children. Please think of the uprooted who have become refugees travelling through Eastern Africa, walking miles on foot in brutal temperatures with hot, dust-filled wind blowing in their faces. She'll thank God if they all arrive at the feeding centre. The baby she is carrying no longer gets milk from her breast; she feels him shrinking in her arms as she walks. The little hands of her other small children clutch at her with a feeling of strength, and their voices have become so weak it's almost impossible to hear them above the howl of the wind. The primary role of these women was to remain silent and obedient and be committed to appeasing their menfolk.

The mother repeatedly tells them that they must put their trust in God and keep moving. One can understand her thirst as she utters words of prayer with every precious drop of water she goes without giving to her children for their survival. She is forced into her suffering by circumstances beyond her control, and she is powerless to mitigate them. She's not thinking of herself. She is thinking of God for His mercy because she knows that her agony could have been worse than this. He has endowed her with abundant patience to be grateful to God for whatever bounties she enjoys. We can have no better description than the one pained by the legendary poet Allama Iqbal in his stirring verse:

"The pangs of motherhood have torn her heart,
Dark, tragic rings have underscored her eyes;
If from her bosom, the community
Receive one Muslim zealous for the Faith,
God's faithful servant, all the pains she bore
Have fortified our being and our dawn."

The intense focus on the *hijab* by its defenders and opponents is intensely myopic. Feminists across the world are talking about the "rights" and "wrongs" of women in a furious social media war instead of joining forces to address the real issues that women and girls are facing around the world. In offering support to Muslim women, all feminists need to be strategic and prioritise the harm those women suffer. Non-Muslim feminists would do well to reconsider the disproportionate weight they are giving to complex symbols such as the veil. The frazzled and stressed women need natural stress-busters and not these ideological wars that can further accentuate their mental health.

There is an agreed-upon international standard of fundamental human rights that all women and girls have the right to enjoy. Where governments will not protect the human rights of female citizens, the global community must work with local activists to keep governments accountable. There is no one-size-fits-all intuitive approach to feminism. A headscarf doesn't preclude empowerment; a bikini doesn't preclude oppression. Social media wars – with one side baring breasts and the other extolling modesty – miss the real issues facing women and girls. Fragile societies, characterised by a lack of institutional and governance capacity, form the front line of this battle for stability and progress.

According to Umar, the second caliph, two things in al *Jahiliyyah* made him cry and laugh. The one that made him cry was when he took a daughter of his to bury alive, and while he was digging the ground, she would wipe the dust off his beard, not knowing what would happen to her. The one that made him laugh was when he used to make gods out of dates and put them by his bed to guard him while he was asleep, but then he ate them in the morning when he woke up.

The advent of the Qur'an

The Qur'an considerably changed women's status from the pre-Islamic (*jāhilīyah*) period and put them on a checkered path. Intending to rehabilitate the status of women in society, Islam denounced the old myth of Eve as a temptress and source of evil, as the cause of original sin and the fall of humankind. Far from being powerless, they make small choices that could lead to significant changes in the Muslim world. Female genital mutilation is fast declining. There is a profoundly spiritual paradigm that affirms the inherent human dignity of women and men. The harrowing trend of women's subjugation is fast reversing. Muslim women are working at a significantly accelerated pace in progressing their development and empowerment agenda.

In the seventh century, the *Qur'an* began as a series of revelations to Muhammad, a caravan trader. These words grew into a spiritual, social, and political force whose impact is now global. As the scripture of the planet's fastest-growing religion— with 1.6 billion followers, Islam is second in popularity only to Christianity— it stands as a moral compass for hundreds of millions. Reading it should be a prerequisite for understanding humanity. The *Qur'an* can refract in dazzling ways.

Before Islam, both polyandrous and polygamous marriages were prevalent and matrilineal, uxorilocal marriages in which the woman remained with her tribe, and the male either visited or resided with her were also quite common. Many women selected and divorced their husbands, and women were neither veiled nor secluded. While these practices do not necessarily indicate the greater power of women or the absence of misogyny, they do correlate with women enjoying greater sexual autonomy than they were allowed under Islam. Islam took away polyandrous marriages and limited the number of female spouses to a maximum of four (Q4:1) as early Arabian Muslims gradually moved from a matrilineal to a patrilineal society. The pre-Islamic practice of female infanticide was declared illegal by the Qur'ān (Q81:8–9). The dower (*mahr*), which in pre-Islamic times was paid directly to a woman's male guardian (*walī*), was now made payable directly to the woman (Q4:3), who also got the right to inherit property (Q4:7).

It has become trite to say that Muslim women are facing persecution. There are several reasons for this assumption. The colonial era has undoubtedly left deep scars. Still, we must understand that rejecting the West and criticizing it for the shortcomings of the Muslim world cannot be a seductive and easy way out. Instead, the gaze should now turn inward. Muslims need to look at themselves realistically instead of their imagined selves.

The Qur'an, the word of God, was revealed to the Prophet Muhammad 1400 years ago. It is the supreme authority in Islam and the living source of all Islamic teaching; it is a sacred text and a book of guidance that sets out the Islamic religion's creed, rituals, ethics, and laws. It has been one of the most influential books in the history of literature. Recognized as the most significant literary masterpiece in Arabic, it hasn't remained easy to understand in its English translations. This new translation is written in a contemporary idiom that remains faithful to the original, making it easy to read while retaining its powers of eloquence. The Arabic meaning continues to protect the essential content by respecting the context of the discourse. The message of the Qur'an was directly addressed to all people regardless of class, gender, or age, and this translation is equally accessible to everyone.

Scholars have devoted much thought to research that is detrimental to women. Muslim women are refusing to accept interpretations of the faith that denigrate women. There is still a robust patriarchal strain – sometimes bordering on misogynistic – within Muslim practice; Muslim men raged and cursed the women with this toxic combination of humiliation, duplicity and abuse, resulting in the contamination of the entire culture, with women finding it difficult to get rid of this stranglehold. It has been painful to know that centuries of a large corpus of Islamic scholarship has affirmed the inherent superiority of men over women, including the right of a husband to punish a "recalcitrant" wife physically. It is a legacy that haunts us still. As long as Muslims don't seriously confront this legacy, there will be more women who question why they should be part of a family, a community, or a system that condemns them as inherently deficient at worst and second-class at best.

The findings of several cross-collaborative studies reveal that an emerging enlightened generation of Muslim women is becoming increasingly independent and determined to assert their right to complete education and a career and to follow their dreams. Many do so in the face of archaic patriarchal cultural traditions on the one hand and discrimination and suspicion from the non-Muslim majority population on the other. These challenges, combined with the relatively low-income family backgrounds of many Muslim women, threaten to limit their social mobility, whatever their aspirations.

Contrary to popular belief, Muslim women have served as sensational and heroic leaders. However, in recent decades, due to the global socio-political climate, the phrase "Muslim woman" might conjure an image of a timid, unempowered woman sheltered by her *burqa* (head-to-toe veil). Yet this image is not what history records or what the present reflects. The early Muslim community recognized and honoured various female roles and responsibilities. A mother was considered the first school for her children. In Islam, a woman is an individual in her own right, an independent person, and not a shadow or adjunct to her husband or any other man. Muslim women are now fighting a protracted and creeping battle and have staked their claim to full entitlement to education, work, business ownership, and inheritance. At the time of Prophet Muhammad, granting women these rights alone was considered sensational. They are not only internalizing these skills, but their pervasive and ubiquitous influence will continue to foster them for the upcoming generations.

The appeasement of men was the primary function of these women. It is true that in societies trapped in poverty, illiteracy and ignorance, women continue to receive abominable and oppressive treatment. But then, this is true of all societies. Muslims cannot be s singled out for such a flawed social order. The pictures we get of wife beating and other retrograde practices imposed on Muslim women are aberrations which we cannot make the usual Muslim stereotype. The wrong practices rampant in some such societies have much to do with illiteracy, ignorance and sometimes dire poverty. In several cases, the plight of Muslim women is a direct consequence of a repressive and highly discriminatory State. A dispassionate analysis will reveal that vested interests in all societies, mainly those driven by patriarchal values, have resisted the uplift of women and have failed to concede them the legitimate rights their faith, community and State have guaranteed them. This distortion, however, should not deflect our focus from some path-breaking and stellar contributions of Muslim women not just to Islamic civilization but to secular society as well. There was a time when divorce was uncommon in all cultures. Parents never trusted their daughters' judgment and didn't care what other people had to say. People did have a lot to say. Divorce may be perfectly allowable according to Islam (the Prophet's first wife was a divorcee), but that doesn't stop the gossip. In a society that prizes virginity, the "value" of the girl with such a record gets depreciated. The patriarchal interpretation of the Qur'an was the critical barrier to the empowerment of women.

Women under Islam

Islam and feminism? Most people consider it a contradiction in terms. We think you can't be a Muslim and a feminist. That's like saying you can be a Ku Klux Klan member and an anti-fascist. Astonishingly, most people usually address "Muslims" and Muslim women as a monolithic block. If you listen to what Muslim women have to say on the subject, you find that many of them have no difficulty reconciling their faith with their feminist approach. We tend to look for structured definitions when we understand something deeply. However, Islamic feminism does not lend itself to easy classification or delimitation.

The overall reaction is a malicious knee-jerk response that demonstrates ignorance and, at worst, bigotry and a lack of desire to look outside a pre-existing, blinkered set of assumptions. Those assumptions are perhaps unsurprising given that the media almost universally portrays Muslim women as victims. They are denied freedom in Afghanistan, but they are also not secure in France, whose government is threatening men from making them wear a face veil (or, in another reading, criminalized for choosing to wear one), which has been having a cascading effect in the domestic life of women. Amongst all this hand-wringing about the oppression of Muslim women, there are remarkably few attempts to solicit the views of Muslim women themselves. Their experiences can transform the upcoming generations. In several cases, the local mullahs have nudged the vernacular media to peddle the maliciously absurd interpretations of the Qur'an.

Suppose you happen to meet some of these women. In that case, you can metaphorically strip away the *burqas* and *hijabs* and start chipping away at the profound misconceptions that have existed in other parts of the world about these women and their culture. Family is a fundamental part of Islam and how effectively women run their families. People, particularly Westerners, should refrain from imposing their definitions of political and social freedom on women in Islam.

These women dispelled the social taboos attached to the public participation of women.

There's this perverse surprise among people that they can't believe that Muslim women can make fantastic progress. It is primarily on account of several misconceptions that have resulted from the media's imagination of pervasive misogyny combined with Islam phobia. When you have a dominant male culture, it allows very little space for the rest of us to be our whole selves. There shouldn't be one idea of a Muslim woman because it is now sanely acknowledged that Muslim women are not monolithic. Some Muslim women would probably disagree with the views of some of the other Muslim women concerning their abilities. This disagreement will always remain prevalent. You can be a feminist, have agency, and choose to wear a *niqab* and *burqa*. Muslim women have clearly articulated why and how they decide to cover themselves and how it's a personal choice and has nothing to do with other influences.

The world is reassessing women's place in society and thereby also focusing on Muslim women: their reproductive rights, safety on the streets, workplace equality, and education. We talk about liberation from the patriarchy, stigma and religion, which has imperilled the lives of these unfortunate women. In the West, women are often on the receiving end of reports that the lives of Muslim women are under threat, restricted and alien to what they know about them. Their knowledge of Muslim female society is superficial and based on secondary sources. The issue of women and Islam is contentious. One view is that the faith oppresses and perhaps even persecutes women; the other looks at cultural authenticity and points out that women in Muslim societies assert their rights in ways that differ from those in the West. Family networks in Islam are strong, and Islamic law privileges the family above other institutions. Women's empowerment had earlier been slower on account of the barrier of the prejudiced theology of Islam propounded by the clerics.

The most common justification for ridiculing Islam is that the religion is "backward", particularly towards women, as a fundamental part of its beliefs. It is another severe misconception with its roots in hearsay, with other women failing to study the essential nature of Muslim female society seriously. Contrary to these beliefs, women's right encompasses many areas, from education to marriage, domestic violence and wife abuse. This phenomenon crosses all boundaries, whatever religious background or culture one may come from, and there seems to be a common misconception that Islam encourages wife-beating. Unfortunately, more often, the practices of some Muslims do not conform to the teachings of the Qur'an and become an issue of culture or simply bad human behaviour. The women have deepened their understanding of the scriptures, and their voices are no longer under-represented.

Under Islam, women got control over their property, especially their dowries and inheritance, but their inheritance was half the rate of men. Islam enforced consent and prohibited marriage by kidnapping. Divorce was possible but difficult for women to attain. Nevertheless, divorce was more feasible than in any faith up to that time. Divorce became clearly defined and humane for women.

The emerging scholarship on Muslim women

Islamic scholars have devoted much thought to reappraising and reconciling the two genders. The most critical elements of Islam are *hadith*, or the collected sayings of deeds, behaviour, practice, and values of the Prophet Muhammad (peace be upon him); *sunnah* (a collection of the Prophet's prescriptions), or the body of Islamic social and legal custom; sira, or biographies of the Prophet; and tafsir, the Qur'anic commentary and explication.

During the last few decades, Islamic feminists have evolved into a revolutionary force that has finally morphed into a vibrant revolution.

The harrowing trend of the struggle of women against patriarchy is fast showing a reversing trend. This movement has gained enormous traction and influenced the intellectual landscape of Muslim communities through activism and scholarship. Different types of feminism have developed in Muslim societies. Their typology provides a foundation for understanding the emergence of "Islamic feminism" as a movement connected to the rereading and reinterpretation of Islamic canonical sources from a woman's perspective. These women are not just pursuing their professional careers but also serving their community to achieve self-realisation and career satisfaction through the uplift of girls by guiding and mentoring them. When you truly want something with all your heart, the universe conspires to make it happen. These women have become catalysts for revolutionary changes in the community.

Scholarship on Islam and women has expanded exponentially, and there has been cross-pollination between other fields and disciplines. Islam empowered Arab women as never before, endowing them with property rights and the right to enter into a contract, even a political contract, with a combatant. Islamic doctrine has enabled women to participate in battlefields, independently carry on trade and business, and sometimes nurse soldiers carry provisions for them. Perhaps the most outstanding accomplishment of early Islam was its strict prohibition of female infanticide, the killing of girl babies, which was commonplace in the Middle East, North Africa, and India. A preference for male babies was evidence of deep-seated misogyny in a society reliant on manual labourers and the belief that girls are a burden for the family.

Surprisingly, it is penetrative women researchers and authors who are tearing down the tiresome tropes of what Muslim women are: what they look like, what Muslim women can wear, what they do or don't do. Page after page of these books, the reader is astonished to read what these women can or should not do. This literature was born out of the frustration of broad-minded writers with the disappointment that the narratives about Muslim women were so one-sided, so narrow, and so unimaginative that real-life Muslim women were troubling all the definitions and boundaries of what it means to be a Muslim woman. Progressive and liberal Muslim women were once under the radar of clerics, but that's all changing.

For Muslim women, these researchers provide an empowering and exhilarating genealogy of strong forebears they can connect to and identify with in their living empowerment journeys. For Western readers, it exposes the untruths that have characterised Muslim women as submissive beings in need of rescue. Collectively, the entire tent of empowered women constitutes a foil against the persistent myth that Muslim women are simpering sorts awaiting rescue. The new crop of authors has effectively countered this Western "rescue" fantasy and the would-be saviours it proposes to create with a worldview founded on solid evidence. It is a pity that the world doesn't know that Muslim women have been crucial players in some of the most defining moments of the faith, and their small and incremental changes have finally morphed into a giant revolution. The women are fighting a relentless battle that has catapulted them to a much better status and position.

Muslim women have undergone a profound transformation and now study in universities, hold positions of power, work and live modern lives and are rulers of their countries. Freedom from religion is not necessarily the antidote to oppression. Instead, we should be encouraging how freedom of religion can overcome inequality. Like many of their fraternity, these women have exposure to primary sources of religious scriptures and are accessing the most reliable authorities. They are in the process of helping the growing understanding that not all Muslim women are silent about the oppression of many of their peers.

An unprecedented migration of women, particularly millennial women, has taken place from home to work across the Muslim world in the last two decades. Millions have joined the workforce for the first time in a movement where economics trumps culture. Muslims are also younger than the global average, with a median age of 23 rather than 28 - a result of the Muslim world's own "baby boom". Young Muslims are now the most educated in their countries' histories, holding new attitudes and using the latest technologies.

The Muslim world is not a monolithic body but comprises diverse economies, cultures, and geographies. Most of the world's Muslims live in 30 emerging markets, in which they are the majority of the population. Together, these economies comprise 12% of the world's GDP and one-fifth of its population. These include countries with high per capita incomes, such as Saudi Arabia, the United Arab Emirates, Qatar and Kuwait; upper-middle-income countries, such as Malaysia, Turkey, Iran, Jordan and Tunisia; and lower-middle-income economies, such as Morocco, Pakistan, Indonesia, Egypt, Bangladesh and Tajikistan.

Contrary to popular belief, Muslim women have served as sensational and heroic leaders, finally morphing into an independent and courageous movement. In recent years, due to the global socio-political climate, the phrase "Muslim woman" has begun to conjure an image of a timid, oppressed woman sheltered by her *burqa* (head-to-toe veil). Yet this image is not what history records or what the present reflects. The early Muslim community recognized and honoured various female roles and responsibilities. A mother was considered the first school for her children. A woman has been independent and not a shadow or adjunct to her husband or any other man. Muslim women are fully entitled to education, work, business ownership, and inheritance. During the era of Prophet Muhammad, granting women even these elementary rights alone was considered revolutionary. The Prophet fostered these women to become active participants in the

Islamic revolution. Women's voices can no longer be under-represented because they have deepened their scriptures' understanding.

Female autonomy in Islam

Women wielded religious titles in Islam; many held political power, some jointly with their husbands, others independently. The best-known women rulers in the pre-modern era include Khayzuran, who governed the Muslim Empire under three Abbasid caliphs in the eighth century; Malika Asma bint Shihab al-Sulayhiyya and Malika Arwa bint Ahmad al-Sulayhiyya, who both held power in Yemen in the eleventh century; Sitt al-Mulk, a Fatimid queen of Egypt in the eleventh century; the Berber queen Zaynab al-Nafzawiyah (1061–1107); two thirteenth-century Mamluk queens, Shajar al-Durr in Cairo and Razia in Delhi; six Mongol queens, including Kutlugh Khatun (thirteenth century) and her daughter Padishah Khatun of the Kutlugh-Khanid dynasty; the fifteenth-century Andalusian queen A'isha al-Hurra, known by the Spaniards as Sultana Madre de Boabdil; Sayyida al-Hurra, governor of Tetouán in Morocco (1510–1542) and four seventeenth-century Indonesian queens.

The status of women in medieval Islam conformed not to Qur'anic ideals but to existing patriarchal cultural norms, which have exercised a negative influence on Muslim thought. Cultural myths, values and customs of a bygone era imprinted the original Islam. As a result, the improvement of the status of women became a significant issue of modern, groundbreaking reformist Islam. Men and women are now defying traditional thinking and are questioning the legal and social restrictions on women, especially regarding education,

Contemporary Muslim scholars suggest that one should distinguish between Islam as a religion and the differing cultural contexts in which Islam descended and was institutionalized, and practiced. Islam as a religion refers to regulations about piety, ethics, and belief. These spiritual aspects of Islam are considered duties of worship (*ʿibādāt*) and hence called "roots" or "foundations" (*uṣūl*) of the faith, and include cardinal beliefs in Allah's uniqueness, the final prophecy of Prophet Muhammad and obligatory practices such as prayer, almsgiving, fasting, and the pilgrimage to Mecca. On this religious level, men and women are moral equals in the sight of God. Evidence for this is in numerous Qurʾānic verses, which render the only distinction between women and men to be their righteousness (*taqwā*), not their sex. Islam as a culture refers to the ideas and practices of Muslims in the context of changing social, economic, and political circumstances. People worship God and interact in social relationships (called *muʿāmalāt*, "transactions"). They make contracts, trade, fight, arbitrate disputes, collect taxes, etc. Collectively, these constitute the *furūʿ* (the branches, or "superstructure").

Women have not received the same equality as men on this cultural level. Such inequality has mainly evolved as an artefact of the preferences and actions of patriarchal authorities after the Prophet's death, including several rulers and administrators, most jurists, and some intellectuals. In many instances, their patriarchal "readings" of the Qurʾānic text resulted from the cultural contexts supplied by the expansion of Muslim rule over former Byzantine and Sassanid territories, where patriarchy was already a well-established social organization which had imperilled the lives of women. Such authorities justified this system of inequality by drawing upon commentaries on certain verses of the Qurʾan and traditions of the Prophet, along with local practices, which later adapted into Islamic law.

Women have published works advocating groundbreaking reforms, established schools for girls, opposed veiling and polygyny, and engaged in student and nationalist movements. Nationalist movements and new states that emerged post–World War II perceived the integration of women and gender issues as crucial to social development. State policies enabled groups of women to enter the male-dominated political sphere and professions previously closed to them, although these policies often caused widespread religious backlash. Many spurious traditions have infiltrated authentic Islam and need purging and filtering to restore to the religion its pristine teachings. There's a bitter feud between liberal women and the orthodox clerics. In due course, the equation will change, and the empowered women will emerge triumphant.

Prophet Muhammad's later teachings and revelations came at a time when he had many wives himself and was much more demanding of women. However, as a much older man with several younger wives and concubines, he had to struggle to control and foster them when revelations restricting women started coming.

Misconceptions about Muslim women

The idea of women's rights in Islam generates voracious interest among Muslims and non-Muslims alike. There is a sharp division of opinion and perspective among scholars. They have devoted a great deal of thought to this theme. One group associates Islam with misogyny and gender oppression, while the other asserts that the religion is a liberatory force for women. Remarkably, despite a surge in female educational attainment and consciousness in Muslim societies compared to their secular counterparts, Islamic women have not taken an extensive part in the discourse of women's rights and feminism. In light of this perception, women must take the initiative for a more nuanced understanding of Islam's gender egalitarian values and to discuss the urgency and efficacy of Muslim women's greater involvement in the discourse on women's rights. Today, there's a lot of dispute about the degree to which Islam can undergo reformation. Some Muslims, especially in the West, are now saying: let's look at these teachings in their context and not take them quite so literally. Their experiences can transform the upcoming generations. In several cases, the local mullahs have nudged the vernacular media to peddle the maliciously absurd interpretations of the Qur'an.

Islam was the first religion to endow women with a status that appeared formally impossible earlier. The Qur'an contains hundreds of exordiums and commandments that apply to both men and women alike. The alignment of moral, spiritual and economic equality of men and women, propagated by Islam, has unquestionably played a pivotal role in the evolution of feminism. These teachings have finally morphed into an empowerment journey for women. The harrowing figures of women's pitiable condition are now showing a reversing trend, thanks to the relentless efforts of women themselves, whose exposure to the primary scriptures has enlightened them and made them are now conduits for assimilating and transmitting the genuine teachings of Islam. Women have accelerated their development pace and surpassed men in several spheres.

In Islam, men and women are moral equals to God and must fulfil the same duties of worship, fasting, faith, prayer, almsgiving and pilgrimage to Mecca. The triumph of Islam in the seventh century codified the position of women with the compilation of the relevant laws of spiritual and civic conduct. Islam limited polygamy to four wives, banned female infanticide, forbade sexual relations outside marriage and spelt out women's rights in marriage and inheritance. But part of this codification placed women, in unequivocal language, below men for various reasons: "Men are in charge of women because Allah hath made one of them to excel the other and because they spend of their property" (in support of women". (Q4:34). Some modern Islamic thinkers believe that, taking the Qur'an as a whole, women have an equal but different status rather than an inferior one. But most Muslim laypeople and scholars who lived in an already patriarchal civilization have not been able to unencumber the original patriarchal legacy and its attendant academic rigidity and have taken such verses the way many Christians take the story of the Creation and the Fall literally.

The specific verses of the Qur'an, which address themselves to men or women, deal with either their physical differences or their role in safeguarding society's moral fibre in the light of Islamic injunctions. The Qur'an affirms that men and women are partners created from one soul. The males and females have the same religious responsibilities, and both genders will receive rewards on the Day of Judgment. It is only in a few instances that circumstances are notably different for men and women in the Qur'an. Passages that seem to affirm male authority over women are on account of the Islamic understanding that men are responsible for the financial support of women. The Qur'an says, "Allah created you from a single soul, and from the same soul created his mate' (Q4; 1). It also says, "O humanity, we created you all from a male and female, and made you into races and tribes, that you may know one another. Indeed, the noblest among you in the sight of God is the most God-fearing of you "(Q49:13). The deep understanding of Islam by women has helped them overcome the barriers that had earlier made their voices under-represented.

Islam allows women to choose whom they marry. In Saudi Arabia, the woman gives her consent at what is called the *shawfa*, which means "viewing." The prospective groom, his father, older brothers, and uncles come to the girl's father's home to propose. It's the first time that a man outside her immediate family will have ever seen a properly brought-up Muslim woman. In Islam, worship is usually strictly segregated by gender. Individual decisions matter: millions of young women have made a slightly braver choice, stretching them a bit more or waiting to get married until after finishing their master's degree. These small gestures have an aggregate effect that can be far-reaching.

A lot of Saudis argue that they get young people married at an early age because it is vital to have an appropriate outlet for their sexual emotions. Courtship doesn't exist in their society the way we understand it. Still, there are as many happily married Muslim women in the same way as married Western women. These developments have finally morphed into a new agenda about Muslim feminism. It, however, doesn't infringe on the fundamental spirit of the Qur'an.

The Arabic term *fitna* refers to sexual temptation. Women's voices are also considered provocative. It is incomprehensible why there is so much hysteria about female sexuality in the Islamic world. It is in many ways considered *fitna*. The literal meaning is chaos. But it is typically used to refer to sexual temptation. It is part of the nomadic culture where the bloodline had to be t low as they lived in a harsh environment.

Women in Islam

A woman is equal to a man in all essential rights and duties; God makes no distinction between man and woman. They are to be equally rewarded or punished for their deeds. The Qur'an says: 'Their Lord answers them: I will deny no man or woman among you the reward of their labours. You are the offspring of one another' (Q3: 194). 'Man' is not made in the image of God. Neither is a flawed female helpmate extracted from him as an afterthought or utility. Dualism is the primordial design for all creation: 'From all (created) things are pairs" (Q 51:49). The Qur'an further says: "Another of his signs is that he created spouses from among yourselves for you to live within tranquility: He ordained love and kindness between you. It further proclaims:" There indeed are signs in this for those who reflect '(Q30:21). It further affirms, "… for women are rights over men similar to those of men over women."(Q2:226). We must appreciate the spirit in which the Qur'an views the congenital differences between the two genders resulting from their creation.

Islam promotes and teaches individuals to practice balance in all aspects of life and lead their lives with moderation. As humans, we are affected by our culture and traditions, and the alignment of economic, political, and psychological experiences has immensely shaped our attitudes and behaviours. Consequently, our world views and religious views differ from context to context, place to place, era to era, and across cultures, thereby leading to different interpretations of Islam and a distorted worldview of genders. The so-called retrograde practices of Muslims take the world's focus away from understanding the overwhelming problems of the Muslim world and the cause of its troubles. It provides an easy scapegoat for those looking to legitimize their illegitimate actions, which are equally detrimental to humanity.

There is a legitimate disconnect between the application of Islamic tenets and the context of societies where they have not been appropriately assimilated, disseminated or understood. If we had to define Islamism, it is the pursuit of the Qur'ānic view of humanity in all aspects of life. One who serves humanity first prevents harm and protects society. At its very core, Islam prescribes the principles of justice and equity for peace and human development and compassion for humanity. The same root word of Islam is the word *salaam* (peace). Islam is a universal religion that speaks to humanity. In his last great address at Arafat, the Prophet summed up his philosophy by decrying barriers between people. Islam, for him, transcended divisions of caste, colour and race. "All mankind is from Adam and Eve, an Arab has no superiority over a non-Arab nor a non-Arab has any superiority over an Arab; also a white has no superiority over a black, nor does a black have any superiority over white except by piety and good action." *(Prophet's Farewell Sermon)*

However, we have to accept that the role of women in Muslim society has changed significantly over the centuries since Islam's birth in Arabia in the early 600s. Their position has varied with shifting social, economic, and political circumstances but has now seemed to stabilize after centuries of injustice and several woes. Although Islam regards men and women as moral equals to God, women have not had equal access to many of the privileges in Islamic life on account of misinterpretations and the integration of ancient cultures into authentic Islam. But their new intuitive approaches are morphing the position of the upcoming generation, who are ably empowered and are leading a stellar role even in male-dominated activities. On account of the relentless efforts of women to climb their way out of oppression, their harrowing tales are now showing a reversal trend. The women's exploration of the Islamic landscape has opened their minds like a parachute and broadened their vision.

The distorted image of Islam

The distorted images of Islam stem partly from a lack of understanding of Islam among non-Muslims and partly from the failure of Muslims to explain them reasonably to other sections of society. The results are predictable: the hatred feeds on hatred. Ignorance of Islam exists both among Muslims and non-Muslims. Non-Muslims, ignorant and misunderstanding Islam, fear it. They believe it threatens their most fundamental values. Fantasy, conjecture and stereotypes replace fact and reality.

Similarly, Muslims have misconceptions. They, reacting to the hate and fear of non –Muslims, create a kind of defensive posture within their societies, and a combative environment soon morphs into militant rhetoric. The voices of peace and tolerance vaporize in this heat and misunderstanding. We need sanity in all spheres to allow truth to prevail. Let us allow the flowers of truth to bloom. That is the right approach to pursuing Islam and making it an egalitarian religion, its original noble mission.

The vast majority of Muslims indeed hate violence and terrorism, and the Qur'an and various schools of Islamic law forbid the killing of innocent civilians. The vast majority of Muslims believe that the central message of Islam is peace. Nevertheless, it is unfair to assume that the Qur'an or Islamic law can be used as a tool to justify barbaric acts. The terrorists are a product of a specific mindset that has deep roots in Islamic history. They are motivated by an Islamic tradition that is intrinsically inhuman and violent in its rhetoric, thought and practice. They assume that it gives them solace and spiritual comfort. Those believing in this agenda and using the Qur'an and Islamic law to motivate people with such ideologies justify these actions and set across a wave of hatred. Their experiences can transform the upcoming generations. In several cases, the local mullahs have nudged the vernacular media to peddle the maliciously absurd interpretations of the Qur'an.

As Muslims, we also have to recognise the Islamic flavour given to the problems the terrorists have thrown up. They are acting in the name of religion; it thus becomes a Muslim's responsibility to examine the tradition that sustains and nourishes them critically. Many of those who define themselves in terms of the totality of a religion or an ideology have demonstrated an innate tolerance for and tendency towards violence. It is the case in all religions and creeds, down through every age. But this does not diminish the responsibility of Muslims to be judicious, to examine themselves, their history, and all it contains to redeem Islam from the pathology of this tradition—the haven of terrorists.

Positive contribution of Muslim women

Muslims feel they are too often associated with extremism, with little attention paid to their positive contribution to society, particularly the recent advances by their women. A generation of neglect, with education failing the religious curriculum, the major religions failing to engage with the broader public – and the media not understanding religion and therefore keeping it at arms' length – has resulted in a society that lacked the confidence to deal with religious subjects and religious people. The most impacted segment is Muslim women. Muslim women have foraged the Islamic landscape so voraciously that men can never serve as barriers to keep the voices of women underrepresented.

The media now recognises that religion matters and needs to be covered, discussed, and examined with knowledge, fairness, and respect. And to carry on mocking it, misreporting it with unhelpful shorthand and careless choice of images, or pretending it is going to go away or that it is only of interest to people who are only intent on destruction is simply not going to wash any more significant increase in the positive portrayal of Muslim women. Still, the media continue to focus on them as victims. The main argument against the veil, for instance, has changed from one of the oppression of women to difficulties surrounding communication with the veil wearer.

Most commentators believe that the way the media reports about the treatment of women in some West Asian countries is making things worse. As in any war, the "rape crisis" in Syria and Iraq is complicated, and the way it is projected shapes the false assumptions and stigma women face.

Anyone who has been following coverage of the conflict in Syria and Iraq will know that the region has seen a significant sexual crisis. Much of the media coverage has focused obsessively on the horrendous violence against Yazidi women and girls escaping from Isis captivity, with details sometimes bordering on the salacious about slave markets, forced marriage, and multiple rapes. It is certainly possible that this is doing more harm than good.

Scholars have argued that the coverage risks being counterproductive: To scholars of sexual violence, these media narratives look typical in three related ways: They are selective and sensationalist; they obscure deeper understandings about patterns of wartime sexual violence; and they are laden with false assumptions about the causes of conflict rape and Islamic vision of women's dignity.

The Prophet's followers accepted his teachings and ushered a revolution in their social attitude towards women. They no longer considered women as mere chattels but acknowledged them as an integral part of society. In the new social climate, women soon rediscovered the truth of their position and the glorious legacy bequeathed to them by Islamic women of the early epoch. They soon became highly active members of society and were instrumental in providing service even during wars which the pagan Arabs forced on the emerging Muslim *ummah*. They carried provisions for the soldiers, nursed them and even fought with them if necessary. It became common to see women helping their husbands in the fields, carrying on trade and business independently, and trying to satisfy their needs. The Muslim women's accelerated pace of development has amazed even the Western world.

The Prophet emphasised and fostered these facets of feminine character. It urged men to marry women of righteousness and encouraged women, in turn, to be faithful to their husbands and compassionate to their children. He said: "' among my followers, the best men are the best to their wives, and the best women are the best to their husbands. Each of such women gets a reward equivalent to the reward of a thousand martyrs. Among my followers, again, the best women are those who assist their husbands in their work and love them dearly for everything, save what a transgression of Allah's laws is." (Riyad as-Salihin 278) The Qur'an repeatedly emphasises this equality by addressing both men and women in its verses.

- "But who so does good works, whether male or female, and is a believer, such shall enter Heaven, and shall not be held wrong even as much as the little hollow in the back of a date-stone". (Q.4:125)

- "And think of the day when thou wilt see the believing men and the believing women, their light running before them and on their right hands, and it will be said to them, 'Glad tidings for you this day! Gardens through which streams flow, wherein you will abide. That is the supreme triumph". (Q.57:13)

- "Whoso acts righteously, whether male or female and is a believer, we will grant him a pure life, and We will surely bestow on such their reward according to the best of their works". (Q.16:98)

The refreshing change in Muslim women

Many of the problems of Islam that jeopardized freedom and women's rights have been a result of obliquely cramped and constricted interpretations of Islamic law. This narrow-minded approach has much truth to it and has the support of many liberal Muslims and Western scholars.

Following Prophet Muhammad's lead, historians of Islam would refer to the pre-Islamic period as the *Jahiliyya* ("the period of ignorance)". For the pre-Islamic tribes, the past was the preserve of poets, who also served as historians, blending myth and fact in their odes, crafted to heighten tribal feeling. The present was all-important, and the future was irrelevant. One reason for the tribes' inability to unite was that the profusion of their gods and goddesses perpetuated a proliferation of divisions and disputes whose natural origins often lay in commercial rivalries. However, on account of the relentless efforts of women in fighting patriarchy, they have been able to consign their harrowing past to history.

Islamic scholars have devoted much thought to the conflicts within the Islamic domain. The predominance of male-dominated interpretations of canonical texts has often caused analysts and others to proclaim the inherently dangerous relationship between religion and women. For example, the abundance of stories (some factual and others fictional) that focus on the unequal status of Muslim women's experiences tend to reaffirm such assessments about the dangers inherent in women identifying with or practising Islam. "Honor"-based violence against numerous Muslim women, the extreme cases of threats, duplicity and violent abuses to the lives of Muslim women and the denial of their fundamental human rights in the name of religious authenticity validate the negative assessments of Islam's interpretations of Muslim women. However, such evaluations focus on Muslim women as the victims of religion and often fail to appreciate the empowerment of several women who experience spiritualism precisely as a result of their faith in the unity of God (*tawhid*) and the belief in Prophet Mohammad as the last messenger of God.

In the last few decades, an unprecedented migration of millennial women has occurred from home to work across the Muslim world. They have joined the workforce for the first time in a movement where economics trumps culture. The Muslim world is not a monolithic block but comprises diverse economies, cultures, and geographies. The past several decades have been a golden epoch for Muslims worldwide. The community's presence and prominence have increased exponentially. When you traverse the overpasses of any big city, you will see metallic domes sparkling below. The number of mosques has also increased considerably. The secular growth of the minority is even more striking. Muslims are one of the most educated religious groups. Exploring Islamic paradigms has given women fresh insights, making their voices strongly representative.

Since the 1970s, however, the formal study of Islamic texts among Muslim women has undergone a significant revival. It is happening even in regions with no prior history, such as South Asia. These movements take different forms, including female madrasas, Islamiyya schools, and informal study circles. However, across various contexts, it is possible to group these diverse platforms into two broad categories: formal and informal. The formal educational platforms, such as madrasas or Islamiyya schools, follow a set curriculum, hold examinations, and issue formal certificates; the informal platforms, which are organized mainly as weekly or biweekly study circles in homes, hotels, or mosques, adopt a looser structure. The teaching across these different platforms is focused primarily on studying the Qur'an (both *tajwid* and *tafsir*), followed by the study of the *hadith*; in the formal platforms, the curriculum also includes primary texts in *aqida* (**Islamic creed or theology**) and *fiqh*.

These movements' emergence and steady spread have led to two critical concerns among scholars. First, what impact do they have on women's agency? Second, as women acquire specialist knowledge of Islam, will they challenge the authority of the ulama and reinterpret Islamic texts through a feminist lens? The evidence suggests that, unlike Islamic feminists, who have sought to reinterpret classical Islamic texts from a feminist perspective, women in these Islamic education movements actively defend the classical interpretations of the core Islamic rulings on gender relations and position themselves against feminist debates. But, equally, while defending the core Islamic rulings, these women reason and discuss and, drawing on the plurality of Islamic legal reasoning, find creative ways to remain loyal to the tradition's core while staying actively engaged with modern realities. These movements are distinct from women's wings of Islamic political parties; they are focused on education and are evident across Sunni and Shi'a contexts.

Apart from professionals, Muslim artists, journalists and politicians are catching up. Credit is mainly due to the women's rights groups that have sprouted worldwide and are instrumental in activating groundbreaking reforms by lobbying with various agencies that exercise influence over reforms for Muslim women. The clerics have obliquely criticised these women and are not aware of the implications of such absurd and flawed approaches on overall Muslim society as women are reworking their networks after strategic patience. With the aggressive stance of women heating up, the position of mullahs appears to be shakier. Most powerful mullahs are shrinking and vanishing in the face of this onslaught. These women leaders obliquely tout them as their adversaries. These women are stalwarts who are steering their fellow women to negotiate challenges from patriarchal societies and build their careers so that the upcoming generations don't have to face such traumatic experiences. When the clerics think from the women's perspectives, society will be able to rise above trivialities and see the future with a broader lens.

The position of women in Islam

Islamic law emphasizes the contractual nature of marriage, requiring that a dowry be paid to the woman rather than to her family and guaranteeing women's inheritance rights and empowerment in owning and managing property. Women have the right to live in the marital home and receive financial maintenance during marriage and the waiting period following death and divorce.

Prophet Muhammad recognized the cognitive intelligence of women. At least one woman, Umm Waraqah, was appointed imam over her household by the Prophet. Women contributed significantly to the canonization of the Qur'an. A woman is known to have corrected the authoritative ruling of Caliph Umar on dowry. Women prayed in mosques unsegregated from men, were involved in *hadith* transmission, gave sanctuary to men, engaged in commercial transactions, were encouraged to seek knowledge, and were both instructors and pupils in the early Islamic period. Prophet Muhammad's wife, A'isha, was a well-known authority in medicine, history, and rhetoric. The Qur'an refers to women who pledged an oath of allegiance to Prophet Muhammad independently of their male kin. Caliph Umar appointed women to serve as officials in Medina's market. Women behaved relatively autonomously in early Islam. In Sufi circles, women were teachers, adherents, "spiritual mothers," and even inheritors of the spiritual secrets of their fathers.

No woman held religious titles in Islam, but several women had political power, some jointly with their husbands, others independently. At one time, when it began to lose its sheen, Islam conformed not to Qur'anic ideals but to traditional culture. However, Islam's image also suffered on account of the stranglehold of clerics and rulers who have obliquely undermined the status of women by their erroneous and flawed assumptions of canonical literature to make it conform to prevailing patriarchal cultural norms. As a result, the improvement of the status of women became a significant issue in modern, reformist Islam. Since the mid-nineteenth century, men and women have questioned the legal and social restrictions on women, especially regarding education, seclusion, strict polygyny, slavery, veiling, and concubinage. Women are retaliating with courage and crafting a strategy to assert them, and they have increased their footprints in Muslim society in several spheres. They have authored works advocating reforms, established schools for girls and engaged in student and nationalist movements. Nationalist movements and new states that emerged post–World War II perceived women and gender issues as crucial to social development. State policies enabled groups of women to enter the male-dominated political sphere and professions previously closed to them, although these policies often caused widespread religious backlash. Based on their understanding of Islamic literature, Muslim women promote a sense of female Islamic ethos and heritage among the upcoming generation.

The practical role model of Prophet's life

The Prophet himself set an example for Muslims to follow. He treated his four daughters with enormous fondness and intimacy. Islam brought radical changes in female society despite the deeply entrenched patriarchy of seventh-century Arabia, which imperilled the lives of these women. The Qur'an provides women with explicit rights to inheritance, independent property, divorce and the right to testify in a court of law. It prohibits wanton violence against women and girls and is against duress in marriage and community affairs. Women and men must equally fulfil all religious duties; otherwise, punishment awaits those who resort to a misdemeanour. Finally, women have assured the ultimate boon: paradise and proximity to Allah:" Whoever does an atom's weight of good, whether male or female and is a believer, all such shall enter into Paradise". (Q40:40). In the period immediately following the death of the Prophet, women were active participants at all levels of community affairs — religious, political, social, educational, and intellectual. They played vital roles in preserving traditions, disseminating knowledge and challenging authority when it went against their understanding of the Qur'an or the prophetic legacy. The Prophet's favourite wife, A'isha, about whom the Prophet said we should learn 'half our religion', was sought after as an advisor to the early jurists.

Prof. Bernard Lewis, known as one of the outstanding Western experts on the history of Islam and the Middle East, comments: "In general, the advent of Islam brought an enormous improvement in the position of women in ancient Arabia, endowing them with property and some other rights and giving them a measure of protection against ill-treatment by their husbands or owners. The killing of female infants, sanctioned by the custom in Pagan Arabia, was outlawed by Islam. But the position of women remained destitute and worsened when, in this as in so many other respects, the original message of Islam lost its impetus and was modified under the influence of pre-existing attitudes and customs."

A need to look inward

The truth and reality is that Muslims can no longer afford to keep wallowing in their past glory and composing paeans and ballads in praise. We have been doing it for centuries, and now the time has come when we must start recognizing these exemplary women's deeds by emulating them instead of turning them into revered monuments of history to be displayed to the world as emblems of our great civilization. They should be honoured living legends so Muslim women emulate them and reach the identical higher pinnacles of glory. If the early Muslim women icons were to serve as role models, Muslim women would have to strive to live up to the ideals. The pride that fills their hearts and minds has to be channelled and harnessed into a potent force that can spur courage and morph into statesmanship, given the civilisation's exponential pace of development.

Muslim women could attain such great merit at a time when they had just inherited a highly demeaned female society with no role models before them around which to fashion their roles. What has gone wrong is that we are now on a journey downhill. The final piece of the puzzle is mullahs. Muslim women always harbour a grievance that the modern feminist society is highly perverted as far as moral values are concerned. It could be on account of the stranglehold of the stonewalling mullahs and patriarchy that imparts a bitter flavour to the thinking on women's roles, rights, obligations and duties and has constantly imperilled the lives of women. In several cases, the local mullahs have nudged the vernacular media to peddle the maliciously absurd interpretations of the Qur'an. Muslims must introspect, emerge out of languishment and forget the euphoria of a great and glorious past. If past glory has significant relevance, it should spur them to redeem their future. It may sound difficult for people to believe that a society which produced such significant figures cannot offer models who may be at least a faint shadow of their predecessors.

The tragedy is that we are just trying to burnish our credentials by projecting our past, which becomes irrelevant if we cannot live up to it. A legacy can last only when it is honoured and consistently nurtured and respected by the custodians of that legacy. It needs consistent and proper moral conduct and character from the inheritors of the legacy. We must understand and delineate those attributes that aided the personalities of yesteryears in attaining such levels of glory. At the same time, we must examine the social and cultural factors that enabled them to use their talents to their utmost value and harness their energies toward their goals fruitfully.

We need to focus on specific vital parameters that can morph this demeaned society and regain the glory of yesteryears. Today, meaningful solutions exist to some women's most complex challenges. However, these solutions are sometimes not measurable, assuredly impactful, and durable, and they never reach women at the last mile to enable fundamental transformation in female society. We need to drive real change and shape concrete outcomes for our repressed females. We must balance risks and opportunities so they can perform multiple roles with more remarkable equipment to scale new solutions and innovations which are impactful and durable. It is the way they can push the envelope.

3. WOMEN IN QURĀN AND SUNNAH

"O People, you indeed have certain rights over your women, but they also have rights over you. Remember that you have taken them as your wives only under God's trust and with His permission. If they abide by your right, then the right to be fed and clothed in kindness belongs to them. Treat your women well and be kind to them; they are your partners and committed helpers".

(Prophet's Farewell Sermon)

The Qur'an enshrined a new status for women and gave them rights that they could only dream of in Arabia. The question naturally poses itself as to why there is a seeming disparity between what once was and what now appears to be. It is more like a mirage. The answer lies in the deterioration of primary Islamic learning after the disasters of the Mongol invasions and the Crusades in the eleventh to thirteenth centuries. The patrilineal traditions in the Middle East that preceded Islam both improved and curtailed women's freedoms in the earliest era. Much of the blame for the regressive interpretations of Islam that led to an obscurantic worldview is a product of the Abbasid dynasty, which ruled from the mid-eighth century onwards and interpreted Islam in a legalistic and rigid manner to serve vested and narrow state interests. It resulted in devaluing much of religion's ethical and normative thrust. It gave rise to distorted practices, overruling the groundbreaking reformist agenda of Prophet Muhammad (peace be upon him). In several cases, the local mullahs have nudged the vernacular media to peddle the maliciously absurd interpretations of the Qur'an.

The Muslim women consistently emphasise two themes, evoked in richly poetic Qur'anic metaphor: first, the equality of the sexes in the eyes of God (the most meaningful equality of all, they argue), and second, the complementarily of the sexes. The Qur'an says, "I created you from one soul, and from that soul, I created its mate so that you may live in harmony and love." (Q7:189). Within the Qur'anic tradition and the life of the Prophet (peace be upon him) lies the rights and inspiration a woman needs to achieve her full potential. The challenge ahead is to educate Muslim girls and women, so they have the necessary knowledge for their religious empowerment. Fortunately, as a result of their exposure to Islamic literature, they are now using the Qur'anic logic to justify wearing the *hijab*, either as a public statement of their spiritual quest or their political identity,

Qur'an's concept of the status of women

Historically, Islam was incredibly advanced in providing revolutionary rights to women and uplifting their social position in the seventh century. Many of the revelations in the Qur'an were by nature reform-oriented morphing, purging the critical aspects of pre-Islamic tradition-ridden laws and practices. The progressive intuitive approach helped eliminate injustice and suffering for women despite the clerics obliquely criticising these women.

The Qur'an interpretation methods have permanently changed and modified throughout history. Textualism is the most accepted approach among traditional exegetes, and proponents of this approach mainly analyze the linguistics of the Qur'an to discover its meaning, which is often assumed to be fixed and unchanging. Unlike textualists, the contextualists in the interpretation of the Qur'an are mostly Muslim reformists who believe that the understanding of the text of the Qur'an should rely on information about the social and cultural conditions at the time of the revelation of the Qur'an. In other words, contextual scholars have not only resorted to linguistic analysis to understand the meaning of the Qur'an but have resorted to various approaches. In the present study, after examining the emergence of a woman-centred approach in the interpretation of the Qur'an, the culmination of a woman-centred approach in the understanding of the Qur'an is focused, and three types of feminine readings of the Qur'anic: understanding of verses is from three perspectives, such as historical contextualization, extraction of general Qur'anic principles and feminist hermeneutics.

Sustenance of Islamic values

It is not enough to merely flaunt these essential values, which must be sustained and conserved by supporting them. The empowered women are now fighting for their rights through ideas, debate, and scholarship. But amazingly, this phenomenon is being propelled by women. The reason is not hard to find. Over the centuries, women have been the first religious teachers in all Muslim homes. When women define and execute a new dispensation for themselves with relentless zeal, society starts changing at its most basic level. These changes permeate the societal order and every sphere of life to bring about everlasting change.

The Qur'an is the immutable word of God, perfect and inimitable in message, language, style, and form. The general tone of the holy Qur'an is sombre and meditative. It is a dialogue between God and humanity. Man and woman enjoy the highest possible status, that of the vicegerent of God on earth. The Qur'an repeatedly points them to knowledge. Knowledge (*ilm*) *is* the second most used word in the Qur'an after the name of God. Humans are encouraged in at least 300 places to contemplate the vast universe created by God.

While Islam solidified as a religious and political entity, a vast body of exegetical and historical literature explained the Qur'an in a progressive worldview and aided the phoenix-like efflorescence of Islam. One of the most remarkable features of the Qur'an, particularly in comparison with the scriptures of other monotheistic religions, is that it has put women on an equal footing with men. Following the spirit of equality in the Qur'an, the Prophet emphasized in his farewell sermon, "All people are equal, as equal as the teeth of a comb. There is no claim of merit of an Arab over a non-Arab or of a white over a black person or a male over a female".

Islamic scholars have devoted much thought to debates that characterize the conflicts within the Islamic domain. While several scholars may consider the spirit of Islam as patriarchal, a profound and contemplative understanding will demonstrate that the Qur'an regards men and women as moral equals. Since a man is technically the head of the household, Islam encourages matriarchy at home. Women may not be equal to men in the manner conceived by Western feminists, but their core differences from men need to be acknowledged. At the same time, women have rights of their own that may not apply to men because the functional roles of both genders are far different. Man has to perform the exterior roles; their responsibility is slightly larger, admittedly, but that does not anyway compromise the equal position of women irrespective of what the patriarchal approach propagates.

Contrary to several popular beliefs, women have played significant roles in the evolution of Islamic civilization; despite having suffered many setbacks during various periods of history, they have fought back steadfastly and are now an empowered generation. It is on account of this development that we now witness a vigorous debate among Muslims over questions as diverse as female imams, modesty in dress, and polygamy. The entire canvas of Muslim women's rights has become very expansive and poses a severe threat to the oblique challenge from clerics whose flawed and absurd assumptions have defied logic. It is primarily on account of the knowledge of scriptures that women have garnered and the misperceived notions of patriarchal leaders who have not been able to comprehend that this approach of women is to evolve meaningful and lasting solutions which are impactful and durable to correcting the aberrations that have crept into the understanding the true holistic spirit of the Qur'an. These distortions have denied the legitimate privileges guaranteed to women, which men misunderstood as amounting to the trampling of their turf.

The Qur'an emphatically and consistently states that men and women are born as equals. "The believing men and women are supportive and protective friends unto each other. They urge the right, forbid the wrong, establish regular prayer, pay the poor due, and are dutifully obedient to God and His Messenger. They will receive the Mercy of God. Surely, God is Almighty, Wise." (Q9:71). This emphasis is the essence of the core Islamic philosophy.

The Qur'anic vision of gender

One of the fundamental aspects of Islamic equality is the story of Adam and Eve. Adam and Eve (Hawa in Arabic) had to share the blame equally for eating the fruit from the forbidden tree. The Qur'an uses the Arabic dual form to illustrate their shared guilt and accountability. The Qur'an emphasizes that Satan caused both of them to stumble. Adam and Eve repented and were pardoned, and a new shared destiny commenced for both of them with a lesson they had learnt. The equality in the Islamic Adam and Eve story undermines the entire discourse that says women are inferior or secondary to men. There is no notion that women were born for men, and the spirit of the Qur'an has repeatedly nullified this assumption.

There are Adamic narratives of the Qur'an which later evolved into hagiographical and theological traditions which serve as a theological fulcrum through which Fatima al-Zahra's roles establish a connection between the tripartite realms of pre-Creation, the earthly world, and the Day of Judgment. Fatima represents the exoteric tradition of prophecy in which her father, Prophet Muhammad, is the seal of the prophets (*khatim al-nubuwwa*), and the esoteric knowledge and spirituality of the Imamate has continued through her role as Mother of the Imamate (*umm al-a'imma*). Fatima's presence, whether physically or implicitly, in the religious imagination, can be discerned through a close reading of several different aspects of traditions and explanation of the story of Adam's creation and the rational knowledge given to him by God, as well as Eve's transgression and physical punishment.

The verse: "Women have the same rights (concerning their husbands) as are expected in all decency from them, while men stand a step above them" (Qur'an 2:228), has created a controversy which has been perceived mistakenly by some men as a reflection of the superiority of the male gender. But, far from comparing the social position of the two genders, this verse specifies the degree of responsibility, not privilege, in a man's role as provider, protector, and maintainer of the family and a woman's role as a caregiver. All enlightened men and women who have appreciated this classification have understood this classification of genders in the right spirit.

Prophet's vision of women

Prophet Muhammad was full of praise for virtuous and chaste women. There are ample *hadiths* to support this approach of the Prophet. He said: "The world and all things in the world are precious, but the most precious thing is a virtuous woman." He once told the caliph, 'Umar: "Shall I not inform you about the best treasure a man can hoard? A virtuous wife pleases him whenever he looks towards her and guards herself when absent from her."

Moreover, Islam decreed women's entitlement to independent ownership of assets, a right that a woman couldn't claim both before Islam and even as late as the 20th century. Islamic law recognizes a woman's right to buy, sell, or lease all her properties according to her will. For this reason, Muslim women have traditionally kept their maiden names after marriage, a symbol of their independent property rights as legal entities. Islam also restored to women the right of inheritance at a time when a female was a commodity in many cultures.

Normative Islam holistically supports gender equity despite the presence of isolated texts that relegate women to subservient roles. Chapter 4, Verse 1 from the Qur'an notes, "People, be mindful of your Lord, who created you from a single soul, and from it created its mate." This verse, along with verses Q7:189 and Q42:11, asserts without ambiguity that men and women have the exact spiritual nature. They were born out of a single soul (*nafsin wahida*), and as mates (*azwaja*), they are a part of us (*min anfusikum*). Given that both men and women have the same spirit; it is only natural that the Qur'ān obligates them to the same religious and moral duties and responsibilities.

It is a fact, however, that a sound administration within the domestic arena is impossible without a unified policy. For this reason, the *shari'ah* requires a man, as head of the family, to consult his family, particularly his wife, and have the final say in its decisions in a manner that respects the wife's feedback. In doing so, he must not be duplicitous or rude, use his prerogative, or cause any injury to his otherwise benign wife.

Islam also recognizes that such equality does not mean that men and women are the same. It notes their different biological and emotional capabilities and, given this, sets out their critical roles in life. The roles do not have any bearing on the superiority or inferiority of the sexes but rely on endowed natural capacities. God emphasises that believers will be rewarded according to their deeds, regardless of gender. The response is emphatic in the Qur'ān: "Anyone who acts rightly, male or female, being a believer, We will give them a good life, and We will recompense them according to the best of what they did. "(Q16:97). The women's movement has gained great traction.

Rights and privileges of women

Perhaps nowhere was Prophet Muhammad's struggle for economic redistribution and social egalitarianism as evident as in the rights and privileges he endowed to Muslim women. The Qur'an is far more egalitarian and protective of women's rights and status than most late Islamic practices in the Middle East. The Qur'an does not urge the obligatory veiling of women, though scholars do mistakenly think that it was necessary for Prophet Muhammad's wives. The verse asking men to speak to these wives from "behind a *hijab*" refers to curtain and veil. Islamic jurists later interpreted this and another verse as requiring veiling, just as other commandments are less favourable to women. Islam's foundational texts have consistently treated women and men as equal believers. However, the Qur'an believes that this repetition reinforces the vital aspect of the Qur'an.

The Qur'an was undoubtedly ahead of its times, but it certainly did not remain entirely egalitarian in its broader outlook, as misinterpretations by scholars distorted the original holistic philosophy. It gives men privileges over women, lets them control their wives and permits them to marry as many as four women. At the same time, the Qur'an offers Muslim women more opportunities to become expansive and take their place alongside men in reforming society. Men and women are created equal, share equally in moral responsibility and have the same obligation to keep the precepts of Islam above reproach. In the words of the Qur'an, the influence of the teachings of Prophet Muhammad is the core objective for advancing civilization. In the history of humankind, no one worked as hard as Prophet Muhammad to protect human rights, especially those women who demonstrated and practiced integrity, strength, strategic genius, beauty and divinity, or to honour humanity by freeing it from the constraints of prejudice, manipulations, personal and social injustice which are markers and emblems of his exordiums for the stability of female society.

Plenty of resources in the Qur'an are more egalitarian than those stipulated in the Western Christian tradition. They came under the strong influence of misogynistic Greek thought. Perhaps the most fundamental aspect is that the Islamic God does not have a gender. Arabic may refer to Him using the Qur'an male pronoun, but He is never described as "father" or "lord", as is the practice in the Judaeo-Christian tradition. Indeed, the Islamic God has expressly feminine characteristics; one of His most important "names" is al-Rahman (the All-Compassionate) from the Arabic *rahma*, which comes from the word meaning womb. In Islamic mysticism, the divinely beloved is female, unlike in Christian mysticism - for example, Bernini's famous statue of St Teresa of Avila in Rome is in love with the male Christ.

Here are a few *hadiths* in which the Prophet encouraged Muslims to be gentle and caring to their daughters:

- "Whosoever has a daughter, and he does not bury her alive, does not insult her, and does not favour his son over her, God will enter him into Paradise." (Ibn Hanbal, No. 1957).

- "If a person has three daughters whom he provides for and brings up, God will surely reward him with paradise" (Abu Hurairah: Kanz al-Ummal:277)

- "If a daughter is born to a person and he brings her up, gives her a good education and trains her in the arts of life, l shall myself stand between him and hell fire" ('Abdullah ibn Mas'ud Kanz al-Ummal:277)

The Prophet's wife, Ā'isha, narrates that once, a woman entered her house with two of her daughters. She asked for charity, but Ā'isha could not find anything except a date. The woman divided it between her two daughters and did not eat any herself. Then she got up and left. When the Prophet came to the house, Ā'isha told him of the incident. The Prophet declared that when the woman would be brought to account (on the Day of Judgment) about her two daughters, they would act as a screen for her from the fires of Hell. (Al Bukhari *Hadith* 2:499)

With parental love and compassion, the Prophet fondled his daughters, looked after them and carried them in their young days. He continued caring for their well-being when they grew up and married. Fatima, the youngest and the only one who survived her father was very close to him, and he used to visit her and invite her with her family to a meal. He would treat them warmly and offer her seat to them. Khadijah was probably in her late thirties when she married Prophet Muhammad and bore him at least six children. Their two sons-Al-Qasim and Abdullah, died in infancy. Prophet Muhammad adored his daughters, Zaynab, Ruqayyah, Umm Kulthum and Fatima. It was a happy household, even though Prophet Muhammad (peace be upon him) insisted on giving the impoverished a higher proportion of their income. He also brought two needy boys into the family. On their wedding day, Khadijah presented him with a young enslaved person called Zayd ibn al Harith from one of the northern tribes. He became so attached to his new master that when his family came to Mecca with the money to ransom him, Zayd begged to be allowed to remain with Prophet Muhammad, who adopted him and freed him.

The women's quest for their rights

In recent years, as debates over Islamic legal interpretations have moved to the forefront, especially in places where the expanded application of Islamic law is on the agenda, the issue of women's testimony has received particular attention. Most jurists arrived at the opinion that women were less trustworthy and less appropriate as legal witnesses than their male counterparts and so have distinguished between male and female testimony in terms of sex.

There is a need to understand the relationship between 'gender' and 'testimony' concerning this sex-based distinction. As such, we will understand why women are sometimes no less discerning than men as witnesses. There is a purpose among genuine scholars to engage in an original interpretation of the law or to judge how others have understood the rules of their religion. Instead, they attempt to approach the topic of testimony, women, and gender from the perspective of a student of the history of Islamic law. The Qur'an deals with women in an egalitarian and non-discriminatory fashion in terms of testimony and legal affairs through reference to certain verses, such as al-Nūr (Q 24:6) and al-Nisā' (Q 4:15). While Ẓāhirisim, including Ibn Ḥazm, and Izzet Derveze follow this egalitarian approach, the four legal schools of the Ḥanafī, Shāfiʿī, Mālikī, and Ḥanbalī do not, and instead claim that women's testimony cannot be acceptable in certain circumstances, such as cases of ḥadd, qadhf (slander), and qiṣāṣ (retaliation)because of the male perspective in such offences...

There is now a subtle but nuanced revolution in female Muslim society. Women are now resolving to find out what Islam has to say about women without a male filter. They are indeed devoting energy towards exploring more profound questions. What is our purpose here? What will happen to us after death? Are there any universal truths? Do women matter in this world and hereafter? Muslim women have wondered all these decades about the response of men. Are they simply unable to think for themselves and, consequently, for their women?

While assimilating the message of the Qur'an, women are finding inherent peace, with the affirmation that their creation was a blessing and came with a defined purpose and meaning. More importantly, no one was inferior – or superior – simply by how a woman was born. Many beliefs and practices of Muslims regarding women were entirely contrary to teachings found in the Qur'an and the practices of the Prophet Mohammed.

Muslim women soon began the painful process of renouncing parts of their original cultural heritage. They refused to accept interpretations of the faith that denigrate women. Instead, they found a profoundly spiritual paradigm that affirmed the inherent human dignity of women and men.

Along the way, Muslim women have come to learn of a robust patriarchal strain – sometimes bordering on misogynistic impulses – within Muslim practice. It has been painful to know that centuries of Islamic scholarship have affirmed the inherent superiority of men over women, including the right of a husband to punish a "recalcitrant" wife physically. It is a legacy that continues to haunt everyone.

As long as Muslims do not seriously confront this legacy, there will be more women who question why they should be part of a family, a community, or a system that condemns them as inherently deficient at worst and second-class at best. Women need to marshal their collective resources to fight for basic human dignity, or else they will continue to suffer. In this battle, they can liberate their fellow women who look to them for inspiration. These women have now been able to gain unique traction.

No verse anywhere in the Qur'an considers a woman's witness half as reliable as a man's. As for verse 282 of Al-Baqarah, which is relied upon to substantiate this notion, it has a logical explanation and different meanings and implications. The conclusion drawn from this verse is not more than a logical fallacy. The proponents of this agenda continue to refer to the above verse in their support. They stress that women are deficient in terms of intellect and prodigious. This conclusion, a natural emanation from this verse, is erroneous and influenced by a patriarchal viewpoint.

The Qur'an has instructed believers that in financial transactions, we must get two male witnesses or one male and two females (Q2:282). However, it is also true that the Qur'an, in other situations, accepts a woman's testimony as equal to that of a man. "The woman's testimony can even invalidate the man's. If a man accuses his wife of unchastity, he is required by the Qur'an to solemnly swear five times as evidence of the wife's guilt. If the wife denies and swears similarly five times, she is not considered guilty; in either case, the marriage is dissolved "(Q24:6-11).

An injunction that emphasizes the preservation of testimony relating to civil transactions, which requires that they become a written document, is sometimes mistakenly interpreted as discrimination of evidence against females. The Qur'an says: "Procure two witnesses from among your men; and if two men be not available, then one man and two women, of such as you like as witnesses, so that if either of the two women should be in danger of forgetting, the other may refresh her memory." (Q2:283).

Diversity of functions

The divine scheme propounded by the Qur'an evokes remarkable wisdom in its typology. Men and women are spiritually akin to one another and are also the recipients of God's favours and bounties in the same proportion. But their functions are not identical. Given this diversity, a corresponding variance exists between their respective faculties:

- "Our Lord is He Who has endowed everything with its appropriate faculties and then guided it to their proper use". (Q20:51)

- "God has fashioned humanity according to the nature designed by Him. There is no altering the creation of Allah". (Q30:31)

The insights into the diversity of the faculties of males and females also demonstrate their divergence of functions as designed by nature. For instance, a woman is well equipped for childbearing, while a man is not. A man is more adept at commanding and fighting in the field; to appoint a woman for command in the field may misfire. It is not a matter of superiority or inferiority; it is a question of the natural capacities of each gender. The proper discharge of the function of child-bearing imposes certain handicaps upon women, from which man is free. The honour of motherhood gives women a unique satisfaction and emotional elevation. Man cannot aspire to it. The upbringing of children during their early years is primarily the mother's responsibility; the father's role is supplementary to that of the mother. At that stage, the child instinctively turns to the mother rather than the father for nurturing, comfort, and security. When a child is rebuked or disciplined by the mother, it doesn't evoke any resentment, while it is aggrieved when it faces any harsh rebuke by the father. The bond between mother and child has far greater tenderness than possible in the father and the child.

Women are vulnerable and need men's support and protection. A woman cannot act against her will; a man enjoys the privilege of this freedom. As a wife and mother, the primary and normal sphere of a woman's activities is the home; as a breadwinner, the normal sphere of a man is the outdoor responsibilities. A social system that relies on wisdom and benevolence helps maintain an accord and balance between the two. Islam is the best exemplification of this distribution of duties and functions. Modern feminism has introduced aberrations that have distorted this balance, and families are undergoing severe strain as a result of this imbalance, which is violative of the natural dispensation.

Ibn Hanbal, the founder of one of the four Sunnī schools of law, notes that at least one woman, Umm Waraqah, was appointed as the *imam* or leader of prayers for her household by the Prophet. Historical and canonical records demonstrate women's important and respected role in Muslim life, as reflected in the story of an older woman who corrected the authoritative ruling (*fatwā*) of the second caliph Umar ibn al-Khattāb on dower (*mehr*).

Women's status in Qur'anic exegesis

The fundamental rule in Qur'anic exegesis is to ensure that the deduced meaning conforms to the integrity of the Qur'an. We find that all the injunctions of the Qur'an concerning women stipulate a social structure that addresses the biological peculiarity of women. The Qur'anic view is, in fact, more humane than the prescription in the scriptures of other faiths or creeds. Wherever patriarchal interests have resulted in the subjugation of women, it is primarily on account of cultural ambiguities and not a result of any Qur'anic stipulation. In a society where all the moral values have alluded to Islam, the social position of women becomes even more holy than what it is in societies that are considered modern. Those who go by the procedure of interpreting the Qur'an verse by verse are missing a crucial point that the Qur'an enunciates a cohesive outlook and is an organic text where each verse has a bearing upon the other.

The practice of quoting verses independently, without examining the overall spirit of the text, has led people to reduce the Qur'an to a checklist of do's and don'ts. A deeper contemplation is needed to understand the Qur'an and its nuances, characteristics, and organic unity. Any segmentation of the Qur'anic text and its coherence will result in obscurity and confusion. Classical Muslim scholars were able to develop systematic approaches to studying the Qur'an. Contemporary Muslim scholars should be able to create suitable approaches to sort out obscurities in contemporary times. Combining classical methods and modern techniques can provide more significant opportunities for our scholars to deal dynamically and systematically with modern challenges.

As a Muslim, you are not supposed to alter the Qur'an because it is a revealed text. Therefore, we cannot just remove verses from the Qur'an. Indeed, we should not read any book that is out of context, nor should we read the Qur'an in a manner that applies the above rules. Islam is a religion of peace. That is its aim and goal. The following powerful commandment in the Qur'an should leave no room for doubt: "Whosoever killeth a human being for other than manslaughter or corruption in the earth, it shall be as though he had killed all of mankind, and whoso saveth the life of one, it shall be as if he had saved the life of all mankind." (Q5:32).

The Qur'an, in its essence, promotes justice, peace, equality, brotherhood, and freedom. Compassion and kindness underpin its core message. One must read the entire Qur'an, not isolated verses. One can understand this by realizing that no verse is a standalone commandment. Each not only has a bearing on the other but amplifies it, too. It is an integrated book, and egalitarianism is its underlying philosophy.

Much of the strife and misunderstanding of the scripture is primarily due to selective reading and the absence of references to the context in which its verses appear. For example, the current modern definition of *jihad* is contrary to the linguistic meaning of the word. Also, it contradicts the beliefs of many Muslims, who equate it with religious extremism. The word *jihad* stems from the Arabic root "J-H-D", which means "strive".

Without recourse to the proper methods of Qur'anic hermeneutics, the literal rendering has importance over the essential. What is effective in one context in Islamic tradition may not be effective in every context. Instead of understanding the nuances of a particular metaphor in its context, the erroneous methods focus on the concrete manifestation that is sliced and grafted on other contexts and forced to fit into the mould of the projected opinion. A better approach would be a subtle but, indeed, not flashy understanding of Muslim thought, and even as it continues to harbour many aggressive strands, we can undoubtedly harmonise these divergent trends.

Thus, by re-reading the Qur'an and leveraging its internal coherence, a more decisive and adaptive criterion for a substantial forward movement for the *ummah* (community, and therefore, women) can emerge, which can help them steer and negotiate the conflicts. Men and women are part of a contingent-pair system. They both must be or are necessary. The relationship is not primary and supplementary, but it is complementary. Islam transcends the evaluations that have come to distinguish males from females in the various contexts in which Islam has spread. It rests on the male and female's equal potential to realise Allah's dictates. The primary and necessary duality in the created world implies mutual necessity and complementarity—not hierarchy.

In general, the determination of human value from the Qur'anic perspective is unspecified in gender: the most noble in the sight of God is the one (they) with the most *taqwa* (piety). *Taqwa* is a crucial Qur'anic idea that implies a confident, pious attitude (consciousness of God) and influences and moulds a particular behaviour. As such, the underlying principle determines Islam's flexibility concerning the roles and status of men and women in society. When people are judged by their *taqwa* and not by their gender, both men and women will be free to strive for greater righteousness to move forward—not only in this life but in the life hereafter.

Many verses of the Qur'an seem to declare male/female equality and have been made a vital centre of solid focus by Westerners who do not realise that there is textual unity in the Qur'ān. By the nature of their procedure, it is impossible to get authentic insights into the cohesive outlook of Islam about the universe and life that is a critical content of the Qur'an. The practice of verse-by-verse interpretation has led to the practice of citing specific verses to justify certain positions, no matter how false these positions may be, when examined against the backdrop of the overall spirit and philosophy of the Qur'an.

4. THE MUSLIM FEMINIST LEGACY

Motherhood is a mercy, being linked.
By close affinity to prophethood,
And her compassion is the prophet's own.
For mothers shape the way that men shall go;
Maturer, by the grace of Motherhood,
The character of nations is the lines
That score that brow determines our estate.
Muhammad Iqbal-*Rumuz-e-Bekhudi*
(Mysteries of Selflessness)

"People are of two types," Ali, the Prophet Muhammad's son-in-law and one of his caliphs, or successors, is reputed to have said. "Either you are brother in Islam, or you are brother in humanity."A section of Muslims are striving to turn word into deed. Women often open services with a prayer. Sermons are in English.

Mosques in the West have come a long way since migrant workers rolled out plastic mats in their back rooms. A new generation of mosques has come out into the public arena. Instead of traditional structures with inward-looking courtyards, their architects are now designing wide staircases that connect to the street. Sports facilities draw in younger Muslims who can pursue sports and distress themselves while remaining rooted in their faith. The most influential section of the community is women, who are essential drivers of this change, and in several cases, they spearhead this transformation. The primary objective is that, apart from uplifting their spiritual souls, they can finally ramp up their physique.

An emerging positive development in Muslim society is the expansive role of women, a movement popularly named Muslim feminism. It is an endeavour evolved by female theologians and activists who aim to generate an egalitarian family law within an Islamic legal framework. Muslim feminism rests on a foundation that combines the teachings and objectives of the Qur'an and the *sunnah* of the Prophet Muhammad with constitutional guarantees of women's equality, international human rights principles and the lived experiences of Muslim women. The last few decades have led to an exponential growth of Muslim feminist organizations that are acting as solid and influential pressure groups by asking governments for legislative reforms, raising public awareness about the discriminatory experiences of Muslim women, and building women's solidarity to expand the idea of egalitarian Islam. Muslim feminist activism is striving to achieve its objectives by supporting the equal rights movement of women in such diverse areas as matrimony, defending women's post-divorce rights and combating all forms of violence against women.

Within the Qur'anic tradition and the life of the Prophet lies the rights and inspiration a woman needs to achieve her full potential - the challenge ahead is to educate Muslim girls and women, so they know that the scriptures empower them with formidable rights. They can justify wearing the *hijab* publicly, expressing their spiritual quest or political identity. In a world where Islamic society and culture perceive themselves as being in danger or under threat of decimation, these women are playing a pivotal role in defending their ethos. They have also been able to gain a sizeable traction.

Specific vital parameters govern women's exposure to entrepreneurial activities:

- Build skills for success in policy and systems, regulation, evaluation and measurement, business strategy, grant writing and leadership.
- They are developing the expertise needed to improve outcomes for their families and delivery for resource-limited populations.

- Learn from industry experts and distinguished faculty from diverse universities.

- The education at various skill development centres has given them more confidence because they have a solid academic background, reinforcing their field experiences and significant virtual interactions with their peer-level classmates.

- Given the dire scenario above, it's no surprise donors weigh numerous factors when distributing aid, from anticipated development outcomes to geopolitical strategies. However, one crucial consideration is Society's susceptibility to natural disasters and human conflicts.

The Qur'ān improved women's status relative to the pre-Islamic period by emphasizing women's and men's ontological and spiritual equality. Although specific social and economic regulations in the scripture seemingly favour men, the conditions prevailing at the time of the revelation, which seemed to justify such inequality, have lapsed. The Qur'ān provides mechanisms for a fresh interpretation of women's roles and status. Modern reforms in personal status law, achieved through recourse to such instruments and arguments, have gradually shifted toward gender equality. Still, a certain degree of backsliding has occurred as a consequence of the rise of ideologies reinscribing patriarchal control over women's dress, comportment, and desired equity before the law in a platform that includes a sometimes unyielding, even violent, confrontation with the state (itself at times co-opted) and reformist groups.

The revered position of mothers

This intensity of emotional commitment of mothers is related to the fact that the Prophet Muhammad (peace be upon him) also stated that paradise lies at the feet of our mothers, that they are the gateway to eternal bliss, and that our bonds with them are of utmost importance to humanity.

The Qur'ān speaks of the mother's rights in several verses. It enjoins Muslims to show respect to their mothers and serve them well even if they are still unbelievers. The Prophet emphasised that the rights of the mothers are paramount, and the rewards for honouring them are extraordinary. They enshrined these injunctions in respect of mothers: "Please do not leave your mother unless she gives you permission or death takes her because that is the most significant (deed) for your reward. " (Narrated by Ibn Abbas. Kanz al-Ummal472)

The Prophet exemplified the best example of health and intimate family relations. His injunctions emphasized the need for kind and caring treatment between husband and wife. The Prophet redefined women's positions and they started exuding confidence in their lives. The Prophet stressed these values for several reasons: The first was that Islam established a norm of marital relations that starkly contrasted with the values that prevailed in Arabian society at the time, and women were treated much inferior to men. Secondly, the Prophet realized that women were always vulnerable to ill-treatment and often unable to find help when their husbands or other male folk abused and were rude to them even in response to their benign behaviours. Thirdly, he clarified that only an evil person could be unkind to women. Fourthly, he wanted to emphasise that the kind treatment of women earned great rewards from God. On his deathbed, the Prophet continued to urge Muslims to treat women compassionately. Prophet Muhammad's first wife, Khadijah, who was the first convert to Islam, makes a striking case against gender segregation. Prophet Muhammad repeatedly insisted before accepting a dinner invitation, "What about her?"

Moreover, the Prophet set an excellent example of a model husband who treated his wives and children with loving compassion and due consideration. He dealt with wives on an equal footing. He devoted a night to each in rotation, helped them with housework, mended his clothes, shared life's ups and downs, listened to their opinions and allowed them to develop their skills and talents. For example, Sawdah developed expertise in tannery and earned a fair income; Zaynab was active in charitable work and was renowned as 'the mother of the destitute'; Umm Salama, enlightened and astute, was a political adviser to the Prophet, while A'isha, the youngest and wittiest, was s a judge, and was often consulted on religious affairs in the absence of her husband. The early generations followed the Prophet's example.

When A'isha had to answer about the Prophet's domestic life, she said: "He used to repair his robes, mend his shoes, and attend to all his family's needs." He believed treating women with inherent dignity ensured their rights were protected and upheld. While advocating for them, they get equitable opportunities to succeed, which is necessary to enforce the Qur'anic vision: "O you who have attained to faith! Be ever steadfast in upholding justice" (Q4:135).

The tragic irony

The Prophet's kindness to women forms the essence of many stories about his character. One concerns his wife, Maria, the Christian Coptic vassal girl sent to him by the head of the Coptic Church in Cairo. His attentiveness towards her provoked his other wives into arguments and ill temper. Life became unbearable for the Prophet. In protest, he withdrew from them for a month, sleeping on the floor of a small mud storeroom and refusing to see anyone. When he finally succeeded in seeing him, Umar broke into a cry of anguish, threatening to cut off his own daughter's head for having brought the Prophet to this point. But by now, the women had learnt a lesson. They promised there would be harmony in the home if he came back.

There are several *hadiths* which encourage compassion and kindness for women:

- "Abu Hurairah reported that the Prophet said: "One who makes efforts (to help) the widow or a needy person is like a mujahid (warrior) in the path of Allah, or like one who stands up for prayers in the night and fasts in the day".

- "Women are the partners of men".(Abu Dawud, Sunan, 1/61)

- "Only a man of noble character will honour women, and only a low, vile man will dishonour them."(Kanz al-Ummal, 16/371)

- "The best among you is he who is best to his family. For my family, I am the best of all of you." (Ibn Majah, Sunan 1/636)

The tragic irony of Islam is that its sacred text, the Qur'an, is mainly concerned with women's well-being and development. Yet, Islamic traditions discriminate against girls from the moment of their lamented births. Islam is proud to have abolished female infanticide, yet one of the most common crimes in many Muslim countries is the "honour killing" of women by male relatives. The Qur'anic description of marriage suggests closeness, mutuality, and equality. Still, tradition defines a husband as his wife's superior in earthly form (despite the Qur'an prohibition against human deification as the one unpardonable sin), her gateway to heaven, and the arbiter of her final destiny. In several cases, the local mullahs have nudged the vernacular media to peddle the maliciously absurd interpretations of the Qur'an.

The Qur'an permits divorce without fault, but Muslim societies have made divorce both legally and socially very difficult for women. The Qur'an stipulates that both parents must concur on the raising of children and not use the children against each other. Still, in many Muslim countries, divorced women automatically lose custody of their children when the boys turn seven and the girls 12. Muslim traditions have misinterpreted the Qur'an's spirit and intentions in the matters of polygamy, inheritance rights, purdah (keeping women isolated and at home), and veiling. These practices were initially meant to protect women and even guarantee women's autonomy; they have become instruments of oppression instead. The Qur'an does not prohibit family planning; a review of the literature suggests ample religious and ethical support for family planning, but there is the mistaken impression that family planning is anti-Islam. The challenge for all women, and especially Muslim women, is to move from a reactive mindset, in which women must assert their autonomy over patriarchal opposition, to a proactive attitude, in which they can speak of themselves as full and independent human beings with minds and spirits as well as bodies. Muslim women must work in full partnership with Muslim men, rejecting Western models of liberation but also, and more importantly, asserting their own.

The view that the Muslim husband enjoys an arbitrary, unilateral power to inflict instant divorce does not accord with Islamic injunctions. The statement that the wife can buy a divorce only with the consent of or as delegated by the husband is also not wholly correct. Indeed, a deeper study of the subject discloses a surprisingly rational, realistic, and modern divorce law: Before Islam, Muslim women had practically no right to ask for a divorce from their husbands; it was the Qur'an that provided for this form of liberation. The Qur'an applies categorical measures to prevent the abandonment and exploitation of wives, who were subject to the whims of husbands in marriage and divorce. Although the Qur'an stipulates conditions for equitable separation, it does not make the rule of uncontrolled power of repudiation for men. The Muslim women's right to divorce is allowed in the Qur'an, and *Khula* is one of the most potent and absolute rights of divorce. The Qur'an gives a reciprocal right to the wife to separate from her husband if she is afraid of cruelty or desertion on her husband's part. Despite the nature of extrajudicial divorce under Indian Muslim Personal law, which is primarily uncodified, this absolute right of Muslim Women has been ignored and wrongly interpreted. The opinion of jurists and interpretation by the court of law insisted on the husband's consent to obtain *khula*, but the Qur'an does not lay down any such conditions.

The testimony of a woman

The wholesale claim those women's witnesses are worth half that of men misses the complexities of Islamic law. In some limited areas of Islamic law, two female witnesses are necessary, whereas one male witness will suffice. However, there are other areas where one female witness is sufficient. Islam believes that all human beings are not equal as far as their physical attributes are concerned. They are equal in so far as they are humans. Therefore, all humans are equal but cannot be treated equally in all practical transactions. Islam allows differentiation among individuals, but this is not based on the gender discrimination of the individuals but on their inherent physiological traits–their inner potential.

In Islam, a woman's testimony is not always half as reliable as a man's testimony. The Qur'an is the only place that speaks of a ratio of one man and two. It has to do with testimony regarding the transaction. Similarly, Islamic law rejects a man's lone testimony in the least significant financial matters, such as lending or borrowing funds and other transactions, since there must be two.

However, many other cases require expertise, knowledge, and experience, which only women can testify to. That is to say that a woman's testimony is not always or necessarily in the ratio of "one man-two women" in all cases. For instance, when it comes to women's issues such as menstruation, confirming virginity, pregnancy, marital consummation, or childbirth, Muslim scholars or judges will, in most cases, agree that a woman's testimony takes precedence over that of a man.

Meanwhile, concerning the verse on transactions, generally, women were not as familiar with contracts and negotiations as men in the past. Hence, the ratio of two women as testifiers was primarily due to a woman's inexperience in transactions, not her ability, intelligence, or lack of trust. However, there is a question: since women are becoming professional businesswomen nowadays, can such an injunction be overturned? The Muslim scholars believe that the Islamic injunctions conform to society's standards, not the exceptions. The fact that some women are becoming experts in specific fields can overturn the rules.

Similarly, it is a false accusation to say that making the testimonies and witnesses of two women equal to one man sometimes insults the woman's intelligence and dishonours her integrity. If that were the case, a single woman's testimony would, likewise, not be acceptable in the other affairs of women.

Islam envisages a sound social environment, which is possible only by strengthening the family setup, which is the basic unit of society. Islam wants the family to become a well-governed institution. God has created man and woman so that they complement each other. In short, they are of the same genre yet are distinct from each other. To be more precise, they are two interconnected poles or two units of a pair. Hence, the difference in their mental, physical, and emotional traits marks the different spheres of roles.

The Qur'an speaks of giving testimony in the context of five specific situations. In only one of these five cases, does it distinguish between witnesses based on gender, namely in the case related to financial transactions, in which two women could testify instead of one man? There is not the slightest trace of discrimination. In the case of a document recording a transaction, which one male and one female witness attest, the female witness would not typically have frequent occasions to meet the male witness and interact with him, so there would be little chance of her memory getting refreshed. It is a wise provision that where only one male witness is available, two female witnesses may be called upon so that the very words of one may refresh the memory of the other. It is more practical for males.

The famous reference about two women witnesses is that if one of them forgets/errs, the other can remind her is a reference not to the inferiority of women's intellect but rather to the fact that women at the time did not engage in borrowing or lending and were moreover mostly illiterate, making them less effective witnesses should a dispute arise. Meanwhile, another one of these five cases outlines when a woman's testimony is worth *more* than a man's, namely when a husband accuses his wife of infidelity—although we never hear anyone mentioning this extraordinary verse or highlighting the principle behind it.

Moreover, women must guard themselves against the contingency of appearing as witnesses in judicial proceedings. A woman should usually not be called upon to attest to a document recording a transaction. In the case of male witnesses, their memory of a transaction that they attest to as witnesses would be revitalized when they meet socially, for one reason or another, and they will be able to remember the transaction. The Qur'ān grants both sexes equality from the perspective of origin and spiritual status. Men and women are equally accountable to God for their faith, actions, and moral behaviour (33:35).

However, from a contemporary perspective, such equality is not reflected in the social sphere, even though in its own time, the Qur'ān significantly advanced women's status. For instance, the Qur'ān entitled women to inherit (Q4:7), but only half the portions received by men (Q4:11); women were considered legal persons (long before they were in the Western hemisphere), but two women's testimonies counted in weight to that of a single male's (2:282). Women had the right to economic security. Still, men "have preference over women" because they were made responsible for women's upkeep (4:34). In Islamic law, women have to remain confined to monogamy, which, while not specified in the Qur'ān, is implied in the injunction that "all married women", are forbidden to men (Q4:24).

Distribution of functional roles of gender

According to the Qur'an, a husband should be the head of the family. In support of this, it presents two arguments:

i) Men have been responsible for earning livelihood for the family, i.e., striving to provide for the family's financial requirements.

ii) Men have suitable mental, physical, and emotional abilities. On the other hand, women have predominantly softer traits that make them ideal for domestic responsibilities.

It is only in this particular relationship between husband and wife that Islam provides a degree of slight authority to man over woman. Beyond this sphere, both remain fully equal. Hence, it would be wrong to say that Islam gives women a lower status as compared to men in the social set-up. In some ways, Islam is more protective towards women and assigns men with more onerous and harsher responsibilities.

The requirement for two female witnesses shouldn't mean women have an inferior position. It is a backward glance at the circumstances of the society that the Qur'an sought to change, a means by which it could transform itself into a conduit for enhancing women's positions. The Qur'an makes Muslim societies sensitised to make the same kind of transformation men make, except that their functional roles for them will vary.

The Qur'an proclaims: "O you who believe! When you contract a debt for a fixed period, please write it down. Let a scribe write it down in justice between you. No scribe should refuse to write as Allah taught him, so let him write. Let him [the debtor] who incurs the liability dictate, and he must fear Allah, his Lord, and diminish not anything of what he owes. But if the debtor is of impoverished understanding, weak, or unable to dictate for him, then let his guardian dictate justice. And get two witnesses out of your men. And if there are not two men [available], then a man and the two women, such as you agree for witnesses so that if one of them [two women] errs, the other can remind her (Q2:282)

However, we must also examine this verse in light of what the Qur'an says elsewhere. The Qur'an does not locate spirituality, morality agency, or individuality in gender. On the contrary, it insists on the equality of humanity, irrespective of men and women, races and nationalities, colour and culture. There is another equally important reason why it is absurd that this verse suggests that "two women equal one man." When it comes to witnesses, the Qur'an indicates that different situations require different kinds of witnesses. When making a bequest, for example, any two men will do (Q5:106). For witnessing a divorce, two witnesses, male or female, will do (Q65:2).

The primary purpose of emphasising different kinds of witnesses is to make the believers reflect on the nature of evidence. What constitutes reliable evidence? Who can you trust? The Qur'an suggests that one should examine the context and decide who would make a viable witness, what kind of experience is needed, and how many witnesses one would need to confirm the validity of a particular event. The witnesses themselves have a severe burden to bear: they cannot conceal their testimony; they must come forward unhesitatingly when needed and be just and truthful in their testimony. They have to bear witness for the sake of God, even though it may be against themselves, their parents, or relatives. The Qur'an proclaims:" O you who have believed, be persistently standing firm in justice, witnesses for Allāh, even if it be against yourselves or parents and relatives. Whether one is rich or poor, Allāh is more worthy of both:" So follow not [personal] inclination, lest you not be just. And if you distort [your testimony] or refuse [to give it], then indeed Allāh is ever, of what you do, Aware". (Q4:135).

This verse does not categorically say that women lack common sense or are feeble-minded or inferior. The issue of two women witnesses relates specifically to commercial transactions. We also have to consider the context in which such transactions would occur in the patriarchal society of 7th-century Arabia. Furthermore, it must be apparent from the context of the principle that the Qur'an is putting forward. It is not a statement on the status of women. The verse emphasizes justice, where the debtors, guardians, and scribes are all urged to act justly. The Qur'an, then, can't proceed to make an unjust statement that accords half of humanity as second-class status.

The restrictions on women

Women in Arabian society had little freedom to choose and did not play an essential part in public life. Of course, there were exceptions, the most notable being Khadijah, the first wife of the Prophet, who persuaded him to go on a business trip on her behalf - a prelude to their romance and eventual marriage. However, on the whole, they were not involved in financial transactions and lacked experience in this regard.

Muslim women tended to stay in their domain and did not go out to bazaars, markets, mosques, and courts as often and as commonly as men. So, the very least we can say is that this advice relates to a specific society in a particular period. The second logic is that a woman can help the other woman if needed to "remind her." The two, between themselves, encourage each other to come forward to do their public duty. They have to be active participants in creating a just and equitable society. If one of the female witnesses is coerced, manipulated, or otherwise forced to change her testimony by some unscrupulous male, we are dealing with two women who could support each other and stand firm.

From the Islamic point of view, education should be freely and equally available to women as much to men. Islam constantly encourages Muslims to read, think, contemplate and learn from the signs of Allah in nature:

- "Are the wise and the ignorant equal? Truly, none will take heed but men of understanding. " (Q39:9)

- Other Qur'anic verses that advocate knowledge and learning are" Allah will raise to high ranks those that have faith and understanding among you. He is conscious of all your actions."(Q58: 9).

- 'Say: Lord, increase me in knowledge'" (Q 20: 113.)

Muslim response to Western feminism

What is the difference between Islamic and Western feminism, or is there no difference? If we go by the definition of feminism as an ideology to empower women, there is no difference. However, historically, Muslim women lost the rights they had as their due on account of the tribalisation of Islam, which was under the influence of patriarchal values.

Muslims resent the appropriation of authority by Western culture to determine what is right or wrong. They believe that most Western notions of feminism are in total conflict with injunctions enshrined in the Qur'an and threaten the value-based society that Islam has fostered all through the ages. Islam equally strongly abhors the aggressive feminism of today that wants to storm male bastions and tear down the gender balance of society. Some of these and Western movements demean the dignity of male folk. The line demarcating exclusive male and female spaces is growing blurred, and we are becoming insensitive to the severe moral consequences and implications of a utopian dream of a gender-neutral society.

The majority of Muslim women who are attached to their religion will not shun conventional Islam through the use of a secular approach imposed from the outside by international bodies or from above by undemocratic governments. The only way to resolve the conflicts of these women and remove their fear of pursuing rich and fruitful lives is to build a solid Muslim feminist jurisprudential structure, which clearly shows that Islam not only does not deprive them of their rights but demands these rights for them. Muslim women have been quite suspicious and resentful of Western feminist concern about "their plight." For one, they note that Western culture has not exactly improved the status of women. It created "super moms "who are eternally exhausted and have turned female sexuality into a commodity.

Contrasts between Islam's and Western ideas of women

The Islamic definition of society is almost the opposite of the Western one, highlighting the norms-based versus the value-free-based difference between the two paradigms, essential to understanding their views on women. The Islamic position differs from the Western position in four different ways:

1. God's revelation provides the best unbiased source of knowledge about how men and women should live and organize themselves,

2. Without guidance and discipline, individuals will pursue greed and self-interest, which will not lead to the benefit of the whole community,

3. That progress comes from sacrifice and cooperation and recognition of the needs of one another and not individualism, and lastly,

4. Society has the right to ask its members to respect and abide by specific moral standards in public, which are unacceptable alternatives.

5. The purpose of society is to safeguard human relationships and the interrelated implications and institutions, especially the family. The idea of injury to another is material, physical, moral, and emotional. Unlike the Western view of society, Islam recognizes certain aspects of human organization, such as faith, family, and interdependence, as universal and necessary for the condition of all communities.

The differences in the Islamic and Western views of women are due to influences of specific ideas in these societies concerning the institution of a family. Islam considers the family the finest outcome of a natural phenomenon and the best institution God could provide for the human race's moral, physical, and social development. It is invested with tremendous responsibility as the provider of values for continuing a norms-based society. Most social injunctions enshrined in the Qur'an protect and promote the family. Small doses of intermittent support can help these societies evolve into full-fledged and vibrant institutions. The Qur'anic injunction, which made men financially and morally responsible for women, was necessary to free women from wage labour so they could concentrate on the more important task of raising the next generation. In the Qur'anic view, women are the keystone to the family; thus, motherhood commands the highest esteem among all possible positions within an Islamic community.

There is a need for a better understanding of the Islamic world and the West. Early Western feminism has made the family the central target of its attack on the organization of society. The concept of patriarchy singled out the family as the leading cause of the oppression of women. The feminist movement saw the family as a social unit which enslaved women for reproduction and the delivery of wage-free services to men, such as childrearing, food preparation, house cleaning, sexual pleasure and nursing the old and sick. Since the family requires sacrifice, feminists claimed that romantic notions were seducing women into making all the sacrifices necessary for the sustainability of society. The feminists did not see the family as a moral institution having any normative value.

The main difference between the Islamic and Western views concerning women is that one is norm-based, and the other is value-free. The Islamic view offers a model for women to follow, intended to be universal and normative in its impact. It takes a stand on many aspects of the life of the individual and the community. While women can struggle with how they will incorporate these values into their lives and lifestyles, general definitions are available as to what constitutes right and wrong and differentiate justice from injustice. Islamic sources outline general principles and guidelines, but it is up to the individual to apply them and give them meaning and relevance according to different contexts. The Western perspective strongly resists any agreed-upon general principles or guidelines for women. It does not see a universal condition-affirming model for the life of women. Making statements about what a woman's life should be like is considered as not leaving her free to make up her mind according to her conscience, with or without reference to any outside source. This essential difference becomes clear when we consider each paradigm's views of society.

The norms-based Islamic approach to women and the supposedly value-free Western-based approach to women can be explained, in part, by each system's very different views of society. The Qur'anic view insists on interdependence, while the Western view encourages atomization and independence. The Western view sees society as a place where individuals should be as accessible as possible to pursue their norms to the extent they like without hurting anyone else. In the Western view of society, injury to another individual usually means physical or material injury. The individual's rights and social, economic and political sovereignty are paramount. Society aims to gain individuals' rights and equal opportunity to make the pursuit of rights possible. To make this possible, society must be defined as value-free to avoid clashes or prevent others from pursuing their definition of happiness, success, fairness, etc. In the Western model, value judgments are 'biased' and an impingement of another's rights. The only value judgment allowed is the one of material equality. No one would argue, for example, that it is right to be impoverished or wrong to be rich. In a value-free society, the norm to measure inequality depends purely on material criteria.

Arab and Muslim women have been spoken about for far too long and must get the space to speak for them. A spate of recent literature on Muslim feminism is rightly putting the issue in proper perspective. They are busting myths of passive women meekly accepting religiously mandated subjugation. We must not overlook the efforts of Muslim women from a multitude of ethnic backgrounds as they fight sexism within their religious communities. There is much more to Arab women than both Islam and reductive Western clichés.

Meaningful change comes from within. Religion itself is not the source of women's oppression, although it serves the purpose in that manner. Refreshingly, there are efforts by women to get rid of the oppressive patriarchy still prevalent in Muslim and Arab communities presided over by those men who have appointed themselves the gatekeepers of religion and have imperiled the social fabric. Female theologians, writers, and activists are trying to tackle the distinction between culture and religion, blaming the former for the sexism they confront. While this is true to an extent, after all these centuries, culture and religion have got so thoroughly tangled that attempting to separate them would be an exercise in futility.

Religion merges with culture, becoming so intertwined that you can't tell them apart. However, justifications of how important Islam is in the lives of Muslims – even many of those who are openly secular– make attempts at upholding this notion. At least part of the answer must be because those born into Islam are not only deflecting sexist interpretations of the texts, but they are also navigating the conflict between the experience of oppression and their deep attachment to their families.

They embrace it so it becomes more manageable or reject it and rebel, which can be painful and destructive. Nothing seems off limits, nor is it used to isolate Arabs and Muslims. Instead, we should examine everything in the context of an enduring global patriarchy that leaves few women without being imperiled and untouched.

Several women are, for example, equally resentful of the double standard in their culture and the assumption that freedom is a uniquely Western pursuit. Ironically, however, while dispelling some myths about

Muslim and Arab women, the *hijab* is something all Muslim women must, if not adopt, and then at least consider.

These are days of agitation in the desert kingdom, and perhaps no group is more determined to push the boundaries of change than the kingdom's well-educated and articulate women. The question for those women is how to alter the ingrained tradition that men must have the last word in how they dress, where they go, and what they study- virtually every aspect of their lives.

Women tried to bring change very publicly once before when Iraq invaded Kuwait in 1990. Some 40 women took to Riyadh's freeways, protesting the unwritten law preventing women from driving. They figured that the pending threat of war would trump the traditionalists' alarm that women behind the wheel would lead to encounters with male strangers.

They were wrong. Conservative theologians denounced the protesters from the pulpit as fallen women, and the ban on driving became law. Now, some women have decided they have a better chance of succeeding if they adopt the methods of their natural opponents, the ultraconservative religious fundamentalists. Those women- a cross-section of doctors, businesswomen, professors, artists, homemakers and social workers- want to return to the ancient roots of Islamic law, viewing the Prophet Muhammad's era as the golden age of women's rights.

Islam's war against patriarchy

Muslim women do not have essential rights spelt out in the Qur'an. Still, access to Western education and feminist discourse is helping them contest centuries of selective male interpretation of the Scriptures. Both the West and Islam saw attitudes toward women as a critical battleground, whether it was non-Muslims focusing on the *hijab* (headscarf) or Muslims focusing on the "decadent and immoral" Sex and the Western lifestyle.

For Muslim women, it's not just their actions but also their very identities that are affected by dual, competing discourses that surround them. There's the fundamentalist, patriarchal narrative, persistently trying to confine the social and public lives of Muslim women in line with the kind of narrow, gendered parameters that are now so pervasive and familiar. Some Western feminist discourses seek to define their identities in ways that are typically neocolonial: backward, oppressed, with no hope of liberation other than to emulate whatever Western notions of womanhood are on offer. This wedging chimes with the women's experience, and it's a problem because both arms deny Muslim women the ability — indeed the right — to define their identities for themselves and especially to do so within the vast possibilities of Islam. It is as though male Muslim scholars and non-Muslim Western feminists have handed down predetermined scripts for women to live by. And it is left to those people and their thoughts not to exist — Muslim women who fight sexism — to rewrite those scenarios and reclaim our identities.

Women have liberation in the West, and men are still getting over it. Many Muslim men believed their piety was demonstrated by how their women behaved. They think, 'if I've got control of my women, I'm a man'. What they do is irrelevant. The patriarchal argument can't tease out two separate strands: women as victims of sexual harassment and women as sexualised people who engage in consensual sex. They can't see these things as different. New voices had begun to challenge the authority of ethnic and religious leadership in the mosque, partly in frustration at the politics and limited capability of ethnic Muslim associations.

Non-Muslims focus on the *hijab* (headscarf), while Muslims focus on the decadence and immorality of the Western lifestyle. New voices in the Muslim community, especially women, are bypassing the mosque as increasingly irrelevant — but the lack of structure also makes space for radical groups to seek recruits. Muslim women are fighting back from "second-class status. New organisations and leaders were emerging through Muslims who responded to "media moral panics" and bypassed Islamic councils to present a moderate, local and English-speaking voice of Islam.

Discrimination against women is rampant in mosques, community gatherings, religious education and membership in Islamic organisations. Women were strictly segregated in mosques and sometimes discouraged from attending at all. Usually, they entered a small door at the back and went to an area cut off by a barrier or wall so that sometimes they could neither see nor hear the speaker. Yet Muslim women work in law, finance, medicine, and engineering and run their businesses. The idea that Muslim women must need protection from the outside world is outmoded.

Social values strongly reinforce orientation towards marriage and children as the normative pattern based on Prophet Muhammad's example. Childrearing, early education, and socialisation of children are among the most important tasks for women in Islamic societies worldwide. Although traditionally excluded from the public male domain, Muslim women are privately involved in the study and oral transmission of texts of Islamic sources (the Qur'an and *hadith*).

In modern times, they have entered both secular and religious forms of education and continue to support their long-standing role as family educators and moral exemplars. Muslim women are now exploring diverse fields and flocking to higher education institutions as their guardians sincerely invest in their education. At the same time, they continue bearing the triple burden of livelihood, child-rearing, cooking and nursing those in the family who are ill. In this manner, they are closely adopting certain features of Western feminism. For Muslim women, their families are their most fascinating and compelling obsession, and they intentionally create opportunities for their children to engage in various roles. They know that all skills aren't just innate traits but can be taught and learnt. Those endowed with leadership skills are laying blueprints for long-term community reforms by translating their field insights into practice and pursuing a hectic path to empowerment. Muslim women have imparted coherence to their community.

Several Muslim women are successful entrepreneurs. Thanks to the ramping of infrastructure, women have inspired bustling hubs of businesses. There is a need for expanding infrastructure so that we can reach more of these women. Education is a tool for Muslim women's activism, and they have used it very usefully. It is essentially a product of the hybridisation of education and business training. Despite facing a steep learning curve, Muslim women have been equal to the challenges and have surmounted several handicaps and attained higher grades in education. Central to Islamic belief is the importance and high value placed on education. From a valid Islamic point of view, education should be freely and equally available to women as much as men.

Muslim women are challenging the elements of patriarchy and imperilment that all women experience around unequal power hierarchies in society. Similarly, they are protesting and influencing their counterparts in other religions against the objectification of women's bodies through various channels. These women have been able to realign their roles and efficiently optimize their outcomes and impacts. Women were starting to take leadership positions through their writing and academics. Women can speak out from the Muslim community into the mainstream, but it's tough to get a platform in the Muslim community to get constructive female voices. It is Muslim women who have imparted coherence to their communities.

5. THE FRESH VISION OF ISLAMIC FEMINISM

"Learn this now and learn it well, my daughter: Like a compass needle that points north, a man's accusing finger always finds a woman. Always." In Khaled Hosseini's novel about life in Afghanistan, A Thousand Splendid Suns, the character Nana, an impoverished, unwed mother, gives this scary advice to her five-year-old daughter, Mariam. In 25 words, she tries to sum up how the world thinks men govern women's lives in the world of Islam.

The position of women in Islamic countries has changed and morphed dramatically in the last few decades on account of access to education and jobs. This acceleration will gain further pace as women become educationally empowered. However, each new advance faces resistance, and it is harder to change human attitudes. However, women in several countries have taken the initiative and changed the women's landscape. From Morocco to Iran, women - secular, liberal and Islamist, sometimes alone, sometimes together - are challenging traditions, demanding greater rights, and reinterpreting the Qur'an and Muslim history.

Although traditionally excluded from the male public domain, Muslim women are privately involved in the study and oral transmission of Islamic source texts (the Qur'an and *hadith*). In modern times, they have entered secular and religious education enthusiastically, supporting their long-standing role as family educators and moral exemplars. They also train for professional careers in the workplace outside the home. Central to Islamic belief is the importance and high value placed on education.

The fully empowered Muslim woman sounds like a self-assured, post-feminist type who draws her inspiration from the example of Sukayna, the brilliant and beautiful great-granddaughter of the Prophet Muhammad (peace be upon him). She was married several times, and, at least in one of her marriages, she stipulated in writing that her husband was forbidden to disagree with her about anything. All these conditions have their roots in the canons of Islam.

The emerging rights of Muslim women

A Muslim woman cannot marry without her agreement; indeed, she has the right to revoke a marriage to which she did not agree in the first place. We now have a curious and empowered female generation of Muslims that will not easily accept rules and codes without reasoning them out and arguing on every strand before embracing them.

Few Muslim women outside the urban areas may want to behave like Western women, but this is a hazardous option and has severe implications for one's morality. A comparison may mean little outside the cultural context, but it is essential to point out that Western women had virtually no rights in law or practice until a hundred years ago. Over 1,000 years before the first European suffragette, Islam gave women far-reaching rights and an empowered status.

Muslim women emerged as the centrepiece of the Western narrative of Islam in the nineteenth century and, notably, in the later nineteenth century as Europeans established themselves as colonial powers in Muslim countries. They simultaneously and hypocritically perpetuated the Victorian English narrative that European men were superior to women while denigrating Muslim culture for being oppressive to women.

Of late, Muslim women have undergone seismic changes. They certainly do not share the Western notion of feminism. These women do not accept that being feminist means being Western and believe that Western women should be respectful of other paths to social change:

- First of all, there are multiple causes of discrimination against women, and religion is but one.

- Secondly, gender relations influence women's options in all societies.

- Thirdly, it is futile to focus on misery elsewhere as an escape from the realities of our own lives.

- And fourth, the issue of power remains crucial for understanding gender inequality in any society.

Women are now elbowing their way into politics, civil society, and universities. Despite cultural and political obstacles, they find opportunities to raise their societies. They believe they should do it within the Islamic paradigm's parameters to preserve their faith's sanctity. We now have female politicians, journalists, entrepreneurs, and educators, urban and rural, making impressive inroads into both social and economic landscapes. It has primarily been due to the ramping of infrastructure. We need to expand this infrastructure further to reach more of these women.

It is time for Western thinkers and practitioners to reconsider their assumptions about the role of Islam in women's rights and approach this theme with a more nuanced lens. They must recognise and consciously accept the broad cultural differences between Western and non-Western conceptions of autonomy. They must respect the social standards that reflect non-Western values.

The distortions in Islam

Historically, Islam was incredibly advanced in providing revolutionary rights for women and uplifting women's status in the seventh century. Many of the revelations in the Qur'an were by nature reform-oriented, transforming critical aspects of pre-Islamic customary laws and practices in progressive ways to eliminate injustice and mitigate. Muslim women have morphed in the Golden Era, and they realised it was insufficient to flaunt these values. They needed to act on them. The reforms that took place in the early years of Islam were progressive, changing with the needs of society. However, the more detailed rules that the classical jurists expounded allowed and reinforced many pre-Islamic customs to get integrated into the progressive Islamic culture. These rules reflected their society's needs, traditions, and expectations, not the progressive reforms that commenced during Prophet Muhammad's time. Hence, the trajectory of reform that began during the Prophet's time slowed down in the medieval period, and it started rolling back through the further elaboration of *fiqh* (Islamic jurisprudence), which was then selectively codified in the last few centuries. Whereas shariah is immutable and infallible, *fiqh* is fallible and changeable. *Fiqh* differs from *usul al-fiqh* in terms of legal interpretation and analysis methods. *Fiqh* is the product of the application of *usul al-fiqh*, the total product of human efforts at understanding the divine will. A hukm is a particular ruling in a given case.

There is no denying that the Muslim world has a significant amount of ground to cover to protect women's rights and freedoms. The quest for gender equality remains paramount, as it can have a transformative effect on women. The idea that all Muslim men are misogynists and women are victims of misogyny is wide off the mark and has turned into a tool for defaming Islam. Contrary to the Eurocentric viewpoint, Muslim women are not a blank slate, and they understand the sociology of all communities. In several cases, the local mullahs have nudged the vernacular media to peddle the maliciously absurd interpretations of the Qur'an.

When given the opportunity, Muslim women participate in civic, economic, and social life while raising children into productive members of society. The distorted picture we get is due to the deliberate attempt of Western media to highlight the negative aspects of Islam and gloss over the positive developments. The Western world must understand that the new generations of Muslim girls are now in the vanguard of a revolution that is propagating the learning and understanding of the Qur'ān. There was a time when primary reading and knowledge of the Qur'ān was discouraged. Whatever Qur'ānic students got exposure to Islamic studies, it was only through secondary sources, much of which was distorted and contaminated. Education had an ideological spin, and the youth grew up with a perverted Islamic worldview. There has been a sea change, and the new generation has been able to access the most authentic sources of their religion, which has helped them to morph into the vanguard of an emerging Islamic civilization that is highly empowered.

The approach of Muslim youth

The youth is trying to understand the conceptualization of gender and its broader relationship with society in the backdrop of Qur'anic insights. We have to encourage the charge of this brigade when they say that several Muslim practices, insofar as women are concerned, are at odds with injunctions enshrined in the Qur'an. There has been no attempt to understand the Qur'an thematically and contextually, which is what the great scholar Fazlur Rehman repeatedly emphasized. Unfortunately, he faced much criticism for his frankness and openness and suffered the heresy charge.

Every Muslim will tell you the Qur'an is eternal. It is timeless, its words unchanged. It is ever-present, permeating every sphere of our lives. The Qur'an addresses us directly, as it has always guided us during the last 1400 years, but religious texts are complex and require a profound and erudite study. One of the most insistent commands in the Qur'an is: Think! Reflect! So, the struggle to understand and interpret the scriptures is our eternal challenge. There is no escaping; it is the only way to keep the Qur'an alive.

Faced with the challenge of modernity, many Muslims today, rather than accommodate them to the age-old fudges that have prevailed in so many Muslim societies, have resorted instead to a kind of textual puritanism. Instead of referring to the things done in colonial Morocco, Ottoman Turkey, or, much further back, under the Abbasid caliphs, they prefer to return to the 'simple truths' of the Qur'an. The Qur'an, however, is not so simple that we can approach it with our finite minds. In many centres in Britain, Pakistan and elsewhere, the standard of training in the basic tenets of Islam, including the meaning and context of the Qur'an, is staggeringly impoverished.

Today, more Muslim women are active in the discussion and reformation of identity than at any other time in human history. By returning to primary sources and interpreting them afresh, women scholars endeavour to eliminate the constraints imposed by centuries of patriarchal encrustations. Questioning the underlying presumptions and conclusions creates a space to help us think about gender and its other interrelated aspects. Drawing upon enduring principles of human rights enshrined in the Qur'an., we can extract meanings that can interact with the reader's changing moral and intellectual circumstances. Women scholars and activists are also busy constructing a system of legal reforms that can help them negotiate the execution of a path towards the complete status of women as moral agents at all levels of human society.

These women embody a spirit of critical enquiry that has led them to raise questions that their predecessors would shudder to ask. Social networking has given these women a collective identity and a transnational network. Critical debates in one corner are creating ripples across the world. Social networking sites have far broader and faster reach than the sermons of the mullahs. It will no longer be possible to subjugate these empowered women, particularly when they are enlightened not just about Islam but all religions and creeds and several modern disciplines. The new Muslim women no longer have to depend on their local mullahs for clarification on religious issues. The internet gives them access to the most authentic information. The intellect of these women has an independent identity; many of them are so prodigious that they can participate in rigorous debates on the varied aspects of Islam. It is these women who are imparting coherence to their communities and their faith.

Young people have varied motivations at different stages of their lives. These are ever-changing and dynamic depending on their socio-economic conditions, geography, age, and peers. The young generation's context, changing needs, and lived realities determine how we harness their talents and empower them for future roles. The youth must be capable of self-organising while being resilient and sustainable so that young people can assume the responsibility of identifying problems and solutions. However, mentoring young people must be provided and is not restricted to community-related work. They want a space to share their feelings, anxieties, and fears about the future with us and with one another. Women organisations are trying to create balance—a few systems and processes can work as a starting point; beyond that, usually, the girls can reach out to their mentors when they need help. It allows room for flexibility and adaptability, making them the decision-makers.

For those working with young people, the most critical piece of the puzzle is to stay aware of their needs and react accordingly. Young people should feel that they are learning something from the community they are a part of. Most people join these communities to develop their skills; some do it for a sense of belonging, and a few others to take up the cause of their community. It is easy to push the cause upon them because that's what the metrics demand. But to keep young people engaged, we have first to prioritise their learning and then attach the cause to this learning.

The backlash against the west

Turkey is the most glaring example of a backlash against Westernization's debasement of social norms. Turkey's liberalism was a legacy of the republic's founder, Mustafa Kemal Ataturk, an aggressive secularist who gave women unprecedented rights in the Muslim world (even if he found it hard to accept women as equals in his life). Men and women have never been considered adversaries by Islam. In 1923, Kemal Ataturk carved the Turkish Republic out of the Islamic Ottoman Empire, abandoning Arabic, initially even in the call to prayer, forcing the Muslim brotherhoods underground, and forbidding religious instruction in the schools. The Turkish republicans blamed Islam for the weakness of its state and for the Ottomans' inability to stand up to the armed might and wealth of the West. Women's subordination and segregation were, for them, emblems of Islam's backwardness. It was the kind of male power the Turkish nationalists wanted to change. The Turkish nationalists saw the Ottomans through Western eyes as too enslaved made passive and feminized by the way they were able to control women. The new Civil Code abolished polygamy and the right of husbands to unilateral divorce. In 1934, the Turkish Republic proclaimed its modernity by granting women the right to vote on the one hand and by forbidding their veiling on the other.

In a climate where Muslims constantly face a 'clash of civilisations' and the West pursues evolving a strategy of perpetual war with Muslim countries, there is a fundamental need to dehumanize the 'enemy'. The overemphasis on Muslim men's perceived misogyny overshadows the complete lack of scrutiny of the West's oppression against Muslim women. The strategies of the so-called Western brigade of women's emancipation are a part of the ideological war that is going on between neo-colonial elements in the West and Islamic societies. The aim is not to emancipate the women from presumed slavery but to reinforce

Western imperialism and mobilise consent for the ongoing wars against Muslim countries.

It is clear that Muslim women's empowerment, like many other accomplishments, cannot be achieved by the imposition of cultural currents and triggering impulses from the outside. Within these conservative communities, men and women must find the justification to allow women a fuller societal role so that they can record noteworthy milestones. Increasingly, they are finding those reasons within paradigmatic Islam. Like men, women deserve to be free because, in today's increasingly global world, everyone has higher stakes than ever to make their lives fuller and more empowered,

Islam teaches humans to promote balance in all aspects of life to lead a life of moderation. As humans, we are affected by our culture and traditions; political, economic, and psychological experiences shape our attitudes and behaviours and separate and divide us. Consequently, our world views and religious views differ from place to place, era to era, and across cultures, thereby continuing to irresponsibly link religion, in this case, Islam, to the oppression of women. The alleged retrograde practices of the community take the world's focus away from understanding the overwhelming problems of the Muslim world and the cause of its troubles. It provides an easy scapegoat for those looking to legitimize their illegitimate actions, which are detrimental to humanity. It is one of the reasons for this unnecessary bitterness over plainly innocuous symbols like *hijab*, which have culturally bonded these cultures over the years.

At its very core, Islam prescribes the principles of justice and equity for peace and human development. The same root word of Islam originates in the word *salaam* (peace). Islam is a universal religion that speaks to humanity. In his last great address at Arafat, the Prophet Muhammad described his philosophy: decrying barriers between people. For him, Islam transcended caste, colour, and race divisions. "All mankind is from

Adam and Eve, an Arab has no superiority over a non-Arab nor a non-Arab has any superiority over an Arab; also a white has no superiority over a black nor does a black have any superiority over a white except by good action."(Farewell sermon of Prophet Muhammad (peace be upon him). Muslim women are not just enlightened and responsive to the new political currents sweeping the world but have the same innovative traits that make them attuned to their Qura'nic obligations. They have been able to evolve approaches that meet both their secular and religious commitments.

The role of Islamophobia

Islam is arguably the most discussed religion in the West today, in both media and society. The plight of Muslim women is probably the most controversial topic of these debates despite women having morphed amazingly. Women are exposed to organized education for the first time and are now enlightened enough to channel their cultural, parental and religious practices and beliefs. Their scepticism on various issues is an understandable reaction from a minority community that has remained pawned in a bewildering welter of ideologies. Muslim communities, and much of the focus on women by those who see Islam as inherently part of the problem If not the whole issue — is contentious and challenging that Muslim women face. Modesty has much to do with clothes and shouldn't be a compulsion. Freedom is about having the choice to do and wear what you want; banning clothing would only counter that freedom and would be counterproductive for all stakeholders.

Women do not accept that being feminist means being Western and argue that Western women should be respectful of other paths to social change. They believe that Western thinkers and practitioners must reconsider their assumptions about the role of Islam in women's rights and must approach this subject with a more nuanced lens that examines the theme at a granular level. They must understand the necessity of recognizing and consciously accepting the broad cultural differences between Western and non-Western conceptions of autonomy and respecting social standards that reflect non-Western values.

They are asserting their Islamic feminists insist that Islam, at its core, is progressive for women and supports equal opportunities for both men and women. These two genders can never be adversaries as they must play contemporary roles. They are arguing for women's rights within an Islamic discourse. Some leading proponents are men—distinguished scholars who contend that Islam was radically egalitarian for its time and remains so in many of its texts. Islamic feminists claim that Islamic law evolved in ways detrimental to women, not due to any inevitability but because of selective interpretation of the Qur'an by patriarchal leaders who wanted to keep the women subjugated. Across the Muslim world, Islamic feminists are combing through centuries of Islamic philosophy to highlight the more progressive aspects of their religion. They seek accommodation between a modern role for women and the Islamic values that reconcile the two ends of the spectrum.

Almost every woman has an unsettling story about the difficulties of being a woman in public — whether it's a stranger walking behind them too closely, verbal cruelty, unwanted sexual advances or physical attacks. But for Muslim women, these isolated incidents of misogyny or violence have taken on an additional, ugly edge amid a surge of anti-Muslim policy proposals, and the year 2015 had the highest number of anti-Muslim hate crimes — five times the pre-9/11 rate. And although the venom of anti-Muslim sentiment is against both men and women, it is a particularly gendered crisis. Women bear the brunt of Islamophobic prejudice.

Women who wear *hijab* and *niqab* are visible representations of Islam. They face a significant risk of exposure to discrimination, harassment and attacks. Although Muslim men and women may both suffer from a presumption of guilt, women experience the additional presumption of victimhood. They're looked upon as recognizable representatives of religion to be feared and passive targets of male dominance. In turn, the r absurd status of Muslims as both villains and victims drives not only discrimination, harassment and hate crimes. Still, it promotes cynical policy proposals crafted to help Islamophobes, which are rooted in stereotypes and anti-Muslim bias.

We have a long road ahead to realize full and equal rights, but it's not Islam that holds us back. Its pervasive prejudice and discrimination permeate all facets of life. Just as it's intellectually dishonest to believe that a posse of police forcing a Muslim woman to remove her burkini on a crowded beach is a sign of progress for women, it's immoral to continue to allow anti-Muslim bias to close the doors of opportunity to Muslims, particularly the females.

Muslim women find themselves trapped between a rock and a hard place — a trap presenting near-impossible obstacles for exposing sexual violence. The Rock is an Islamophobic right wing in other cultures that is all too eager to demonize Muslim men. The media typically jumps to reports of misconduct by Muslim men to their Muslinnesss and Islam as a faith rather than to their maleness and the power with which patriarchy rewards it around the globe. Many Muslim women have been reluctant to discuss this Tariq Ramadan case because, in part, they don't want to feed into elements of the media's Islamophobic and racist framing of these allegations,

It is the harassers and assaulters who make women look bad, not the women who have every right to expose crimes against them. Muslims continue to venerate Muslim male scholars who give them incredible and often unchecked power. As a feminist, a woman's life should not be allowed to be influenced by the belief that religion and culture mustn't justify the subjugation of women, Even when women are held guilty of giving ammunition to the Islamophobic right in the struggle between "community" and "women", Muslims always choose the women. It is exhausting those Muslim women's voices, and their bodies are reduced to proxy battlefields by the demonises and defenders of Muslim men.

Muslims need to look inward

Muslims need to look at themselves realistically instead of focusing on their imagined selves. The Prophet was centuries ahead of the men of his time in his attitudes towards women, and not surprisingly, after he died, men started rolling back his reforms. The Prophet may have been too advanced for the mindset of seventh-century men. Still, his compassion for women is the model Muslims must emulate today. Like their counterparts in other creeds, Muslim women have undoubtedly emerged as an empowered community and have dramatically morphed to incredible levels of accomplishment. They believe that Islam empowered them with foundational Islamic texts, but their interpretation through patriarchal lenses has disallowed men to see what is suitable for the entire Islamic society.

Women are now elbowing their way into politics, civil society and universities. Despite the present cultural and political obstacles, they are finding opportunities to raise their voices and steer their societies. They feel the key is to do so within Islamic paradigms. There is a need to engage in Islam from a position of Western feminism to ensure that Muslim women have access to the knowledge that can help them negotiate their paths within the Islamic paradigm.

Through their knowledge and understanding of their scriptures and modern sciences, women can assert their rights and challenge patriarchal interpretations of Islam. While giving priority to a literal, puritanical reading of the Qur'an, they are relentlessly working to discard the historical reality of the Muslim world in favour of the ideal society of Prophet Muhammad and his companions. Their unifying vision has made it possible for them to morph into collective action.

It is clear that Muslim women's empowerment, like many things, cannot be imposed on a country or a culture from the outside. Men and women within these conservative communities must find their reasons and justifications to allow women a fuller societal role. Increasingly, they are finding those reasons within Islam. Like men, women deserve to be free. In today's increasingly global world, the stakes are higher for everyone. Societies that invest in and empower women are on a virtuous cycle. They become more prosperous, stable, better governed, and less prone to fanaticism. Countries that limit women's educational and employment opportunities and their political voices get stuck in a downward spiral. They are impoverished, more fragile, have higher levels of corruption, and are more prone to extremism.

A most unforeseen development of modern history is the positive and seismic changes in Muslim women who have bolstered their position in several spheres. The women are not shunned by Muslim men nor prohibited from areas that are purely Muslim domains. Muslim women are no longer consenting to embrace a restrictive, seemingly sexist religious lifestyle. It is possible to reclaim the positive messages in the Qur'an and Islamic history and craft an indigenous Muslim feminism that can serve as a riposte to its Western counterpart.

Liberal women are no longer endangered and are far from becoming extinct; they are spawning in droves. The brightest hope for positive developments in this direction comes from black chadors of devout Iranian women who are camouflaging themselves and whose unquestioning adherence to religious rules gives them high ground to present their case for women's rights even though they have leveraged that position sparingly. Across South Asia, they are slowly becoming resilient through skill development and livelihood generation to stand up to patriarchal practices undermining their dignity in literate societies. We must give them sufficient leeway to pursue their objectives and emerge as wage givers rather than just wage earners. They are imparting coherence to their faith.

The performance of these women is no longer suboptimal, nor do they remain confined to being part of the supportive structure for men. Muslim women are an empowered community like their counterparts in other creeds. Several women are encouraging their philanthropic husbands to channel and expand the reach of capital into women's menstrual hygiene products targeted at feminine hygiene. Women entrepreneurs amplify their marketing reach for low-cost, women-friendly products for overall hygiene to create more impact outcomes. It has mainly been possible due to the ramping of infrastructure. We need to activate logistics and infrastructure further so that we are in a position to reach more such women.

The localisation of Islam

Cultures that arose since then have been characterized by customs and localized leanings more than genuine Islamic values. The lives of the first Muslim women represent valuable models, transcending time and physical boundaries; therefore, these models can serve as powerful, culturally authentic tools in advancing the human rights agenda toward increased female empowerment in the political, social and economic spheres in Muslim communities. The contributions of these women to the Muslim community are undeniable; to some, they even appear almost mythical. They are mistakenly subscribing to the erroneous notion that contemporary Muslim women cannot attain such stature. However, these women represent others who lived, fought, learned, worked and led during Islam's foundational period and beyond. Their male companions, the caliphs who assumed Muslim rule following the demise of Prophet Muhammad, treated them with respect, admiration and appreciation as equals. Society needs to actively pursue female society's progress; otherwise, complacency can lead to regression.

Muslim women have proven resourceful, creative, and dedicated to claiming ownership of and responsibility for their faith individually and communally. It is despite the challenges they have often faced in gaining access to the appropriate religious training facilities and establishing credibility with the conservative male religious establishment. Today, Muslim women are active in Qur'anic study circles, mosque-based activities, community services sponsored by religious organizations, and Islamic education as students and teachers. There are a bolstering number of female Qur'an reciters, Islamic lawyers, and professors of Islamic studies. This dynamism has found a morphic force in their commitment to building a healthy and cultured family.

Even in its nascent stages, Islam sought to elevate women and delineate them as independent agents of free will. Twenty-four women appear in the Qur'an in various forms and for multiple purposes; 18 of those women appear as minors, the primary five being: Mary, mother of Jesus; Bilquis, the queen of Sheba, Mary's mother Hannah; Hawa (Eve) and Umm Musa, the mother of Moses. All of them are potent examples of the tremendous potential of women.

Women empowerment

Contemporary Muslim women's activism now plays an interpretive role within the Islamic tradition. It focuses on three key aspects of religious life: reciting, teaching and interpreting the Qur'an. There is a diversity of voices in debates concerning a more empowering role for women, some conservative, others self-crafted "progressive," who claim an equal position for both sexes and others affirming specific unique roles for men and women. Vibrant, passionate, and often contentious, these debates are among the most important in defining Islam and the place of women in the future. They consider men and women as equals, not adversaries.

Although there have been significant strides in including women's voices in Islamic debates, challenges remain, particularly in widely accepted conservative approaches that have diluted the vitality and vibrancy of the reformist zeal, which has already ceased the broadening trajectory. Muslim women have successfully fought back, networked and are now engaged in global dialogue and cooperation with other women. However, the ultimate success of grafting women's voices in interpreting Islam requires their acceptance by society as equally capable interpreters alongside their male colleagues. Many Muslim men support and encourage this dialogue within Islam, which they believe is critical for the overall Islamic civilization. Several male groups motivate women in this endeavour.

The advancement of women has taken place in almost all spheres. In Egypt, women comprise a more significant percentage of engineering and medical faculties than in the US. Their newly acquired freedom has complemented their concerted efforts in several fields. Women have already pushed the envelope so far and are certainly on the cusp of a gradually evolving revolution. There have been sincere efforts to bring more diverse yet unique perspectives and unearth fresh ideas to synthesise the existing approaches of women in nurturing ecosystems to deliver change.

In the present century, the combined spread of literacy, the availability and promotion of public education for both girls and boys, the expansion of job opportunities for women and the rising number of conversions to Islam from other religious traditions, particularly in the West, have added to the desire of Muslim women for greater empowerment in the practice and interpretation of their faith.

As in other areas of life, Muslim women have proven to be resourceful, creative and dedicated to claiming ownership and responsibility for their faith individually and communally. In the face of challenges, they are gaining access to the appropriate religious training facilities and establishing credibility with the male religious establishments. We are witnessing the onset of a new Muslim feminist revolution. Their unsavoury past is now far behind.

Modern Muslim women are active in Qur'anic study circles, mosque-based activities, and community services sponsored by religious organizations. They are dominating Islamic education as students and teachers. There are many female Qur'an reciters, Islamic lawyers and professors of Islamic studies worldwide. This process also helps to shake up some traditionally held cultural misconceptions. All Muslims can further activate the reform process by re-examining the lives of the very first Muslim women who lived during Islam's formative period, not just as historical figures but as modern Islamic models. While many Muslims around the world learn about such exceptional Muslim women in school, their relevance to the contemporary context is undetermined. Most critical aspects of their lives have not been remodelled or replicated to keep their character and roles alive. Through learning and celebrating their examples, men and women can better understand and build upon notions of the role of Muslim women icons in a culturally authentic paradigm.

The empowerment of Muslim women

The Qur'anic description of marriage suggests closeness, mutuality, and equality, but ancient tradition defined a husband as his wife's god in earthly terms. The Qur'an provides rights that address the common grievances of women, such as the lack of freedom to make decisions for themselves and their inability to earn an income. That can make them financially independent. The challenge for all women, and especially Muslim women, is to move from a reactive mindset, in which women must assert their autonomy against patriarchal opposition, to a proactive attitude, in which they can speak of themselves as independent human beings who can articulate their thoughts emanating from their minds and spirits as well as bodies.

Muslim women have surmounted many complex challenges, and several of them have assumed strategic roles in giant corporations and have been instrumental in handling several vital political roles.

Although traditionally excluded from the male public domain, Muslim women are now privately involved in the study and oral transmission of Islamic source texts (the Qur'an and *hadith*). In modern times, they have entered both secular and religious forms of education with extraordinary devotion and commitment, supporting their long-standing role as family educators and moral exemplars, as well as training for professional careers in the workplace outside the home. Muslim women are now an empowered community, and they can't be able to retreat from any deterrent as they are negotiating from a position of strength.

A comparison may mean little outside the cultural context, but it is essential to point out that, until 100 years ago, western women had virtually no rights in law or practice. Over 1,000 years before the first European suffragette, Islam gave women far-reaching rights and a defined status. However, these Western attitudes have undoubtedly helped to stimulate discussions of the problem in Muslim urban society, thereby revealing the gap between the talk of the Islamic ideal and the actual situation of women.

Women emerged as the centrepiece of the Western narrative of Islam in the 19th century and, notably, in the later 19th century as Europeans established themselves as colonial powers in Muslim countries. Their narratives simultaneously and hypocritically perpetuated the Victorian English narrative that European men were superior to women while denigrating Muslim culture for being oppressive to women.

Muslim women do not certainly share the Western notion of feminism. First of all, there are multiple causes of discrimination against women, and religion is but one. Secondly, gender relations explain women's options in all societies. Thirdly, it is futile to focus on misery elsewhere to escape from the realities of our own lives. Fourth, the issue of power remains crucial for understanding gender inequality in any society. It is these women who are imparting coherence to their faith.

An empowered generation

We now have a curious and empowered generation that will not easily accept rules and codes without reasoning and arguing on every strand before embracing the entire culture. A heartening development is that, unlike earlier times, when only those who had finally retired from all worldly responsibilities would make the hajj pilgrimage, the youth actively participates in this most potent Islamic exercise.

Hajj is a revolutionary experience that radically transforms one's mindset and provides a correct perspective of Islam. Exposure to a composite global culture gives a refreshing perspective to the pilgrim. Few Muslim women outside the urban areas may want to behave like Western women. The high rate of divorce and sexual frustration are expected consequences of the reckless drive to equate the sexes and "free" sexual relationships.

Muslim women maintain a respectful distance from males as a part of their modesty, but that does not compel them to be defensive in their vibrant dynamism. They are no longer victims of timidity and have overcome their earlier vulnerability to prejudicial social norms. They also often shrug off the disrespectful annoyance of strangers. They were once quite hesitant and reticent but are now swift and decisive in their life. They have sparked their inner abilities and are pushing the frontiers of possibilities.

The controversy around women's dress

Women's dress is a favourite subject of religious bigots of all hues with their notions of morality. Everyone wants to talk about the "moral values" attached to women's dress or the "purity" of their attire that "go against the parameters" laid down by the moral police. Nobody is interested in discussing the more critical issue — the morality or purity of one's conscience. Today, a woman's character is identified d by her clothes. Natural markers like piety and morality have lost their relevance.

Modesty is a virtue for both men and women. A connection between spiritual life and modesty exists because that virtue is not just about outward appearances. Instead, it is tolerance, first and foremost, about the inward state of having modesty before God – awareness of divine presence everywhere and at all times that leads to propriety (within oneself and in one's most private moments). Outward modesty means behaving in a way that maintains one's self-respect and the respect of others, whether in dress, speech or behaviour. Inward modesty means shying away from any character or quality offensive to God.

When it comes to women's clothes, everybody seems to be obsessed with them. More than a means to cover one's body, women's clothes have become a symbol of oppression for some and a mark of liberation for others. But, more peculiarly, garments are often used as a benchmark by conservative Muslims to judge the morality of a Muslim woman and her "Muslimness". There is still no such benchmark for Muslim men who owe a duty of modesty to the Qur'an, whose injunctions are as vital for men as they are for women. Indeed, judging by the discourse, one would assume that the primary religious duty of Muslim women is to observe "the dress code".

In the context of proper attire and conduct, the Qur'an forbids modesty on men, too and only when the men have attained that level of modesty should they feel justified in talking about the modesty of others. "Tell the believing men to lower their gaze (avoiding its concentration on a person's body, or a specific part of it) and to be mindful of their chastity; in this, they will be more considerate for their well-being and purity, and indeed God is fully aware of all that they do "(Q24: 30-31).

From certain imams insisting that earthquakes are caused by women not wearing proper dresses to muftis excommunicating Muslim women, the intellectual level of discourse that surrounds Muslim women is excruciating and is more or less concerned only with notions of modesty. By reducing Muslim women to their bodies and pretending that modesty is their primary religious duty, we strip them of their personhood.

In the view of the great liberal Islamic scholar Mohammad Asad, what the Qur'an requires of women is that they should be clothed "decently". Elaborating further, he states: "My interpolation of the word 'decently' reflects the interpretation of the phrase 'illa ma zahara minha' by several of the earliest Islamic scholars, and particularly by Al-Qiffal (quoted by Razi, one of Islam's greatest high priests), as 'that which a human being may openly show following prevailing custom (al-'adah al-jariyah)'."

Today's world is in a state of great upheaval. With gnawing problems such as toxic combinations of superstition, sectarianism, bigotry and patriarchy in Muslim-majority states, we cannot afford to divert all our attention to pedantic details of how to worship God "correctly". Suppose we are serious about preventing the so-called fitna (spiritual affliction). In that case, we must start addressing the issues that have long been glaring at us —society's attitude towards women.

Modesty permeates most monotheistic faiths

Modesty is not uniquely an Islamic requirement. It's also part of other monotheistic religions. For example, ultra-orthodox Jewish women wear wigs to cover their hair. Nuns wear apostolic as a sign of their religious consecration. Episcopalian women are supposed to wear hats to church. The Qur'anic view of an ideal society is that social and moral values have to be upheld by both Muslim men and women, and there is justice for all, that is, between men and women. The Qur'an asks women to behave with dignity and decorum, befitting a secure, self-respecting and self-aware human being rather than an insecure female who feels that her survival depends on her ability to attract or persuade those men who are interested not in her personality but only in her sexuality.

For women who observe *hijab*, it is not merely a piece of cloth or a symbol of defiance. Instead, it is a path that aids self-purification and nearness to their creator. It is a means to teach modesty. A veil is a genuine expression of a woman's religiosity. Paradoxically, women engaging in the modern world rely on the veil to signal to others that they will express their freedom. Veiling among Muslim women is modelled as a commitment mechanism that limits the temptation to deviate from religious norms of behaviour. The analysis suggests that veiling is a strategy for integration, enabling women to take up outside economic opportunities while preserving their reputation within the community. It accounts for the puzzling features of the new veiling movement.

Several university graduates, all in their mid-twenties and with careers ranging from journalism to teaching, have chosen in the past few years to wear the *hijab* (a scarf wrapped tightly around their heads to conceal every wisp of hair). Most strikingly, however, these women fluently and cogently articulate how they believe Islam has liberated and empowered them. The Islam they describe is a million miles away from that of the Taliban, let alone the Islam practised in many Muslim countries from Pakistan to Saudi Arabia. Still, they insist -and back up their points with Qur'anic references - that the Islam they first discovered when they were teenagers is faithful to the Prophet's teachings. They don't need Western feminism, which, they argue, developed as a reaction against the particular expression of Western patriarchy.

All women agree that this is one of the most significant sources of misunderstanding between Western feminists and Muslim women. They do not wish to express their sexuality in public and believe that its proper place is in the privacy of an intimate relationship. Sexuality is not to be used to assert power but to express love, they add. They hotly deny that veiling and modesty in public is a form of repression. It is not about the shame of the female body, as Western feminists sometimes insist, but about claiming privacy over their bodies. The Moroccan writer Fatima Mernissi ponders on how, in the West, women reclaiming their bodies have led to the public expression of their sexuality.

In contrast, in Islam, it is about modesty. The associations with shame and repression stem from the influence of the Christian tradition's hostility to sexuality and, hence, women and the legacy of confusion and guilt that has bequeathed Western society. Islam, on the other hand, has a healthy honesty and acceptance of human sexuality, which is evident in a wealth of detail in Islamic jurisprudence, they argue. Muslim women are straddling several roles without compromising their traditional modesty.

The unrelenting discourse that focuses only on the veil worn by Muslim women gives an oversimplified version of Islam's teachings. A woman can wear a *hijab* in the West as a sign of modesty yet embrace all of the rights and opportunities Western women enjoy. National policies and media discourses aside, there are endless millions of Muslim women who believe that covering their hair is religiously mandated, so they demonstrate their loyalty to Islam and their relationship with God.

To insist otherwise is to deny the agency, autonomy, and choice of these Muslim women. We can't cast the choices of the hundreds of millions of women who have worn the headscarf as somehow invalid, irrational, wrong, or backwards. Just as women should be free and empowered to choose not to wear the *hijab*, they must also be free and empowered to wear it if that's what they want. Through this knowledge, women can assert their rights and challenge patriarchal interpretations of slam. While giving priority to a literal, puritanical reading of the Qur'an, they want to discard the historical reality of the Muslim world in favour of the ideal society of Prophet Muhammad and his companions. Their unifying vision has made collective action possible.

Muslim society needs gender parity

The Qur'an's messages of equality resonated in the teaching that women and men have emerged from a single self and are each other's guides who have the mutual obligation to enjoin what is right and to forbid what is wrong. Women scholars taught judges and imams, issued fatwas, and travelled to distant cities. Some made lecture tours across the Middle East. None of the inspired women who were strong, vocal, and fighting for their rights during the era of the Prophet felt that their faith was at odds with their conviction that they, as women, should be equal citizens and not adversaries. Their message resonated with the broader society.

We must understand the necessity of recognising and consciously accepting the broad cultural differences between Western and non-Western conceptions of autonomy and respecting social standards that reflect non-Western values. Muslim women must work in full partnership with Muslim men, rejecting Western models of liberation but also, and more importantly, asserting their own. There is no denying the fact that the Muslim world has a significant amount of ground to cover to protect women's rights and freedoms, and the quest for gender equality remains paramount. There should be even the faintest thought that they can be adversaries. However, the idea that all Muslim women's liberation is a result of misogynist Muslim men is wide off the mark. After all, women's oppression manifests itself in several ways. Not all Muslim men are the oppressors.

The principle of equality has faded or erased over centuries of exegesis, and we need to contextualise our understanding of revelation to place ourselves in our postmodern era. Islam is constantly evolving and must participate in postmodernity. The Muslim religion will regain its dynamism through ijtihad (the effort to interpret the Qur'an).

There is a need for f "radical reform" and a dynamic conception of *sharī'ah* law, bearing in mind that the original revelation was grounded in a profoundly patriarchal context. The universality of the Qur'an is what allows for this approach. The "hermeneutics of the oneness of God" clearly underlines that inequalities between men and women are contrary to the message of Islam.

Muslim women's right to education

Education is universally accepted as the most potent and effective tool to achieve empowerment in any section of society. Although it is true that economic well-being also makes a significant contribution in this regard, the nature of positive change brought about by education ensures a position of dignity for the individual and the community, instilling a sense of confidence and self-worth. Social and economic status evolution is usually a natural outcome of good education.

Islam strongly encourages the education of women both in religious and social domains. There is no priority for men over women concerning the right to education. Both are equally encouraged to acquire education. Indeed, all the Qur'anic verses relate to education and advocate acquiring knowledge for t men and women alike.

According to the Qur'an, learning is an unending process. The entire universe is made subservient to man, the agent of God, who has to abide by the truth and not narrow notions of hereditary customs and beliefs:" We did not create the heavens and the earth, and all between them merely in sport. We made them only for just ends, but most of humanity does not understand.'(Q15:85) The verses in the Qur'an that urge people to learn and observe nature outnumber all those related to prayer, fasting, and pilgrimage. Indeed, the first verse of the Qur'an was a command to the Prophet to read (Iqra):

"'Read! In the name of your Lord, who created man from clots of congealed blood. Read! Your Lord is the Most Bountiful One, Who taught by the pen, taught man what he did not know' (Q 96: 1).

The Qur'an exhorts Muslims to ask God to increase their knowledge (Q20:114). It underscores the importance of knowledge: "God elevates by several degrees the ranks of those of you who believe and those who know.'" (58:11). The Qur'an even asks rhetorically in one passage, "… Say: Are those equal, those who know and those who do not know?' It is those who endowed with understanding that receive admonition." (Q39:9.)The Prophet emphasized the importance of knowledge and education. Among his most famous statements on the subject are the following:

- Scholars are the heirs of prophets (Al-Bukhari),

- All that is in heaven and earth asks God's forgiveness for a scholar (Ibn Majah),

- Pursuit of knowledge is the duty of every Muslim

- Safwaan Ibn 'Assal Al-Muradi came to the Prophet in the mosque and said, "Oh Messenger of Allah, I have come seeking knowledge." The Prophet told him: "Welcome, O seeker of knowledge! Truly, the angels surround the seeker of knowledge with their wings, gathering around him in ranks one above the other, until they reach the first heaven, out of love for that which he seeks."

Following the all-embracing idea of tawhid– oneness – when Islam elevated women physically by abolishing female infanticide, it could not overlook the need for their mental and spiritual elevation. By contrast, Islam would view the neglect of these dimensions as virtually equivalent to murdering their personality. The Qur'an says: 'They are losers who besottedly have slain their children by keeping them in ignorance'. (Q 6:141)

Both the Qur'an and the *Sunnah* (a collection of the Prophet's prescriptions) advocate the rights of women and men equally to seek knowledge. The Qur'an commands all Muslims to exert effort in the pursuit of knowledge irrespective of their sex. It constantly encourages Muslims to read, think, contemplate and learn from the signs of Allah in nature: 'Are the wise and the ignorant equal? Truly, none will take heed but men of understanding. (Q 39: 9) 'Allah will raise to high ranks those that have faith and knowledge among you. He is conscious of all your actions. (Q 58: 9). 'Say: Lord, increase me in knowledge'. (Q 20: 113).

Women's eligibility for judicial roles

In Muslim history, there have been three juristic interpretations of textual sources regarding the appointment of women as judges:

1. The majority Sunni view (*jumhur*) among the founding jurists (*mujtahid mutlaq*) of Imam Ash-Shafe'ii, Malik and Ibn Hanbal was that women couldn't become judges. Because of an interpretation of Surah a Nisa'4:34, men are *qawwamuna*, or protectors of women.

However, there was also a minority view among the Malikis, led by Ibn al-Qasim al-Maliki, who believed that women could be appointed judges. The Ash-Shafe'iis also allowed the idea of women that women could act as judges when required in exigencies. Only the Hanbali School unanimously decided that women should not be appointed judges.

2. The minority Sunni view of Imam Abu Hanifah was that the authority of a judge is not valid unless the judge possesses the qualifications necessary for a witness. This opinion allows women to be judges in all cases involving capital punishment. It flows from Imam Abu Hanifah's interpretation of Surah al-Baqarah (Q2:228) on women's eligibility to witness commercial transactions.

3. The individual views of jurists such as al-Tabari and Ibn Hazm stated that a woman can be a judge in all cases without exception

as long as she fulfils the requirements for the position. It would appear to flow from reading the following verse: "Behold Allah bids you to deliver all that you unto those entitled to that, and whenever you judge between people, judge with justice. Verily most excellent is what Allah exhorts you to do: Allah is all-hearing, all-seeing" (Q 4:58).

6. THE QUEENS OF ISLAM

Oh, what a woman! Having all the virtues
Of the pious women, humble to their Lord;
Of the women who have memorized the Qur'an by heart
and who do extraIn prayers, alms-giving,
then recitation of the Qur'an,
defending the unjustly treated,
carrying the burdens of many responsibilities
She was a guardian of orphans and widows,
a pillar of the community, ensuring harmony.
– Nana Asma'u, *Lamentation for A'ishah*

In a few circles, Islam evokes an image of anti-feminism. It goes ignored that its first believer and financier was Khadijah, and its first martyr was Sumaiya. The first wave of feminism centred on demands for women's role in legislation and leadership in the early 19th century. Still, history fails to notice how Zainab binte Ali, a granddaughter of Prophet Muhammad, assumed the leadership role at Karbala centuries ago. Two of the few believers who took the pledge of allegiance at al-Aqabah were women, meaning they were part of the decision-making and pursuance. Women believers also accompanied men at wars, right on the battlefield and in assistance or planning. Muslim history is replete with women who have left their mark in their respective societies' religious, political or social spheres. They managed to do so not despite their Muslim identities but precisely because they believed in Islam.

The significant contribution of the Prophet's wives

Women are prominent figures in the history of Islam, from Prophet Muhammad's (peace be upon him) wives to his transformative policies about women that have made seismic changes in their lives, and women became increasingly expansive in their breadth as the empire grew. Muslim women transitioned to leadership positions in the Golden Age and were essential to early Islamic religious thought. As in most monotheistic religions, women were the first converts and were close to the Prophet, whose teachings are central to the faith.

From the beginning, women were at the heart of Islam, as the Prophet Muhammad's wife, Khadijah, an older divorcee and financially independent businesswoman became "the first Muslim." She was the first to believe in her husband's revelations. Their daughter, Fatima bint Muhammad, commonly known as Fatima al-Zahra, was also very close to the Prophet, who fondly loved her and was very intimate with her. He considered her the most outstanding woman of all time, and she is a paradigmatic example of Muslim womanhood because of her compassion, generosity and ability to mitigate their enduring suffering.

Legal scholars often consulted women because they memorized the teachings of Prophet Muhammad, wrote petitions, entered opinions in the public sphere, and served as valuable resources for biographers, compilers of dictionaries, and debates of the day. To establish authenticity and authority, scholars kept track of lineages, noting which scholars mentored which schools and recorded "chains of transmission." Oral histories that retold these chains strengthened the legitimacy of Islamic history.

Women transitioned and contributed significantly to the early development of the Muslim community. Women were the first to learn of Prophet Muhammad's initial revelation. They later played an essential role in compiling all the revelations from written and oral sources into a single, authoritative text. Women were custodians of vital secrets, including the location of the Prophet's hiding place when he was terrified of his likely surrender during his plans to attack Mecca. The Prophet often consulted women and gave serious attention to their opinions seriously. His first wife, Khadijah, was his chief adviser and first and foremost supporter. His third and youngest wife, A'isha, was a well-known authority in medicine, history, and rhetoric. Together with Umm Salama, she played a crucial role in compiling the traditions of the Prophet, considered one of the primary sources of Islamic jurisprudence. For a considerable time, she acted as a judge, correcting and guiding the leaders of her time.

During the lifetime of the Prophet Muhammad, women endured persecution, exile, and martyrdom side by side with their male counterparts. On the battlefield, women carried water to the wounded, tended to the injured, and even participated in the fighting. The most sacred place on earth for Muslims, Makkah (Mecca), was founded by Hagar, the wife of Abraham. Her diligence and faith were as remarkable as her celebrated husband. The Prophet and his companions sought their advice (*mashwara*) before making the most critical decisions.

Islamic tradition praises Asiya, Mary, Khadijah, and Fatima as the women who provided monumental examples of excellence in faith. Imam Ahmad recorded that Ibn Abbas said: "The Messenger of God drew four lines on the ground and said, 'Do you know what these lines represent? The best among the women of Paradise are Khadijah bint Khuwaylid, Fatima bint Muhammad (peace be upon him), Maryam bint Imran, and Asiya bint Muzahim.'"

Asiya: The daughter of Muzahim, wife of the Pharaoh

Mary: The virgin mother of Prophet Jesus, peace be upon him

Khadijah: The first wife of Prophet Muhammad,

Fatima: The fifth child of Prophet Muhammad and Khadijah

While Mary, the mother of Jesus, is the only woman eluded to by name in the Qur'an, the other three are alluded to in the sayings of the Prophet Muhammad. Asiya was Pharaoh's wife and the one who protected Moses in the palace from the wrath of her furious husband.

Mary is the epitome of purity and submission; she gave birth to Jesus miraculously, and she stood firm against all kinds of slanders and accusations. Khadijah was the first believer in the Prophet Muhammad (peace be upon him). She spent all her fortune on her husband's cause, including her life. Fatima, the Prophet's daughter, is the person through whom the Prophet's generation continues.

In Islam, God is not gendered, physically located, or carnal. There is no original sin – the two genders were "created from a single soul", which is entirely pure and good. To know God, at least 99 attributes or names of both genders are equally critical in learning about and approaching the divine. Both genders have their own free will and have their minds and must make their contribution. Qur'anic and Islamic narratives have plenty of examples of such women: Mary's Immaculate Conception is a strong vision of a woman raising a child as the head of the family without any men present. Hagar raises her son while her husband is away, and Aasiya, the wife of Pharaoh, stands up to her dictatorial, bloodthirsty husband. All of them are role models for both men and women. Neither is marriage supposed to be subjugation for women, but completion and partnership for both man and woman. Every man held up as an example has a woman by his side (or you could argue it is vice versa) who is exemplary in her own right: Adam with Eve, Rachael with Moses and Prophet Muhammad with his wife, Khadijah.

Biographies of distinguished women, especially in the Prophet's household, show that women enjoyed autonomy in early Islam, and they relentlessly pursued this freedom to recharge the Islamic revolution. The women about whom substantial details are available are Khadījah, the Prophet's first wife; ʿĀʾisha, his favourite wife; Fāṭima, his youngest daughter; Zaynab, his granddaughter; Sukaynah, his great-granddaughter; and ʿĀʾisha bint Ṭalhah, the niece of her namesake. Women gave sanctuary (*jiwār*) to men. Women owned and disposed of property and engaged in commercial transactions, and wealthy women in the Islamic medieval period patronized large-scale architectural projects. Like men, women were encouraged to seek knowledge, which they pursued in the Prophet's home. Women were instructors and pupils throughout Islamic history. The Prophet's favourite wife, ʿĀʿisha, was a well-known authority in medicine, history, and rhetoric and is noted for the number of *hadīths* that cite her as a source.

The feminist approach of the Prophet

Women played a pivotal role in the canonization of the Qur'an. The community sought women's endorsement and allegiance during the nomination of the successors to the Prophet. They exercised influential roles in advising Muslim rulers on issues such as military leave for soldiers or even admonishing them if a particular policy contradicted the spirit of the Qur'an. We consistently see brilliant examples of accomplishment by Muslim women throughout Islamic history and worldwide. Women from Africa to India to the Persian Gulf distinguished themselves as foremost Islamic scholars, controllers of gargantuan public endowments, and even ruling queens of their countries. Their legacies, at several epochs of history, acquired global stature. These women represent many others who lived, fought, learned, worked and led during and after the foundational period of Islam. Their male companions and the caliphs who assumed Muslim rule following the demise of Prophet Muhammad treated them with respect, admiration, and appreciation -- and as equals. They relied on these able women's knowledge, wisdom and valuable insights in various spheres of governance.

Indeed, the unique privilege of being the first Muslim goes to Khadijah al-Kubra, the Prophet's first wife. She was older than him, wealthier, and from an aristocratic background. Previously widowed, Khadijah initiated the marriage proposal, too. She remained the ideal wife, consoling Mohammed in loss, encouraging him in his great mission, and never doubting him when he announced his message to the world. He was inconsolable when she died.

Of Khadijah, the Prophet said:

The best of the world's women (Al Bukhari)

A'isha's scholarship and valour matched Khadijah's munificence and steadiness. She was a highly respected authority in Islamic jurisprudence. A'ishah was the daughter of Abu Bakr, one of Prophet Muhammad's (peace be upon him) closest companions and one of the first converts to Islam, and the first to assume leadership as part of the close circle of the caliphate over the Muslim community.

A'isha has inspired Muslim women for centuries. She was a scholar, a poet, a jurist, a politician and a military commander who led armies. She was the one woman whom the Prophet was closest to, the one he chose to spend his final hours with, the one who cradled the Prophet's head as he passed away. It was in A'isha's arms that he died in 632 CE.

A'isha enjoys a highly deferential status in Islamic history. She combined spirituality, activism and knowledge and remains an ideal role model for Muslim women. Some of A'isha's protégés were extraordinarily brilliant. Among her women pupils was Umrah bint Abdur Rahman who is one of the trustworthy narrators of *hadith* and is said to have acted as A'isha's secretary.

Wives of the Prophet

According to the biographer Ibn Hisham (d. 834), the Prophet Muhammad married thirteen women. Khadijah bint Khuwaylid, Sawdah bint Zama, A'ishah bint Abi Bakr, *Hafsah*hh bint Umar, Zaynab bint Khuzaymah, Hind bint Abi Umayya (known as Umm Salama), Zaynab bint Jahsh, Maymuna bint al-Harith, and Juwayriyah bint al-Harith were Arab; six of them were from Quraysh, and the rest were from other tribes. Safiyah bint Huyay was from a Jewish tribe. Rayhanah bint Zayd was from a Jewish tribe as well, although there is some doubt regarding her marriage to the Prophet; Asma bint al-Numan and Amra bint Yazid were both divorced by the Prophet before consummation. At his death in 632, the Prophet left nine wives and a consort, Maryam the Copt. The wives of the Prophet are called "Mothers of the Faithful" (Umm al-Muminin) in the Qur'an (Q33:6) and are prohibited from marriage to other men after the Prophet's death (Q33:53). They are rare moral exemplars for Muslim women. A'ishah and Umm Salama, in particular, reported numerous *hadiths* from Muhammad and thus played a decisive role in shaping the *Sunnah*. These divinely inspired men became what they

Prophet Muhammad's first marriage was to Khadijah bint Khuwaylid in 595, when he was 25, and she was either 28 or 41. She was his only wife until her death in 619 (the Year of Sorrow) ended their 24-year-long marriage. After Khadijah, Muhammad went on to marry ten women: Sawdah bint Zam'ah in 619; A'isha bint Abu Bakr in 623; *Hafsah*h bint Umar, Zaynab bint Khuzayma, and Hind bint Abi Umayya in 625; Zaynab bint Jahsh in 627; Juwayriya bint al-Harith and Ramla bint Abi Sufyan ibn Harb in 628; and Safiyya bint Huyayy and Maymunah bint al-Harith in 629. Among the Prophet's wives were those who brought him the enviable gifts of political alliances, social prestige, enchanting beauty and mature charm: A'isha, the young and vibrant daughter of Abu Bakr. Prophet Muhammad's right-hand man and Islam's first caliph made her way more profound than any of the rest. With her faith and support, Khadijah steadied Muhammad's (peace be upon him) troubled spirit on the threshold of his prophetic career.

1. Khadijah bint Khuwaylid (556 – 619 CE)

The first wife of the Prophet was Khadijah bint Khuwaylid. Khadijah was born in Mecca some 68 years before the Hijra. Her father was Khuwaylid b. Asad was from the clan of Asad, the sub-clan of Quraysh. Her mother, Fāṭima bint Zāida was from the clan of ʿAmir b. Luʾayy. Before her marriage to Prophet Muhammad, she had been married twice from her first marriage with Abū Hāla Hind b. Nabbāsh had two children named Hind and Hāla from her second marriage with ʿAtıq b. ʿAidh, she had a daughter named Hind. After her second husband's death, some of the notables of Quraysh offered proposals for marriage because she was rich, beautiful, and noble. But she did not accept these proposals.

Mecca was unsuitable for agriculture due to its hot climate, rocky terrain, and lack of water. For this reason, the Quraysh population traded to earn a living. Having inherited much wealth from her deceased husband, Khadijah was also a part of the Meccan business elite. She would hire men to work for her or partner with trusted people. She made a partnership agreement with Prophet Muḥammad, a reliable person and put her vassal, Maysara, to assist him. The trade caravan led by Prophet Muhammad went to Damascus and returned with significant profit. Khadıjah learned about Prophet Muhammad's work ethic, reliability and honesty from her vassal, Maysara. Impressed by these traits, she proposed to Prophet Muḥammad, who accepted the offer. The Prophet was barely twenty-five when they married. Khadijah, on the other hand, was forty years old.

Nevertheless, some rumours would downgrade her age to thirty-seven or even twenty-eight reasonable numbers. Their marriage lasted for about twenty-five years. They had two sons named Qāsim and ʿAbd Allāh and four daughters named Zaynab, Ruqayya, Umm Kulthūm and Fāṭima. The marriage of the Prophet and Khadıjah rested on love, respect, and devotion; Khadijah supported her husband in all adversities. She cared for Prophet Muhammad and supported him during his periodic contemplating sessions in the Cave of Ḥirā' before the Qur'an commenced revelation.

Prophet Muhammad may not have received a visit from the angel Gabriel without his wife's business acumen. Khadijah ran a successful caravanning business which supported The Prophet throughout his regular spiritual retreats. According to tradition, the Prophet returned to his wife in shock after his divine revelation. Khadijah wrapped him in a blanket, calmed his nerves, and told him, "You will be the prophet of your people." She continued by his side, despite her husband's teachings threatening their family's lives and livelihood.

Khadijah comforted the Prophet with the following words: "I swear that Allah will never embarrass or upset you. Because you take care of your relatives and speak the truth, help the incapable, supporters, entertain guests and assist the oppressed." Khadijah then took the Prophet to her cousin Waraqa b. Nawfal is a rare scholar of both the Bible and the Torah (The New and the Öld Testaments). Waraqa believed that the angel who appeared to Prophet Muḥammad was none other than the angel of revelation who served the last awaited Prophet. According to tradition, Maawfal assured Prophet Muhammad that his call to prophecy and message were genuinely from God. He acknowledged that Prophet Muhammad's recitation of revelation was identical to the revelation given to Moses. He prophesied that Prophet Muhammad, like other prophets before him, would be rejected, fought against, and slandered.

Khadijah was the first person to believe Prophet Muhammad's message. Moreover, she consulted her cousin Waraqah ibn Nawfal, who likened Prophet Muhammad's revelations to Moses's, further providing Prophet Muhammad confidence in his revelations. Khadījah provided instrumental support in Prophet Muhammad's early prophethood. Her wealth allowed him the leisure to meditate, and she reassured him of the authenticity of his first revelations.

Khadījah provided instrumental support in Prophet Muhammad's early prophethood. Her wealth allowed him the leisure to meditate, and she reassured him of the authenticity of his first revelations. She never left the Prophet alone in the face of the ruthless persecution of the polytheist population of Mecca. During the years of boycott when

Muslims suffered under the cruel pagan embargo, she stood firmly by Muslims and did not hesitate to spend her wealth assisting them.

Khadijah died three years before the Hijra. The Prophet lost two crucial supports since his uncle Abū Ṭālib died three days before Khadijah's death. The Prophet did not marry another woman until Khadijah died. Although he married many women after Khadijah, he never forgot her. He commemorated her sacrifice and sincerity throughout his life.

Khadijah, perhaps, best defies the popular perception of a Muslim woman. A prominent businesswoman, she was neither oppressed, submissive, nor subjugated. On the contrary, she was a source of immense intimacy, strength, and comfort for Prophet Muhammad A'ishah, and her lively temperament and pert charm brought a refreshing romance. A'isha, the Prophet's favourite, served at various times as a judge, a political activist and a warrior. An eminent traditionalist, she transmitted *Hadith* to several of the foremost early Muslim traditionalists. She has narrated around 2,210 *hadiths*.

2. Sawdah bint Zam'a (b.unknown – d.674)

Sawdah was the daughter of Zam'a b. Qayyis from the clan of 'Amir b. Lu'ayy, the sub-clan of Quraysh and her mother was Shamūs bint Qayyis from Banū Najjār of Medina was one of the early converts to Islam. She first married Sakrān b. 'Amr, her uncle's son, was one of the first Muslims like herself. Both were subjected to torture at the hands of Meccan polytheists and forced to immigrate to Abyssinia with the second caravan. Sakrān passed away as a Muslim after the couple returned to Mecca. At the time, Sawdah, over fifty years old, was left alone with her five children. Meanwhile, the Prophet had lost his beloved wife, Khadijah, with whom he had happily married for many years. He needed someone to look after his children and care for the household. On the advice of a female companion, he ruefully proposed to Sawdah. They married in Mecca, three years before the Hijra, in the tenth year of his prophetic mission. Sawdah had been the Prophet's only wife for three years until he married ʿAʾisha. During this time, she was also a mother to Umm Kulthūm and Fāṭima.

Being a household member and having an intimate relationship with the Prophet, Sawdah narrated only five *hadiths*. She was a tanner who had been an early convert to Islam. Prophet Muhammad married her when he was unpopular and bankrupt. He considered divorcing her when, as the oldest and plainest of his wives, she no longer attracted him, but she persuaded him to keep her in the house (she gave up her turn to Aʾisha).

Sawdah remained loyal to her husband, giving him all he needed: love and care. Nor did she ever express any jealousy or ruefulness when she realised that the Prophet's heart leaned towards a particular one of his wives. On the contrary, she demonstrated sublimity as she realized that the Prophet's heart favoured Aʾishah above all others, but he had to maintain fairness between all his wives. He would not allow himself to give Aʾishah an hour more than he would give every one of his other wives.

Sawdah was kind to others and enjoyed giving them what pleased them. She wished to remain married to the Prophet and be remembered by Muslims worldwide as a 'mother of all believers' as his wives earned this title. Sawdah handled every crisis so diplomatically that there was no space for escalatory impulses. At the same time, she wanted to give greater pleasure to her husband and the one he loved most among his wives. Hence, her gift became a model for any woman who wished to forego some of her rights to please her husband. Sawdah died toward the end of Umar's reign, about ten years after the Prophet passed.

The Prophet married several other women in the following years. Sawdah, kind-hearted and naïve, got on well with all the ladies, especially 'A'isha. 'A'isha loved her, too. She even said about her: "The woman from these expressions, it is possible to deduce that 'A'isha loved Sawdah, as well as that Sawdah was a woman who expressed her feelings and demands without hesitation. In the case of honey syrup, causing the revelation of the first verses of Sūrat al-Taḥrım, Sawdah implemented what 'A'isha told her but later regretted it. In the later periods, the Prophet wanted to divorce Sawdah. But she wanted to get reinstated to her status as the Prophet's wife in the hereafter; otherwise, she granted the alignment of spending the night with the Prophet to 'A'isha. This way, she remained as the Prophet's wife. In this regard, the following verse was revealed: "If a wife is worried about her husband's disagreement or turning away from her, there is no blame on them to make peace between them" (Q4:128)

3. A'isha bint Abu Bakr (612 –678 CE)

A'isha was the daughter of Prophet Muhammad's best friend and head evangelist, Abu Bakr. She remained his favourite wife and contributed significant information to Islamic law and history. 'A'isha was born in Mecca in the fourth year of prophethood. Nevertheless, some sources indicate a prior date claiming that she was fourteen or eighteen when she married the Prophet. Her father, Abū Bakr 'Abd Allāh b. Abı Quḥāfa of the clan of Taym of the tribe of Quraysh was a close confidant of the Prophet and his first successor. Her mother, Umm Rūmān, was of the tribe of Kināna. The Prophet and 'A'isha were married in the month of Shawwal in the first or second year of the Hijra.

If there was ever proof that a pious Muslim woman need not be a submissive wife and mother, it is the life of Aisha, the third of the Prophet's eleven wives. She has divided opinions ever since the seventh century, among both Muslims and non-Muslims. Her marriage proposal to the future Prophet was forthright: "I like you because of our relationship, your high reputation among your people, your trustworthiness, your good character and truthfulness."

A top Islamic scholar, an inspiration to champions of women's rights, a military commander riding on camelback, and a fatwa-issuing jurist, Aisha's intellectual standing and religious authority were astonishing by the standards of our own time and hers. Aisha is not the only wife of Prophet Muhammad whose life explodes notions of what constitutes a "traditional" Muslim woman. Khadija ran a caravan business in Mecca. A wealthy and successful trader, she was also a twice-widowed single mother, fifteen years Muhammad's senior, and his boss.

There has been a controversy about A'isha'a's age at the time of her marriage to the Prophet. Critics allege that A'isha was just six years old when she was married to the Prophet, who was in his 50s, and she was only nine. The Prophet consummated the marriage when there was a significant age difference between them. This fact is in a saying attributed to A'isha herself (Sahih Bukhari volume 5, book 58, number 234), and the debate on this issue became complicated because some Muslims believe this to be a historically accurate account. Although most Muslims would not consider marrying off their nine-year-old daughters, those who accept this saying argue that since the Qur'an states that marriage is void unless entered into by consenting adults, A'isha must have entered puberty early.

They point out that, in seventh-century Arabia, adulthood was considered the onset of puberty. (This is true, and this was also the case in Europe: five centuries after Muhammad's marriage to A'isha, 33-year-old King John of England married 12-year-old Isabella of Angoulême.) Interestingly, of the many criticisms Muhammad made at the time by his opponents, none focused on A'isha's age at marriage.

According to this perspective, A'isha may have been young, but she was not younger than was the norm at the time. Other Muslims doubt the very idea that A'isha was six at the time of marriage, referring to historians who have questioned the reliability of A'isha's age as given in the saying. In a society without a formal birth registry, people estimate their age and that of others. A'isha would have been no different. What's more, A'isha had already been engaged to someone else before she married Muhammad, suggesting she had already been mature enough by society's standards to consider marriage for a while. It doesn't seem easy to reconcile this with her being six.

A'isha was renowned for her knowledge of medicine, history, and philosophy. She was an essential transmitter of *hadith*. When there was an accusation of adultery against her, Prophet Muhammad ruefully received a revelation vindicating her. She opposed Ali's bid for the caliphate and led her forces against him in the Battle of the Camel, but she lost. It was the first time one Muslim army opposed another—this incident was evidence of the logic of conservatives as proof that women should shun politics. A'isha participated in several expeditions, such as the Uḥud, Ḥudaybiyya, the farewell hajj and the conquest of Mecca. But one of the most critical expeditions she participated in was the Banū Mustalik Campaign, which took place in the fifth year of the hijra.

While returning to Medina after the war, ʿA'isha got off her camel to meet her needs and left the camp because the army was also camping there. When she returned to camp, she realised that she had dropped her necklace and went out to look for it. The army had to move, considering that ʿA'isha was in the palanquin on her camel. When ʿA'isha found her necklace and returned to the camp, she discovered that the army was gone, and no one was left. She began to wait, hoping they would notice and come for her. Ṣafwān b.al-Muʿaṭṭal, a member of the army coming from behind, saw her and brought her back to the next camp. Hypocrites in the military, however, began to slander and tattle, to which some unfortunate Muslims also succumbed. The Prophet was very upset because of the slander and rumourous gossip. ʿA'isha, who fell ill after returning from the expedition and could not recover for a month, cried for days after hearing this slander. Finally, verses 11-21 of Sūrat al-Nūr descended, and Allah absolved her. ʿAʾisha lost her necklace again on another expedition, and the army lost time in a waterless place. Since the time for the fajr prayer was approaching and there was no water for ablution in sight, Muslims got upset. Then, the verse of tayammum descended. Those initially mad at her started expressing their gratitude and appreciation.

The Prophet died with his head resting in ʿAʾisha's lap and then interred in her room. She lived another forty-seven years after him and died in Medina. She was the Prophet's favourite among his wives, except for Khadijah. He answered "ʿAʾisha" to ʿAmr b. al-ʿAs, when asked who he loved most in his life. The Prophet enjoyed talking to her and answering her questions. She gained an exceptional place in his heart thanks to her outstanding qualities, such as her sharp intelligence, comprehensive understanding, strong memory, powerful rhetoric and oratory skills, and zeal for the perception of the Qurʾan and the *sunnah* of the Prophet. Among his wives, ʿAʾisha was most jealous of the Prophet and made a lot of effort to win his intimacy decisively. As a result of this jealousy, ʿAʾisha led the other wives of the Prophet, causing the Prophet to swear not to drink honey syrup, and the first verses of Sūrat al-Taḥrım descended during this episode.

4. *Hafsah* bint Umar ibn Al-Khattab (605 – 665)

Ḥafṣah, born in Mecca five years before Muhammad received the prophetic mission, was the daughter of Kumar, a close friend of the Prophet and who would later become the second caliph of Islam. She was from the clan of Adı, the sub-clan of Quraysh. Her mother was Zaynab bint Maẓʿūn Ḥafsa's first husband was Khunays b. Ḥudhāfa was one of the first Muslims to migrate to Abyssinia, escaping the persecution of the Meccan Polytheist. Their marriage took place after his return from Abyssinia. Ḥafṣa migrated to Medina with her husband. Khunays participated in Badr but fell ill on the way back and died in Medina. To marry his widowed daughter to a virtuous person, 'Umar first made an offer to 'Uthmān and then to Abū Bakr. But he did not get a positive response from either of them. Offended at these developments, 'Umar complained to the Prophet. The Prophet said that Ḥafṣah would marry someone better than 'Uthmān and 'Uthmān would marry someone better than Ḥafṣah, and he married Ḥafṣah in the third year of Hijra. Later, 'Uthmān married the Prophet's daughter, Umm Kulthūm.

Hafsah was also active in public affairs. The companions very often sought her insight and guidance. For example, once, her father consulted her before deciding the time limit for a husband to be away from his wife. Hafsah ruefully expressed her concern about the political situation following the assassination of her father. While he was on his deathbed, she urged her brother Abdullah to discuss the issue with her father and ensure a smooth and peaceful transition of power. Also, she played a crucial role in persuading her brother, who was unwilling to get involved in the conflict between Ali and Muawiyah, to attend the arbitration to discuss the conflict and solve the problem peacefully and amicably.

Ḥafṣah mostly agreed with 'A'isha in the Prophet's house. There were times when both of them collaborated against the other ladies. Ḥafṣah was also alluded to among those who cooperated with 'A'isha in the honey syrup incident alluded to above. In another incident related to Ḥafṣah, the Prophet told her a secret, but she did not keep this secret and informed A'isha. In addition to that, God informed the Prophet about this situation. When 'Umar heard about the incident, he fell into deep mourning and sadness. The Prophet returned to Ḥafṣah after Gabriel told him that: "Ḥafṣah is a woman who fasts and prays a lot, and she is your wife in paradise."

In another incident related to Ḥafṣah, the Prophet told her a secret, but she did not keep this secret and informed A'isha. Probably because she failed to keep secrets, the Prophet divorced her. When 'Umar heard about the incident, he fell into deep mourning and sadness. The Prophet returned to Ḥafṣah after Gabriel told him that "Ḥafṣah is a woman who fasts and prays a lot, and she is your wife in paradise. 'Umar kept in his custody the copy of the Qur'ān collected during the reign of Abū Bakr. Thence, it was with Hafsah, his daughter. Thus, Hafsah had the honour of preserving the muṣḥaf. Sources claim that Ḥafṣah was an unpliable person like her father and that she had some impulsive outbursts against the Prophet in some cases.

For this reason, she was warned frequently by her father, 'Umar. She was the daughter of Prophet Muhammad's wealthy friend, Umar. Hafsah was the custodian of the compiled text of the Qur'an, which is somewhat different from today's standard Qur'an.

Ḥafṣah could read and write. Shifā bint 'Abd Allāh, one of the female companions, taught him to read. Hafsah died in Medina. Sixty *hadiths* owe their lineage to her. Sources claim that Ḥafṣah was an unpliable person like her father. She had some impulsive outbursts against the Prophet in some cases. For this reason, she was warned frequently by her father, 'Umar.

5. Zaynab bint Khuzaymah (595 – 624)

Zane Bent Khuzayma was the daughter of Khuzayma and the fifth wife of the Holy Prophet. She was born in 595 CE and was the first wife of the Prophet, who did not belong to the Quays tribe. An early convert to Islam, Zaynab was the wife of Muhammad's (peace be upon him) adopted son Zayd ibn Harithah. She was also the Prophet's biological cousin. To justify marrying her, Muhammad new revelations that an adopted son did not count as a natural son, so Zaynab was not his daughter-in-law. Zaynab excelled at tannery -craft. Zaynab was the first of Prophet Muhammad's wives who did not come from the tribe of Quraysh. She died less than one year after her marriage, and as a consequence, very little is known about her. Before this marriage, she had earned the title of Mother of the Impoverished because

Her last husband died in battle, and her marriage to Prophet Muhammad set a precedent for others to follow. Muslim men no longer feared that their deaths in battle would mean starvation and neglect for their families. It became honourable to marry the widows of the deceased. When 'Ubaydah had died after his single combat with 'Utbah at the beginning of the battle of Badr, he had left a widow who was very much younger than himself, Zaynab, the daughter of Khuzaymah.

Zaynab Bint Khuzayma had married twice before marriage to the Prophet, divorced and widowed in both, respectively. She was very generous; before Islam, she was titled "the mother of the impoverished". A year after being widowed, she was still unmarried, and when the Prophet asked her to marry him, she gladly accepted. The title of 'Ummul Masakeen' knew her due to her kind-heartedness and compassion for impoverished people. Prophet She died soon after her marriage and was interred in Jannatul Baqi. She was the first wife after Khadijah to die before Prophet Muhammad.

She was one of the companions known for their accurate understanding and rigorous preservation of the Qur'ān and the *sunnah* of the Prophet. She was also one of the seven companions famous for issuing many fatwas. Thanks to her strong memory, the number of *hadith*s she narrated is 2210. She was childless.

6. Umm Salamah bint Abu Umayyah (596 – 680)

Umm, Salamah married Prophet Muhammad at the age of twenty-nine, after her first husband died from the wounds in the battle of Uhud. Umm Salamah and her husband were part of the migration to Abyssinia. She was an example of patience in the face of trials and tribulations. She was extremely patient, and she and her husband were among the first to leave Mecca, bound for Medina when she endured separation from her husband and the abduction of her son. At the death of her husband, she supplicated to Allah: "O Lord, reward me for my affliction and give me something better than it in return, which only You, the Exalted and Mighty, can give."

Although her name was Hind, she was tagged with the name of her eldest child, Salama, and was known as Umm Salama. She was from the Makhzūm clan of the noble tribe of Quraysh. Her father was Abū Umayya Hudhayfa B.Mughira, and her mother was Atike bint Amir. Umm Salama first married her cousin, Abū Salama ʿAbd Allāh b. ʿAbd al-Asad. Abū Salama, the son of the Prophet's aunt, was among the first to convert to Islam. Umm Salama and her husband accompanied the emigrations of Muslims to Abyssinia. Later, she set out with her husband to migrate to Medina, but her family did not allow her. Thereupon, Abū Salama migrated alone, leaving her behind. She received another blow when her husband's family separated her from İbn Saʾd, at-Ṭabaqā.

The supplication of marriage to the Prophet, recited by Umm Salama, materialized soon. She narrated more than 00 *hadiths*, many of them concerning women. She accompanied the Prophet on many expeditions and married him for seven years until his death. Umm, Salamah outlived all the other wives and died at the age of eighty-four.

Abū prayed for Umm Salama to marry someone better than himself. When Salama passed away, Umm Salama cried for several days. When her iddah (the period to be waited by a woman after divorce or the death of her husband) was over, she received marriage proposals from Abū Bakr and ʿUmar, respectively, but she declined both. Later, the Prophet proposed to her. Salama said there was jealousy among women in the prophet's home. It was after the Prophet assured her that he would pray to God to remove her ill feelings and take care of her children that she accepted the proposal.

Umm, Salama was a prodigious woman. Hence, the Prophet consulted her on several issues. For example, when the Muslims felt disappointed in Ḥudaybiyya, they demonstrated reluctance to slaughter the animals they brought for sacrifice. They thought that the Meccans were given significant concessions because of the treaty. Umm Salama advised the Prophet to sacrifice his animal first. Following her advice, he did so, and the believers followed suit.

Umm Salama was the latest to pass away among the Prophet's wives. She died in Medina at the age of eighty-four. She narrated 378 *hadiths*. Umm Salama's name appears among the Qur'ān memorizers. Umm Salama was a charming woman, so ʿA'isha was very jealous of her. She was also a calm, understanding and experienced woman. Umm Salama was interested in science and asked the Prophet many questions, particularly about the revelation of some verses. Umm Salama had four children from Abu Salama but none from the Prophet.

7. Juwayriyah bint al-Haarith (608 – 673)

Juwayriyah came to the Prophet's attention when she became captive in the battle against the tribe Banu Mustaliq. She was the 20-year-old daughter of the chief of Banu Mustaliq, and her marriage brought about an alignment between her tribe and the Muslims. When Prophet Muhammad married Juwayriyah, it allowed the tribe to enter Islam with honour-removing the humiliation of their defeat. During the formalisation of the proposed marriage, the Prophet returned the war booty of Banu Mustaliq, and the captives also got freedom. Juwayriyah was married to the Prophet for six years and lived for another thirty-nine years after his death. She died at the age of sixty-five.

One of the captives from the skirmish with the Banu Mustaliq was Juwayriya bint al-Harith, who was the daughter of the tribe's chieftain. Her husband, Mustafa bin Safwan, had been killed in the battle. She was from the Banū Mustalik tribe. She first got married to her cousin Musāfi' b. Ṣafwān. Many individuals from this tribe were captured during the Banū Mustalik Campaign and brought to Medina. Juwayriya, whose husband died in the war, was among those captives. She applied to the Prophet for help to pay her ransom. The Prophet did so and proposed marriage to her. She married the Prophet at twenty in the fifth year of Hijra. Immediately after the marriage, Muslims released their captives because they became relatives of the Prophet. Not much later, Banū Mustalik converted to İslam collectively. Juwayriya had narrated seven *hadiths* from the Prophet. She passed away in Medina at the age of sixty-five. Juwayriya, a very charitable woman, didn't have any children.

She initially fell among the booty of Muhammad's companion, Thabit ibn Qays ibn Al-Shammas. Upon being enslaved, Juwayriyya went to Muhammad requesting that she - as the daughter of the lord of the Mustaliq - be released. However, he refused. Meanwhile, her father approached Muhammad with ransom to secure her release, but Muhammed still refused to release her. Muhammad then offered to marry her, and she accepted. When it became known that tribals of Mustaliq were relatives of the prophet of Islam through marriage, the Muslims began releasing their captives. Thus, Muhammad's marriage resulted in the freedom of nearly one hundred families he had recently enslaved. The daughter of an Arab chief, she was taken prisoner when Muhammad (peace be upon him) attacked her tribe. Muhammad (peace be upon him) did not make a habit of marrying his war captives, but A'ishah claimed that Juwayriyah was so beautiful that men always fell in love with her at first sight.

8. Zaynab bint Jahsh (590 – 641)

While her real name was Barra, the Prophet changed her name to Zaynab. Prophet Muḥammad gave her in marriage to his freedman and adopted son Zayd b. Ḥāritha. With this marriage, the Prophet wanted to show that there was no harm in the marriage of free and enslaved people in Islam, to establish the idea of equality among believers, and to make people adopt the fact that superiority was due to righteousness, not lineage. However, Zaynab was peevish, and there was no love between the spouses. The marriage turned out to be incompatible.

Their marriage was short-lived and stormy, and to please both of them, Prophet Muhammad allowed them to divorce. It caused a dilemma because divorce was frowned upon and left the woman in a difficult situation. To remedy the dilemma, she married Prophet Muhammad. This episode appears in the 37th verse of Sūrat al-Aḥzāb. With this marriage, the *Jahiliyyah* custom forbade the divorcee of an adopted son was rendered obsolete. This book explores and helps in decoding this abominable concept. It transpires that it was a powerful tool in the hands of men for subjugating and humiliating women. The Prophet and Zaynab got married in the fifth year of Hijra. By marrying Zaynab, Prophet Muhammad demonstrated that in Islam, an adopted son differs from a natural son. Zaynab joined the growing family of Muhammad and was known for her generosity and charitable works. She died at fifty.

Zaynab boasted to the other wives of Muhammad, saying, "Allah arranged my marriage in heaven". The Prophet loved her because she was very fond of worship. For this reason, his other wives, especially Aisha, were very jealous of her. She was jealous of them too. When Ṣafiyya's camel fell ill while on pilgrimage, the Prophet asked Zaynab to give her spare camel to Ṣafiyya. However, Zaynab said he did not want to give her camel to a Jewish girl. This condescending reply offended the Prophet so much that he abstained from visiting Zaynab for about three months. When ʿAʾisha suffered humiliation, the Prophet asked Zaynab what she knew about this subject. She replied: "I do not know anything but goodness about ʿAʾisha." ʿAʾisha said about Zaynab ", I've never seen a better woman of pious qualities than Zaynab." Zaynab mastered handicrafts such as leather tanning, sewing, and beading.

Moreover, she was magnanimous, giving away most of the money she earned from handwork. Zaynab was the first wife of the Prophet to die after his death. She died in Medina at the age of twenty. She narrated twenty *hadiths*. Her first husband was one of the Qurayza men whom Muhammad beheaded. He enslaved all the women and selected Rayhana for himself because she was the most beautiful. She died shortly before Muhammad (peace be upon him) in 632.

9. Umm Habibah bint Abu Sufyan (589 – 666)

Ramlah, also known as Umm Habibah, was the daughter of Abu Sufyan, a leader of the Quraysh and an enemy of Islam at that stage. She declared her faith without fear of the consequences to herself, and she stayed fast to her faith when she was under enormous pressure. After converting to Islam and mitigating suffering from persistent oppression, Umm Habibah and her husband joined the migration to Abyssinia. Her husband died after that. She was alone in a strange country with a young daughter and no visible means of support.

When the Prophet heard of her predicament, he offered to marry her. She accepted. The king of Abyssinia, who had secretly converted to Islam and was a good friend to the fledgling Muslim community, provided her *mahr* and witnessed the marriage contract. It was some years before she could join her husband in Medina. She was married to Prophet Muhammad for four years until he passed away.

She was the daughter of Abu Sufyan, the Meccan chief who led the resistance against Muhammad (peace be upon him), but she had been a teenage convert to Islam. This marriage offset some of Prophet Muhammad's political humiliation in the Treaty of Hudaybiya by demonstrating that he could command the loyalty of his adversary's daughter. Ramlah was devoted to Muhammad (peace be upon him) and quick to pick quarrels with people who were not.

Umm Habibah was born seventeen years before the advent of İslam. She was nicknamed Ramlah. Her father was Abū Sufyān b. Ḥarb, one of the notables of Quraysh and her mother, was Ṣafiyya bint Abū al-ʿAṣ.

His mother and father were of the 'Abd Shams of the Quraysh clan. Umm Habiba was initially married to 'Ubayd Allāh b: Jaḥsh, the son of the Prophet's aunt. Among the first Muslims, umm Habiba and her husband migrated to Abyssinia with the second caravan. Umm Habiba, pregnant during this journey, gave birth to her daughter, Habiba, in Abyssinia. After a while, her husband converted to Christianity and died as a Christian in Abyssinia. Since the Prophet knew Umm Habiba's troubles, he decided to marry her. He sent an invitation through 'Amr b. Umayya to Abyssinia or Najāshı to embrace Islam. He also proposed his marriage to Umm Habiba. She was overjoyed when she received the offer. The marriage of the Prophet and Umm Habiba took place in absentia in Abyssinia. Afterwards, she went to Medina, to the Prophet's side. She was thirty-five years old when she came to the Prophet. This marriage of the Prophet made it easier for Banū Umayya to sympathize with Islam.

10. Safiyyah bint Huyayy ibn Akhtab (610 –670)

Safiyyah was born in Madinah to Huyayy ibn Akhtab, the chief of the Jewish tribe Banu Nadir. Banu Nadir had been expelled from Madinah and settled at Khaybar. Ṣafiyya, whose lineage is traceable to Hārūn, was born in Medina. Her mother was Barra bint Samaw'al who was of the Banū Qurayẓa. She married first to Sallām b—Mishkam, one of the leaders of Banū Naḍır, and then to Kināna b.al-Rabı' after divorcing him. On leaving Medina, the Banū Naḍır Jews settled in Khaybar. Ṣafiyya, whose husband died during the conquest of Khaybar by the Muslims, was taken prisoner.

Ṣafiyya, whose real name was Zaynab, was called Ṣafiyya when she fell to the Prophet's share of the spoils of war. She had the option of returning to her tribe or converting to Islam and marrying the Prophet. She opted for the second one. Thus, the Prophet married her in a stopover while returning from Khaybar to Medina. Prophet Muhammad suggested that Safiyyah convert to Islam, and she agreed and became Muhammad's wife. Despite her conversion, Muhammad's other wives teased Safiyyah about her Jewish origin. Prophet Muhammad once said to his wife: "If they discriminate against you again, tell them that your husband is Muhammad" Safiyyah was twenty-one years old when the Prophet died. She lived for another 39 years, passing away in Medina at 60.

Prophet Muhammad married her on the same day he defeated the last Jewish tribe in Arabia, only hours after he had supervised the slaying of Kinana, her second husband. His earlier victims had included her father, brother, first husband, three uncles and several cousins. This marriage was of no benefit to Safiyah's defeated tribe, who were banished from Arabia a few years later; its real political significance was that Safiyah's presence in Prophet Muhammad's household was an open demonstration that he had defeated the Jews.

Ṣafiyya, a beautiful, intelligent, virtuous, mild-tempered, and pious woman, had no children. She was the beautiful daughter of a Jewish chief, Huyayy ibn Akhtab. Ṣafiyya was influenced decisively by the rivalry between the Prophet's wives. They were constantly using her Jewish origin against her. Ṣafiyya was very upset when ʿAʾisha and Ḥafṣa took pride in their pedigree, stating that they share the same lineage with the Prophet.

Safiyya chose to wed Prophet Muhammad and become a Muslim rather than be free and return to her tribe. Safiyya, although honoured by the Prophet as a "Mother of the Believers", sometimes faced hardship among the Arabs, including her co-wives. They sometimes would call her "the Jew". Instead of becoming angry at the others, Prophet Muhammad helped Safiyya stand up to those who were sarcastic towards her. He said: "If they repeat it, give them this response:

My father is the Prophet Aaron, my uncle is the Prophet Moses, and my husband is, as you see, the Prophet Muhammad, the chosen one. What do you have more than me to be proud of?'"

When she would garner whispers while they were together, the Prophet would firmly say:

"She is my wife," to ward off ill-intentioned speculation or gossip, Ṣafiyya, who narrated ten *hadiths* from the Prophet, died in Medina.

11. Maymunah bint Al-Harith (594 –674)

Maymunah was a middle-class widow from Mecca who proposed marriage to Muhammad. A serene woman who kept a tidy house, Maymunah was utterly obsessed with rules and rituals. She was one of several enslaved people whom the Governor of Egypt sent as a present to Muhammad (peace be upon him). Mariyah bore Prophet Muhammad (peace be upon him) a son, Ibrahim. Maymūna, whose original name was Barra before the Prophet changed it to Maymuna. Barra was the daughter of al-Ḥārith B. Hazn from Barra. Among her maternal sisters was the Prophet's wife, Zaynab bint Khuzayma. Maymūna first married Mas'ūd b. AmrThakafi, and after he divorced her, she married Abū Rukm b. 'Abd al-Uzza. After her husband's death, she told her sister, the wife of 'Abbās b. 'Abd al-Muṭṭalib,

The Prophet and Maymūna got married in the seventh year of the hijrah, on the way from Mecca to Medina, returning from the 'Umra al-Qaḍā'. Maymūna, who narrated seventy-six *hadiths* from the Prophet, died in Mecca. 'A'isha honoured her posthumously with the following statement: "Maymūna was the most pious of us and the most looking out for the ties of kinship".

When the third caliph, Uthman ibn Affan, was assassinated, the political system was affected by internal division and conflict. A'ishah led a vocal public protest against Ali, the fourth caliph, in 656. She delivered a public address at a mosque located in Mecca, where she swore to avenge the death of the murdered caliph. She garnered the support of many Muslims across Arabia and eventually led an army into the Battle of the Camel. Her speeches during the battle cast a spell on the accountant of their force and sincerity. Following her defeat on the battlefield, she withdrew from public life and dedicated herself to intellectual pursuits. A'isha's life represents a powerful model for Muslim women and exemplifies cardinal Islamic values: excellence in scholarship, political engagement and even military leadership. F

The female companions of the Prophet

Sumaiyyah bint Khayyat has a rare honour in Islamic history. She belonged to the first batch, which embraced Islam. She did not enjoy the benefit of wealth or political stature. She lived with her husband and son under the control of an influential pagan family. Her pagan owners demanded that she renounce her newfound faith, yet she blatantly refused. She had to undergo severe persecution for her convictions ruefully. She was systematically tortured and eventually killed by a spear driven through her heart by Abu Jahl, the arch-enemy of the Prophet, resulting in the dreadful end of a legendary woman. The story of Sumaiyyah's sacrifice is well known to Muslims and undermines misconceptions—in the East and the West— of women as weak beings.

Abu Sufyan ibn Harb could not conceive of anyone among the Quraysh who would dare challenge his authority or go against his orders. He was, after all, the Sayyid or chieftain of Makkah who had to be obeyed and followed. His daughter, Ramallah, known as Umm Habibah, however, dared to challenge his authority when she rejected the deities of the Quraysh and their idolatrous ways. Together with her husband, Ubaydullah ibn Jahsh, she put her faith in God alone and accepted the message of His Prophet. The Prophet had stationed her with the army during the early Muslim battles against the Arab pagans. She helped supply water to the soldiers and nursed the wounded. She participated in the Battles of Uhud and Khyber, assisting the injured.

Safiyya, an aunt of the Prophet, was among the many women who actively participated in the battles. She defended a fortress in Medina at the Battle of the Trench. She noticed an intruder who had penetrated the defences of the fortress; she managed to manoeuvre and kill him before he was able to do any harm to the women and children. Umm Atiyyah, whose name was Nusaybah bint Al-Harith, was a dedicated servant of Islam. When the Prophet went on a jihad expedition, he usually took some women with him. He would take one of his wives and some women who could serve in the army. Umm, Atiyyah was always ready to join a Muslim army. She reports: "I went with God's messenger on seven expeditions: I would watch over their belongings, cook for them, treat the wounded and nurse the ill." (Muslim).

Umm, Atiyyah had very close relations with the Prophet's household. She was also close to the Prophet's daughters. She was the one who prepared the body of his eldest daughter for burial when Zaynab died early in year 8. She reports: "When Zaynab, the Prophet's daughter, died, he told us: 'Wash her odd number of times, three or five. Use camphor with the last wash. When you have finished, let me know. When we finished, he gave us his robe to cover her with." (Related in all six authentic anthologies of *hadiths*). She also prepared the body of the Prophet's other daughter, Umm Kulthoom, for burial.

Rehanah bint Zaid was a beautiful and young Jewess of the Banu Nadir. She had married into the tribe of the Banu Quraizah and had lost her husband and other male relatives in the wholesale massacre of the latter tribe. Tradition is undecided as to her proper status in the prophet's household. Another Jewess to join Muhammad's (peace be upon him) household was Safiya, the beautiful seventeen-year-old widow of Kinanah, chief of the Jews of Khyber, who lost his life on the unhappy occasion of the Muslim reduction of that town. Unlike Rehanah, Safiya seems to have been a fickle opportunist who readily accepted Islam and flattered the prophet. The third girl to catch Prophet Muhammad's fancy was the young and curly-headed vassal girl, Mary the Copt. Strangely enough, she and her sister were the gift of the Christian governor of

Egypt sent to Prophet Muhammad (peace be upon him) in the seventh year of *hijrah*. She was a young and comely widow of twenty-six who had assigned her personal affairs to her brother-in-law, the influential Abbas, uncle of Prophet Muhammad. She was the aunt of Khalid bin Walid, the recently converted general and the future 'Sword of Allah'.

Asma' bint Abu Bakr (694--695) was another of the Prophet's companions with a notable contribution to Islam. Asmā', nicknamed Dhat an-Nitaqayn (meaning she with the two belts), was one of the companions of the Islamic prophet Muhammad and half-sister of his third wife, A'isha. Her nickname, Dhat an-Nitaqayn, was given to her by Prophet Muhammad during her migration to Medina. She is regarded as one of the most prominent Islamic figures, as she helped Prophet Muhammad during the Hijrah from Mecca to Medina. Prophet Muhammad) and Abu Bakr were among the last to leave Mecca. On their way to Medina, they stopped at the Cave of Thawr. Asma used her waistbands to tie food supplies for her father and the Prophet in the cave. For this courageous act, Prophet Muhammad (peace be upon him) told her she would be among the privileged ones in paradise. Her courage did not end there. When Abu Jahl, one of the Makkan leaders, came to her searching for the Prophet and her father, Asma refused to betray them and, as a result, suffered a severe wound.

Prophet's wisdom in marital life

The wives of the Prophet Muhammad were vibrant, outspoken, dynamic, influential, enterprising community members and fully involved in Muslim public affairs. The women were Muhammad's intellectual partners. Accompanying him on his raids and military campaigns, they were not just background figures but shared with him his strategic concerns. He listened to their advice, which sometimes became the deciding factor in thorny negotiations. In the city, they were leaders of women's protest movements, first for equal status as believers and then regarding economic and sociopolitical rights, mainly in inheritance, participation in warfare and booty, and personal (marital) relations.

Scholars and writers about the Prophet and his character often explain his marriages in terms of political, social, and even legislative needs. While such reasons were undoubtedly present in many of his marriages, they are not the overriding reasons for any. Each of his marriages expressed a desire to unite with the lady in question. In Sawdah's case, we read explanations that he wanted to compensate her for the loss of her husband. The fact is that the Prophet needed a new wife after Khadijah had passed away, and the qualities he needed in his new wife were maturity, kindness and being a believer in his message. Sawdah answered all these. She was the one to take care of his two unmarried daughters, Umm Kulthoom and Fatima.

Leading by example

Through leading by example, Prophet Muhammad's wives denounced worldly attachments and chose Prophet Muhammad and the Hereafter. Prophet Muhammad led such a basic life that he only slept on thin bedding on the floor, used water sparingly, and, on many days, had very little to eat. Imagine living in these conditions and being directed by God to marry many women (with most of them raising their children from previous marriages), treat them equally and provide for them and their children.

At one point in time, the wives of Prophet Muhammad, in their humanness, did ask for a little more than they had. They were not indecent requests, and Prophet Muhammad was not angry with them. Instead, he chose solitude to express his sadness; his wives also felt grave regret.

When Abu Bakr and Umar (both of whom had daughters married to the Prophet) heard of this incident, they were angry at their daughters for causing pain to the Prophet. However, the Prophet cautioned not to be mad at his wives as he felt the grief of being unable to meet their requests.

In turn, God advised the Prophet:

"O Prophet! Say to your wives: If you desire this world's life and its adornment, I will give you a provision and allow you to depart a goodly departing. And if you desire Allah and His Messenger and the latter abode, then Allah has prepared a mighty reward for the doers of good among you."} (Q33: 28-9)

Despite the special status of the wives of the Prophet, they were reminded of their need for patience and humanness, as some ill feelings like jealousy and misunderstandings could always arise in domestic lives.

7. THE FADING FEMALE MUSLIM SCHOLARS

Did you know that a Muslim woman founded the world's first university? Maybe you did not. No popular sources beyond academic history books concerning the golden age of Islamic civilization have ever alluded to such a fact. Instead, people are generally inclined to think Islam would never allow women to attend classes in madrasas (schools), founded as early as the ninth century.

Muslim women were very active in the academic studies of early Islam. Many scholars have explored both the continuities and changes that have occurred in seminal moments in history and how those changes have defined the fortunes of women and their position within the crucible of Islamic civilization. However, it seems necessary at this juncture, when the mere mention of the word 'Islam' conjures up a whole array of negative stereotypes, to try to capture the very different atmosphere of the classical Islamic era. It is not to suggest that any single person or civilisation is better than any other but to depict Islamic civilization as self-confident, tolerant of the time's standards, and open to outside influences. It was nowhere better evident than in the role of the feminist society in that blooming civilization of Arabia. The Middle East has always been the physical bridge between Europe and Asia, but it has also been an essential link between the past and present. As inheritors of at least a portion of the cultural wealth of antiquity, Muslims presided over a new period of synthesis and creativity, the fruits of which the Western Europeans came to share through various Mediterranean meeting points and frontiers before embarking on their age of discovery and creativity.

The subject of female Islamic scholarship has slowly gathered more attention over the last decade, spearheaded in many ways by the incredible work of Shaykh Muhammad Akram Nadwi and his groundbreaking research. Tragically, in several ways, the discussions about female scholarship have remained confined to theoretical or historical areas, with little recognition or acknowledgement of what female Islamic scholarship and leadership look like in modern times. Although numerous historical examples attest to women serving as muftīyāt (interpreters of Islamic law), faqīhāt (jurists of Islamic law), muḥaddithāt (transmitters of *hadith*), and scholars of Islam across the centuries, women are rarely accepted as authoritative interpreters of Islamic law today. In recent times, there have been various legal and educational barriers for women who seek to acquire Islamic religious authority on par with men. Notably, the contemporary situation is often more restrictive for women than injunctions of the schools of Islamic law (madhhāhib) allow for. It is mainly on account of the narrow-minded interpretation of the Qur'an by the clerics, even though the holy book has a much broader outlook and a particular focus on women.

Most Muslim societies define women's role in the purely domestic sector. Some people consider that Islam stands against women's role in the public sector, believing that it has roots in the context of the prophet's time. There is no prohibition for women to participate in public and social affairs, including in political roles. It was the case that some women companions of the prophet participated in the political role, including Aisyah, the wife of Nabi Saw, Asma binti Abu Bakr, Ummu Athiyah, Ummu Hani' and Rubayyi' bint Mu'awidz. In this paper, the writer focuses on female companion *hadith* transmitters wrapped up in the missionary work with the prophet. In addition, the relation between women companions transmitter activities and their *hadith* transmission under the assumption that the woman's role would influence the texts of the transmitted *habits*. It is because, as a text, *hadith* had a particular context and condition. Accordingly, every transmitter had different *hadith* transmission based on her context, status, profession, and even gender construction. Therefore, this is the woman companion transmitters who play their role in politics and their influence in their transmitted *hadiths*.

The study of women in Islam has expanded broadly and rapidly in recent times. A review and analysis of normative Islamic injunctions about gender roles provides insights into a framework for situating specific practices within diverse regions and societies and at differing historical epochs. At the same time, increased academic attention has focused on the broad picture we get about actual Muslim women. New texture and complexity in the field have been achieved, for example, in the case of historical studies, by examining documents such as court records. In anthropological, sociological, and development-oriented studies, scholarship on gender increasingly exhibits more excellent cultural knowledge and lived fieldwork experience by researchers, many Muslim women.

During the colonial period, the depiction of Muslim women as confined and oppressed was used to support an imperialistic project of changing and controlling Muslim cultures. Several scholars have subsequently critiqued the persistence of such attitudes and rationales. In addition, particular works on women and gender in Islam may reflect an apologetic approach or reformist trends within contemporary Islamic thought, or the trends may need a profoundly deep understanding of the subtle nuances of an experience from an academic perspective. The development of Western feminist activism inspired similar approaches and methods among Muslims. Theorizing gender as culturally constructed has also led to studies of many elements of Muslim contexts, including masculinities, queer theory, and other dimensions of sex roles as represented and enacted in Islamic thought and societies. Postmodern and postcolonial theories have similarly generated critiques of how Muslim women have been defined in both popular and academic settings and have attempted to expose the power relations and ideological agendas driving and sustaining such constructions.

Muslim female scholarship

Many scholars have explored both the continuities and changes that have occurred in seminal moments in history and how those changes have defined the fortunes of women and their position within the crucible of Islamic civilization. However, it seems necessary at this juncture, when the mere mention of the word 'Islam' conjures up a whole array of negative stereotypes, to try to capture the very different atmosphere of the classical Islamic era. It is not supposed to suggest that any single person or civilisation is better than any other but to depict Islamic civilization at a moment when it was self-confident, tolerant by the time's standards and open to outside influences. It was nowhere better evident than in the role of the feminist society in that blooming civilization of Arabia.

The Middle East has always been the physical bridge between Europe and Asia, but it has also been an essential link between the past and present. As inheritors of at least a portion of the cultural wealth of antiquity, Muslims presided over a new period of synthesis and creativity, the fruits of which the Western Europeans came to share through various Mediterranean meeting points and frontiers before embarking on their age of discovery and creativity. Ā'isha, one of Prophet Muhammad's (peace be upon him) wives, was among the prominent Islamic jurists of her time. She was also involved in several political events after the death of the third caliph, Uthman ibn Affan. She was also the initial source of many habits, thanks to her well-known intelligence and memory. There are other examples, like Umm Waraqa, who knew the Qur'an by heart and was praised by the Prophet or al-Shifa, "the Healer" bint Abdullah, the first Muslim woman to teach literacy and was also a practitioner of folk medicine.

Muslim women did not stop learning after the first generation, though the feudal dynasties succeeding the great caliphs applied several unnecessary restrictions, which resulted in the rolling back of the rights and status given to Muslim women. It was the beginning of the stagnation of Muslim women's scholarship. On the other hand, during the feudal dynasties, the majority of rich men's daughters and wives, though restricted socially to some extent, were allowed to receive education, teach others and even sponsor educational institutions. Medieval Muslim women were not only patrons of academic establishments. They were also academics. A 15th-century Egyptian biographical dictionary lists over 1,000 prominent female scholars.

For most of Western civilization, men wrote history, and they wrote what they knew. Until feminist historians began unearthing women's achievements after the 1960s, women's contributions were left unsung. In the context of Islamic culture, the erasure of women was somewhat more complex. "Muslim society prizes female modesty. Traditionally, many Muslim families didn't want the names of their wives or their daughters published."

Keeping women's names out of the classroom, madrasa, or Islamic seminary records was just a broad interpretation of the concept of *hijab*. The term, commonly used to refer to women's head coverings, referred more generally to the modesty required by men and women. The lives and works of learned women were left unrecorded to shield them.

The religious education of women in early Islam proceeded hand in hand with that of men. Consequently, women would debate with men about the proper interpretation of a specific verse in the Qur'an, a *hadith,* or the significance of a particular event. A famous incident occurred in the mosque between Caliph Umar and an unknown woman. The Caliph wanted to limit the amount of *mehr* (dower) a woman may demand from a man. But *mehr* was not intended as consideration for the woman's entry into a monogamous sexual relation with a man, but rather to provide the woman with a precautionary safety net which she may decide to exploit during the life of the marriage or later, either by investing it or by using it to start her own business. That money is to be her personal property, one to which the husband may have no access even if he were in need. Thus, the importance of this safety net cannot be over-emphasized. By arguing for placing a ceiling on the amount of the *mehr* to facilitate the marriage of young men, the Caliph was taking away from women their right to determine the size of the safety net that makes them comfortable.

A woman understood the significance of this proposal and stood up in the mosque, taking issue with the Caliph. She said: "You shall not take away from us what God has given us." She then cited a passage from the Qur'an which supported her argument. The Caliph realized his error, saying: "A woman is right, and the Caliph is wrong." (Ibn Hajar al-'Asqalani, Fath al-Bari.). This story is remarkable not only because it illustrates women's participation in the religious activity of interpretation (*ijitihad*) but also because it reveals the degree of democracy in the early days of the Islamic state. The woman was unknown, but through her Qur'anic knowledge, she successfully made the Caliph withdraw his proposal.

Women teachers of Islam

Islamic literature abounds with stories of women who dialogued with men about proper Islamic practices or the preferred interpretation of an Islamic text. Furthermore, great female Islamic scholars taught many great male Islamic scholars. Unfortunately, the latter's contributions were not as quickly recognized by their contemporaries or as meticulously preserved by male historians. Among the male scholars who studied under female scholars are al-Ash-Shafe'ii', Ibn Khillikan and Abu Hayyan.'Ibn 'Asaker, a prominent *hadith* scholar, alluded that his female mentors and teachers numbered more than eighty.

Apart from well-known figures, including A'isha, the grandeur of forgotten scholars is remarkable. Fatima Al Batayahiyyah, an 8th-century scholar, taught the celebrated work of *Sahih al Bukhari* in Damascus. She was known as one of the most outstanding scholars of that period. Her classes enjoyed large crowds during the *hajj* when leading male scholars of the day flocked from afar to hear her speak in person. Whenever she tired, she would rest her head on the Prophet's grave and continue to teach her students as the hours wore on. Any woman visiting the Prophet's mosque now will know the frustration of not even being able to see the blessed Prophet's grave, let alone rest their head on its side wall. Another scholar, Zainab bint Kamal, taught more than 400 books of *hadith* in the 12th century. Her "camel loads" of texts attracted camel loads of students. She was a natural teacher, exhibiting exceptional patience, which won the hearts of those she taught.

An inspiring example is Umm al-Darda, a renowned jurist and scholar from the 7th century. Imam Bukhari refers to her as a faqiha, an authority in his Sahih. She would divide her time between lecturing in the Grand Ummayad Mosque in Damascus and Masjid al-Aqsa in Jerusalem. She regularly lectured in the men's section (and shockingly enough, even prayed shoulder to shoulder with them for a bit). Her students included prominent scholars, jurists, and the Caliph Abdul Malik ibn Marwan. In her advanced years, a witness recounts, the two would often talk at the entrance to the Dome of the Rock, and when the call for dusk prayers sounded, Abdul Malik would offer her his arm for support on her way to the mosque.

After a gruelling study session, a student asked Umm al-Darda, "Have we wearied you?" She responded: "You weary me? I have sought worship in everything. I found nothing more relieving than sitting with scholars and exchanging [knowledge]."

This exchange — apart from encapsulating an entire worldview precious rare in this day and age — also hints at an everyday reality in those days: study sessions were often extremely long and very demanding because students would travel from distant lands and would try to compress as much exposure and learning as they could in the shortest possible period.

The presence of female teachers alone does not do justice to the importance of women in Islamic history. The Qur'an, as recorded initially on parchments and animal bones, was assigned to the custody of Hafsah, daughter of Umar. With the help of these preserved records, caliph Uthman disseminated six standardised versions of the Qur'an to the Islamic kingdom's significant political and cultural centres. He ordered that all copies of non-standardised editions be burnt, thereby vindicating his immense trust in Hafsah's competence and character. Since then, the companions have never doubted the validity of women's teachings on account of their gender or by any respected scholar.

Another shining example is Karimah bint Ahmad ibn Muhammad ibn Hatim al-Marwaziyyah. An authority on Sahih al-Bukhari, she was critical in transmitting the text. A notable scholar of the day, Abu Dharr of Herat, urged his students to study that book under no one else. The Orientalist Goldziher comments, "Her name occurs with extraordinary frequency in the *ijaza*hs for narrating the text of this book." She travelled extensively for her vocation, visiting Sarakhs, Isfahan, Jerusalem and Mecca. Her accomplishments led the scholar Al-Samani to wonder if anyone had ever witnessed a woman of her like before.

Gender parity in Islam

The Prophet taught that believers have no difference in worth because of their gender. Both have the same rights and duties to learn and teach – from memorising and transmitting the words of the Qur'an and *hadith* to the interpretation of these sources and giving counsel to fellow Muslims through *fatwas* (legal opinions). Women have the same duty as men to encourage the good and restrain the evil. It follows pretty logically from this that if they cannot become scholars and be capable of understanding, interpreting and teaching, they cannot fulfil their duty as Muslims. Relegating the Muslim woman only to the role of a mother and housewife is a relatively modern phenomenon.

A confident woman called Nasibah once came to the Prophet Muhammad and said: 'O Messenger of God, Men have excelled in meriting the rewards of the Hereafter. They join the Friday prayer, attend congregations and perform *jihad*. Then what is left for us women to do?' The Prophet replied, 'O Nasibah, if your manner of living with your husband is proper and obedient, such conduct is equal to all the actions performed by men, which you have just alluded to.' (Kanz al-'Ummal, 16/411.)

There is still an enormous amount of work required to unearth Muslim feminism. The Aghlabid dynasty ruled Qayrawan under the Abbasid Caliphate during the eighth and ninth centuries. They brought peace to the region of Ifriqiyya and conquered Sicily. Aghlabid palaces were also famous.

When Imam Zuhri, a famous scholar of the *sunnah* (a collection of the Prophet's prescriptions), indicated to Qasim ibn Muhammad, a scholar of the Qur'an, a desire to seek knowledge, Qasim advised him to join the assembly of a well-known woman jurist of the day, Amara bin Al-Rahman. Imam Zuhri attended her community and later described her as "a boundless ocean of knowledge." Amra tutored several famous scholars, such as Abu Bakr Muhammad ibn Hazama and Yahya Ibn Said. Amra was not an anomaly in Islamic history; it abounds with famous female narrators of jurisprudence, starting with. Ä'isha, the youngest wife of Prophet Muhammed. Women scholars taught imams and judges, issued fatwas, and travelled to distant cities. They went on lecture tours across the Middle East.

Iqbal considered it crucial for developing a Muslim society where women expend their energy on being good wives and mothers. To him, as to most Muslims, Fatima, threefold blessed on account of being the Prophet's daughter, Ali's wife and Hussain's mother, is the perfect role model for women. Her unlimited love, willingness to render selfless services, self-surrender to her husband's will and pleasure. Patience and fortitude inspire all women, irrespective of Muslims or non-Muslims.

The sad comparison with their present situation raises many questions. It is almost as if a catastrophe took place to alter their status so dramatically. The drastic change in Islamic women's status occurred in the 19th and 20th centuries when European powers colonised Muslim lands—this period of colonisation affected society both internally and externally. There was a loss of confidence, which resulted in a loss of tolerance. Muslim men reacted to this loss, not unnaturally, by doing what they thought was necessary for the protection and integrity of their families. They secluded their women from the prying eyes of foreign troops. *Burqas*, the black, tent-like attire women wear, became common. Women were now allowed to go no farther than their front yards.

This image provided fodder for orientalist scholars to depict Muslim harems as characteristic of the decadence of Islam itself. It was a time of retreat and confusion. When the Europeans left in the middle of the 20th century, Muslim women once again emerged in public in varying degrees. Still, they were left to fight now-entrenched local traditions and male views and prejudices. Some of these have virtually nothing to do with Islam. For example, unmarried or widowed women do not inherit property in some parts of the Muslim world. Their male relatives make excuses and pass their greed off as Islamic law. A woman demanding rights or insisting on her career could be in trouble. There is an old proverb understood in Pakistan and Afghanistan: "For a woman, either the *kor* (house) or the *go* (grave)." In traditional homes, the wife's primary role appears to be to serve her husband. It is rooted in another proverb: "Husband is another name for god."

Islam can empower women, as evidenced by numerous religiously observant Muslim women who strove to achieve professional, financial, and social success following their understanding of religious scriptures. As for those Muslim women who do not have similar opportunities, Muslim educationists can create awareness of these rights and sensitize both Muslim men and women to each other's obligations in the Islamic paradigm.

The reversing trend

However, there are few notable women in the modern era. These include Noor Inayat Khan, a British spy and the first female wireless operator who went into occupied France during World War Two, as well as the recently passed Dame Zaha Hadid, a prestigious architect and the first woman to be awarded the Pritzker Architecture Prize in 2004,

It is a pity because women have been crucial players in some of the most defining moments of the faith. There is the Prophet Muhammad's daughter, Fatima, who chastised his feuding followers after his death: "You have left the body of the Apostle of God with us, and you have decided among yourselves, without consulting us, without respecting our rights.

The earlier trend is now history. We hardly ever encounter female Islamic jurists. Women are all but absent from Islamic public and intellectual life. If we scan the centuries of Islamic history records, we find many women active in all areas of life, only to see them marginalized dramatically later. So, what happened? In the last 300 years, finding women involved in Islamic sciences has been unusual. Unlike in the past, significantly few Muslim men would even consider being taught by a Muslim woman.

Many female figures throughout Islamic history have attained glory for their knowledge and morals. The history of women's movements, collected under three waves, manifested in various ways in every field, from politics to art. Therefore, the issue of Islam and women comes to the fore frequently. It is also one of the often-studied themes in culture and art. Many highly respected female figures are among the Prophet Muhammad's companions. These friends, called companions, saw or met the Prophet during his lifetime and followed and continued his path as Muslims. In Arab cinema, some productions have shed light on these women.

In Ottoman literature, a biographical study titled *"Meşahirü'n-Nisa"* stands out. The work *"Meşahirü'n-Nisa,"* which means famous women, contains the biographies of women that Islamic scholars have examined. It is a vital publication of some prominent women in Ottoman literature. The Islamic historiographical texts about the biographies of people living in the same period or region, dealing with the same discipline and performing the same art, are called *"Tabakat."* These books present relevant biographies of successive generations according to their chronological order. They feature thousands of figures, especially poets, artists and scholars. It is where we initially meet famous women.

Unique to the Islamic world, these works exclaim about the first Muslims, so they developed parallel to the first century of Islam. In this deep-rooted tradition of work, we do not come across a remarkable book written only for women. When a substantial section of devout and enlightened women feel that we are trying to give a patriarchal spin to certain crucial verses of the Qur'an that have a critical bearing on the status and rights of Muslim women, we owe a responsibility to respond to their valid concerns. We cannot snuff their voice by simply casting them as anti-Islamist. It is not a sign of our strength; it only exposes our shallowness and reinforces the charge of misogyny against us.

Nadwi's compendium of female *hadith* scholars

Modern research is bringing to light some of the rarely known facets of Muslim women down the ages. First, women deserve a more central place in the historical narrative of Islam, and second, the examples in this book can perhaps foster a more visible and effective role for women in the present and future.

Islamic scholar Sheikh Mohammad Akram Nadwi's epic work al-*Muhaddith lat*: The Women Scholars in Islam stands as a riposte to the notion, peddled from Jakarta to Morocco, that Islamic knowledge is men's work and always has been. "I do not know of another religious tradition in which women were so central, so present, and so active in its formative history," Nadwi writes. Nadwi has pieced together in this epic book the lives and work of hundreds of Muslim women scholars and researchers. Nadwi sheds light on the tradition of female scholarship in Islam, revealing their research contours' deep and broad roots. Nadwi's commentary chronicles the lives and work of thousands of Muslim women researchers. He paints a vivid picture of these transformative women, exploring the motivations that spur them to crucial phases in Islamic scholarship.

A magnum opus spread over a 43-volume biographical dictionary containing 10,000 entries detailing the lives of female *hadith* scholars written by renowned Islamic scholar Shaykh Mohammad Akram Nadwi. As *hadith* narrators, teachers, jurists, wives, mothers and daughters, these women have contributed to the growth and development of the Muslim community on a social, moral and intellectual level. Nadwi has unravelled the previously unexplored history by meticulously analysing documents such as class registers and *ijazah*s from women authorizing men to teach and the glowing testimonies from the most revered 'ulema about their female teachers.

The profound 43-volume dictionary, titled "Al-Wafa Bi Asma Al-Nisa" (Biographical dictionary of women narrators of *hadith*) (also known as al–*Muhaddith lat* — the female *hadith* transmitters) is the result of more than two decades of commitment that took Nadwi scouting biographical dictionaries, classical texts, madrasa chronicles and letters for relevant citations. A conservative count would reveal at least 2,500 extraordinary women jurists, narrators of Prophet Muhammad's sayings (*hadith*), and poets. There is no other religious tradition where women were so central, present, and active in its formative history. Surprisingly, their stories have not been actively researched or adequately acknowledged.

Nadwi's work reveals the high public standing and authority enjoyed by learned women in the formative years of Islam. For centuries after that, women travelled extensively to seek religious knowledge. They routinely attended the most prestigious mosques and madrasas across the Islamic world, teaching, learning, and making significant contributions to the study and transmission of Prophetic *hadith*. This history had previously been unexplored. Nadwi makes a thorough and detailed analysis of documents such as class registers and *ijazah*s from women authorizing men to teach and the glowing testimonies from the most revered 'ulema about their female teachers.

Nadwi also has a few exciting stories to tell. Take Tea, a prominent legal scholar in 7th-century Damascus. As a young woman, she not only studied with the men but also prayed with them in the men's area of the mosque – something that would be unthinkable in the vast majority of mosques today. Or Karima al-Marwaziyya. She lived in Mecca in the 11th century. Her copy of the most critical *hadith* collection, the al-Buhari collection, is still considered definitive.

Altogether, Nadwi estimates women handed down about a quarter of all *hadith*s. What's more, they were not only diligent but also thorough. "When it comes to the Prophet's traditions, many men have been accused of making up *hadith*s. Yet all the *hadith* scholars confirm that lying about one of the Prophet's *hadith*s is not something a woman has ever been accused of, which is amazing."

Female scholarship

Al-Dhahabi praises his teacher, Sitt al-Wuzara bint Umar ibn al-Munajja, as one who was "steadfast, patient for long sessions of teaching".

She taught Bukhari's Sahih in Damascus and Cairo, lived for over 90 years, and was teaching on the last day of her life. Until the 20th century, women scholars were few and far between. If there were any, their work was limited to the confines of their homes.

Nazirah Zein Ed Din (1908-1975) was a Lebanese woman who wrote 'Removing the Veil' and a book on veiling when she was only 28 years old. The book caught the attention of scholars in Muslim and non-Muslim countries alike and led to fierce debates by a small group of men in Egypt. Nazirah argued for social reform, led by women's liberation, which removed barriers to women's education and social participation. She said: "A woman's mind is inherently better than a man's. He surpasses her with his physical strength, and she surpasses him with her reasonable and noble character." Her book came to be widely read and honoured for its sheer force of argument and religious reasoning.

Nusret Begüm Emin of Iran and Aisha Abd-ur Rahman of Egypt wrote well-researched tafsirs. Aisha believed that Eve and Adam were born from the same nafs (spirit) as opposed to the notion that Eve was born from Adam's rib, a view widely propagated over the centuries. Zaynab Al Ghazali was the first woman scholar to interpret the Qur'an through contextual reading. Laleh Bakhtiar was the first American woman to translate the Qur'an into English. Asma Barlas and Riffat Hasan have written extensively about women-specific verses. They use hermeneutics based on the sacred text and provide a holistic basis instead of piecemeal readings for their arguments. Their writings are markedly different from the beliefs propagated by men, focusing on how the Qur'an addresses women and men in society and their mutual responsibilities.

After the Qur'an, the *hadiths* were the second most important source for many Muslims. They have documented records about the life of the Prophet Muhammad – things he is said to have said or done. They are vitally important to Muslims because they translate the abstract message of the Qur'an into everyday specifics. During the early years of Islam, Muslim scholars concerned with establishing *hadith* authenticity handled their source material critically.

In Islamic history, women travelled extensively to seek religious knowledge. They routinely attended the most prestigious mosques and madrasas across the Islamic world, teaching, learning and making significant contributions to the study and transmission of Prophetic *hadith*. The dictionary's diverse entries include a 10th-century Baghdad-born jurist who travelled through Syria and Egypt, teaching other women; a female scholar — or *muhaddithat* — in 12th-century Egypt whose male students marvelled at her mastery of a "camel load" of texts; a seventh-century Medina woman who reached the academic rank of a jurist, issued vital fatwas on hajj rituals and commerce; and the biographies of prominent jurists like Umm al-Darda, in seventh-century Damascus, whose students included the caliph of Damascus.

Author Hossein Kamaly's book is an act of reclamation on several fronts. For Muslim women, it provides an empowering and exhilarating genealogy of strong forebears they can connect to their contemporary empowerment journeys. For Western readers, it exposes the untruths that have characterized Muslim women as submissive beings in need of rescue. Kamaly clarifies that Muslim women have shaped the course of Islam. Instead, when reading through the different eras of Islamic history, we encounter the knowledge that our history has only been half told - that it's women who have shaped the fate of Islam. Whether it's deciding to follow the Prophet Muhammad's biological lineage through Shia Islam or Muhammad's last wife, A'isha, into what is known today as Sunni Islam, if we're moving away from the Prophet Muhammad's time, the impact of Terken Katun's prosperity as the Empress of the Khwarazmian Empire or Nana Asma›u, the princess, poet and founder of the Sokoto Caliphate in West Africa is predominant.

Islamic feminism is an extensive topic, as complex as the lives of women that it encompasses. Several Muslim and non-Muslim scholars have provided cutting-edge scholarship on, among other things, Qur'ānic hermeneutics and ḥadīth studies; women's legal and social rights; women's scholarly, cultural, economic, and political activities in the premodern and modern Islamic societies; the rise of Islamic feminism and women's activism and movements in several contemporary Muslim-majority countries and regions—including Egypt and North Africa, Turkey, Iran, Palestine, Lebanon and Syria, Saudi Arabia and the Gulf region, and South and Southeast Asia—and Muslim-minority contexts in western Europe, the United States, and China.

The politicized portrayals of Muslim women, especially of those who wear the headscarf (ḥijāb), in the global Western-dominated media and the weaponisation of their bodies have been active parts of contemporary feminist discourses. Modern researchers address a broad spectrum of views on critical issues that are prevalent inside and outside academia and provide a sophisticated and careful analysis of textual sources and broad sociological and political trends. They emphasize, above all, the diversity present in Muslim women's lives, both in the premodern and modern periods. They also pay close attention to the historical and political contexts that shaped their lives and framed the thinking and actions of key female figures throughout Islamic history. This approach results in fine-grained macro-and microstudies of Muslim women's lives that problematize reified assumptions of gender and agency in the context of Muslim-majority societies.

There are widely alluded arguments that the male gender bias in Islamic scholarship has affected the interpretations of the Qur'an and *hadith*. However, the historical records show examples of fatwas issued by male jurists that were materially adverse to men and in favour of women. Furthermore, their male students have recounted many of the testaments of excellent female scholarships. Imam Dhahabi noted that among female narrators of *hadith* were fabricators. Women's scholarly integrity and independence were unimpeachable. Naturally, any sexist male would have a problem admitting to these facts. Since women today participate so little in the teaching of *Hadith* and the issuing of fatwas, there is a wide misconception that they have never played this role. When Akram started, I thought there may be thirty to forty women." Still, as the study progressed, the number of females in the account grew, and more than 8,000 accounts have emerged till now. Such vast numbers genuinely testify to the enormous role that women have played in evolving and developing Islamic learning since the time of the blessed Prophet Muhammad.

Apart from well-known figures, including Ayesha Siddiqa, the daughter of Abu Bakr, the grandeur of forgotten scholars is rekindled in the work. Fatima Al Batayahiyyah, an 8th-century scholar, taught Sahih al Bukhari's celebrated work in Damascus. She was known as one of the most outstanding scholars, especially during the Hajj, when leading male scholars of the day flocked from afar to hear her speak in person. Her beautiful picture was painted and displayed but has long disappeared – a distinguished, older woman teaching her students for days in the Prophet's mosque. Whenever she tired, she would rest her head on the Prophet's grave and continue to teach her students as the hours wore on. Women visiting the Prophet's mosque know the frustration of not even being able to see the blessed Prophet's grave, let alone rest their head on its side wall.

A famous scholar, Zainab bint Kamal, taught more than 400 books of *Hadith* in the 12th century. Her "camel loads" of texts attracted camel loads of students. She was a natural teacher, exhibiting exceptional patience, which won the hearts of those she taught. With such a towering intellectual reputation, her gender was no obstacle to her teaching in some of the most prestigious academic institutes in Damascus.

The new approach

Muslim women have morphed into significant advances in many fields, from being literal queens and leaders of their communities to being mathematicians. These women are independent, outspoken, brave, intelligent, and so much more. It was refreshing to see this and not the usual media narrative, which perpetuates stereotypes and always shows Muslim women as weak and submissive. This book, amongst others I have read this year, is the beginning of us taking back the narrative of who we are.

Then there is Umm al-Darda, who used to sit with male scholars in the mosque as a young woman. "I've tried to worship Allah in every way," she wrote, "but I've never found a better one than sitting around debating with other scholars." She became a teacher of *hadith* and *fiqh* and lectured in the men's section. One of her students was the caliph of Damascus. The sheer hard work and dedication to Islam by these women are unfathomable by standards today – but they also had some biological advantages over men. Female *muhaddith lat* students are referred to as learn *hadith* because of their longer lifespan - which shortens the links in the chains of narration.

Umm al-Darda was a 7th-century scholar who taught students in the mosques of Damascus and Jerusalem. The caliph Abd al-Malik ibn Marwan was one of her students. One of the most outstanding 8th-century scholars was Fatima al-Batayahiyyah, who taught in Damascus. During the Hajj, leading male scholars flocked to her lectures. She later moved to Madinah, where she taught students in the revered mosque of the Prophet. Fatima bint Mohammed al Samarqandi, a 12th-century jurist, advised her more famous husband, 'Ala' al-Din al-Kasani, on how to issue his fatwas; she also mentored Salahuddin.

In many Muslim countries, women are already involved in issuing fatwas or legal rulings. Still, frequently, these are confined to "female issues "A woman who is learned and trained in issuing fatwas is not limited in her role to issuing fatwas that relate to women only, but rather, she is qualified to issue on matters of worship, jurisprudence, morality and behaviour".

It will be noted particularly in Egypt, where Soad Saleh, professor of comparative jurisprudence at Cairo's famed al-Azhar University, has been campaigning for ten years for a female mufti to be appointed. As a prominent authority on religion, Saleh says Egypt's Grand Mufti was enthusiastic when she first mentioned it, but nothing has happened since.

With such a towering intellectual reputation, gender was no obstacle to teaching in some of Damascus's most prestigious academic institutes. Then there was Fatima bint Prophet Muhammad al Samarqandi, a jurist who advised her more famous husband on how to issue his *fatwas*.

This line — that it is man-made rules that need to change, not religion — is strengthened by the UAE being the first place where these first muftis will be appointed. However genuine the image of the Emirates as an easygoing boom state may be for expats, it is still a highly traditional society which observes a conservative form of Islam.

If the Grand Mufti of Dubai blasted for being a liberal or a reformist, he would probably be mightily offended and repudiate such descriptions in the strongest terms. Islam needs no "liberalising" or "reforming", he would say. He merely removes the clutter and accretion of male-dominated tradition and culture. It is an important pointer for the future, as Western critics of Islam tend to assume that women's rights in Muslim countries can only be safeguarded and increased through secular means by pushing religion aside. But in Islamic states, it is much more likely that women's emancipation will come from within their religion, from enlightened individuals.

Those who say this is not enough or ask why it has taken so long for Islam to accept women in such positions should perhaps turn their thoughts to the Catholic Church. It has, after all, been around for over 600 years longer than Islam, and it is still nowhere near letting women into the priesthood. The reason for this is that Christ's disciples were all men crucially. In contrast, Muslims can look to several examples of women in positions of religious and political authority in and around the time of the Prophet. Let us hope that more people like him choose to do so.

8. MARRIAGE AND DIVORCE AMONG MUSLIM WOMEN

O you who believe! You are forbidden
to inherit women against their will.
Nor should you treat them with harshness,
that you may take away part of the dowry
you have given them - except when
they have become guilty of open lewdness.
On the contrary, live with them
on a footing of kindness and equity.
If you take a dislike to them,
it may be that you dislike something
and Allah will bring about through it
a great deal of good.
(Qur'an 4:19)

Religions often articulate worldviews that attempt to replace a morally corrupt social order with a purer, if utopian, counterpart. In the Abrahamic tradition, the time of corruption is contrasted with when an agent of God, or prophet, arrived (or will arrive) to lead the people into a new era of righteousness, virtue or guidance. For instance, in Christianity, the world was corrupted by the primordial parents of humanity, Adam and Eve, who sinned in the blissful Garden of Eden and corrupted the world and their countless human descendants (i.e., Original Sin). One day, this world of imperfection and sin will be perfect when Jesus Christ, who sacrificed himself to redeem humanity from Original Sin, returns to the world and ushers in the eternal Kingdom of Heaven. In a world intent on demonising Islam, positive stories about Muslims are all rarefied.

How refreshing it is, then, to see such initiatives to combat the pervasive stereotype of the passive Muslim woman. Most of the positive stories are now coming from women who have a far keener understanding of Islamic marriage and divorce and no longer consider them as taboo and are handling these once contentious issues confidently.

In Islam, marriage is not just a legal contract; it's a spiritual one, too. This spiritual covenant is, perhaps, most beautifully described in the Qur'an when God says that a wife is like a garment for her husband, and a husband is like a garment for his wife (2:187). If we think about what a garment does – it beautifies, elevates, comforts, covers and completes a person. Likewise, this spiritual covenant calls us to be this for each other. Just as a garment hides our nakedness, so do husband and wife. By entering into the marriage relationship, we secure each other's purity of character. The garment comforts the body; the husband finds comfort in his wife's company and her in his. Islam does not consider a woman "an instrument of the devil", but rather, the Qur'an calls her *muhsana* - a fortress against Satan because a good woman, through marriage to a man, helps him keep to the path of righteousness in his life.

A generation ago, Arab divorcees used to be considered objects of scorn. Today, they are often heroines, confronting bastions of patriarchy in courtrooms, mosques and marital beds. A big hit across the Arab world last Ramadan, the Muslim month of fasting (and feasting on television), was an Egyptian soap opera about a mother escaping from her abusive ex-husband. The women believe that pop culture had more impact than decades of fighting for their rights. The pattern of divorce is changing, too. Once, it was almost exclusively a male prerogative. In Morocco, nearly as many women as men initiate a split. Sheikhs may once have quietly rotated their favourites within harems. But polygamy —the practice permitted by the Qur'an whereby a man may have up to four wives simultaneously, provided each is "fairly" treated—is increasingly restricted. In many Muslim countries, it is now not allowed.

Even among royalty, what is novel is that divorced wives are hitting back, even in public. Most Arab rulers have gone with the social flow, curbing the old custom whereby a husband could get rid of a wife merely by declaring talaq, the Arabic term for divorce, three times over. After it became easier for Egyptian women to file for divorce, Algeria, Jordan and Morocco followed suit.

As social influence has shifted from extended families to nuclear ones, with couples marrying more often for love, the relatives are much less able to perpetuate unhappy unions. Marriage has gone from a collective decision made by the family and immediate relatives to an individual choice. Islam has always been pragmatic about marriage. Most of the Prophet Muhammad's wives were widows or divorcees.

Gender parity

Muslim women are showing the world that gender justice is a fundamental principle of Islam. That equality for Muslim women is not a mirage but a distinct possibility. Reforms are being led directly by women, based on their reading of holy texts that emphasize spiritual equality and accountability of men and women. The next step is codifying Muslim family law to eliminate spurious practices.

Such progressive efforts are reminiscent of a formidable woman in early Islamic history, Khawla bint Tha'labah. Given the title of al-Mujadilah ("the one who disputes") in the Qur'an, bint Tha'labah fought against instant divorce in seventh-century Arabia. At the time, a husband could end a marriage by simply telling his wife: "Your back is as the back of my mother." This practice of "dhihar" (literally "back") was widespread, ingrained and unchallenged. Until bint Tha'labah, a devout Muslim woman, came along.

During a heated argument, her husband, Aws, pronounced dhihar. Rather than crumble, bent Tha'labah vented outrage – first at Aws and then to Prophet Muhammad (peace be upon him). "I gave him the best years of my life, bore and raised his children. And now he throws me away. It is wrong!" she pleaded. The Prophet counselled patience. But bint Tha'labah refused to budge. She stood her ground and argued respectfully with the Prophet of Islam to ban the practice. She then prayed directly to God for relief.

Relief came swiftly, decisively, unequivocally in bint Tha'labah's favour. According to historical records, four remarkable Qur'anic verses descended in response to bint Tha'labah's pleading. There was no rebuke against her for arguing with the Prophet. On the contrary, God affirmed her logical stand. "Dhihar" was considered a vile practice and subsequently banned. God prescribed Harsh measures for husbands who indulged in these terrible practices. Those who changed their mind after pronouncing "dhihar"(divorce) were required to pay a steep penalty for the harm they had caused. Husbands can be held accountable for their abuse, duplicity and cruelty.

Bint Tha'labah's example has stood for 14 centuries. Unfortunately, she has remained largely ignored by Muslims in contemporary discourse. Here is an example of a devout Muslim woman who challenged the Prophet, no less, and God unequivocally affirmed such bold steps of women in the Qur'an. She reminds us that we must confront abuse – even when that abuse is sanitized by prevailing cultural norms or sanctioned by religious authority.

Contemporary female Muslim scholars -- are challenging patriarchal interpretations of the Qur'an, thereby providing women with exegetical tools to confront male privilege rooted in theology. Muslim women are realizing that piety does not mean submissiveness. They are finding moral clarity within their spiritual tradition to address contemporary challenges.

The Qur'anic vision of marriage

Marriage was a virtuous act in the eyes of the Prophet Muhammad. He said: "When a man marries, he has completed one-half of his religion."

He enjoined matrimony on Muslims by saying: "Marriage is part of my way, and whoever keeps away from my way is not from me (i.e. is not my follower)." The Qur'an has given the raison d'être of marriage in the following words:

"And among His signs is this that He has created for you mates from among yourselves, that you may dwell in tranquillity with them; and He has put love and mercy between you. Verily in that are signs for those who reflect". (Q 30:21)

Marriage has a genuine and high purpose. The Qur'an puts it this way: "so that you may dwell in tranquility" (Q30:21). It is a serenity that gives one a taste of the spiritual home that we came from and the house to which our soul yearns to return– the abode of the hereafter that will have gardens for the righteous. To grow this garden, God gives us as a wedding gift two seeds with which to plant our flowers and trees: "And God places between (your hearts) love *and* compassion" (Q30:21). Love means commitment and loyalty. Compassion is striving to be and remain empathetic towards each other throughout life and never allowing apathy to settle between ourselves. It means listening to each other and being there for each other during times of ease and difficulty. And it means forgiving each other for shortcomings often and readily.

Life is not always easy, and being in a relationship is not always fruitful. It takes struggle, sacrifice and hard work. The Qur'an offers prayers for the safety and security of women: "We pray, then, that when people walk through the garden of tranquility and eat the fruits thereof, they say this is undoubtedly "from among the signs of God…for those who ponder" (Q30:21)". And we pray as God asks the righteous to pray, "O our Guardian-Sustainer! Grant that our spouses and our children are a coolness for our eyes, and make us foremost among those who are God-conscientious and righteous" (Q 25:74).

Many men who deny their wives and daughters fundamental freedoms hide behind their *Qur'ans*. A favourite passage for patriarchs is the famous thirty-fourth verse of "The Women," the *Qur'an's* fourth chapter. These six lines must surely rank among the most hotly debated in Muslim scripture. The women's group Musawah has called them the "DNA of patriarchy" for the Islamic legal tradition. It is here that many scholars have claimed to find Allah setting out men's superiority and authority over women, a rule that can be mandatory. One popular translation, by the early-twentieth-century English translator Muhammad Marmaduke Pickthall, reads:

"Men are in charge of women because Allah hath made the one of them to excel the other, and because they spend of their property [for the support of women]. So good women are the obedient, guarding in secret that Allah hath guarded. As for those from whom ye fear rebellion, admonish and banish them to beds apart and scourge them."

Debates on how to translate the verse continue to rage. New translations suggest less sexist meanings than earlier ones. One casts men as women's "protectors and maintainers," and another says that "men are to take care of women because God has given them greater strength. One thing remains certain: men's interpretations of the verse have made millions of women miserable.

Purpose of marriage

The ultimate purpose of marriage in Islam is to win the pleasure of God through virtue, fulfilment, contentment and continuation of the species. For instance, among the characteristics of true believers, the safeguarding of chastity through marriage is stressed along with strict and humble observance of prayer, the shunning of all that is vain, the payment of the *zakat* and watchfulness of trusts and covenants:

- "Marry those among you who are single, or the virtuous ones among yourselves, male or female: if they are in poverty, Allah will give them means out of His grace: for Allah encompasseth all, and he knoweth all thing." (Q 24:32)

- "He is the one who created man from water; then, He made a blood and marriage relationship for him. And thy Lord is ever Powerful"1(Q 25:54)

- "One of His signs is this: He has created mates for you from yourselves that you might find the quiet of mind in them, and He put between you love and compassion. Surely, there are signs in this for people who reflect." (Q30:21)

- In the context of praising the prophets preceding the Prophet Muhammad, the Qur'an proclaims:

- And surely We sent Messengers before thee and appointed for them wives and children. (Qur'an 33:38)

- And in praising the habits of good believers, it reads:

- And those who say, "Our Lord, grant us in our wives and our offspring the joy of our eyes . . ." (Q 25:74)

- These true heirs will inherit Paradise, wherein they shall abide. (Q23:11-12)

- Then there is the exordium:

- Arrange the marriages of widows among you and the righteous among those under your control, male and female. Allah will grant them means out of His bounty if they are impoverished. (Q24:33-34)

The Qur'an directs:

- Consort with them graciously. If you dislike them, you may dislike something in which Allah has placed much good. (Q4:20)

- And how could ye take it when ye have gone in unto each other, and they have Taken from you a solemn covenant? (Q4:21)

- Corrupt women are for corrupt men, and corrupt men are for corrupt women. Good women are for good men, and good men are for good women. The latter are innocent of what they say. They will have forgiveness and generous provision. (Q 24:26)

God demands that both spouses be protective of and supervise each other. The Qur'an proclaims this duty in the following words: "They cover you and you for them" (Q2:187). A woman can regain custody of her children if the courts initially ruled in favour of the husband but failed to fulfil his responsibilities. There is also provision for the child to get suitable accommodation consistent with their living conditions before the parents' divorce. This requirement is separate from the other alimony obligations, which conventionally consist of a paltry lump sum. The new law also protects the child's right to acknowledge paternity in cases where the marriage remains to be registered officially, or the child was born outside wedlock. The new law also requires that husbands and wives share the property acquired during the marriage. Husbands and wives can have separate estates, but the law allows the couple to agree on managing and developing assets acquired during marriage in a document other than the marriage contract. The Qur'an is also equally emphatic about the status of women and the obligations to which they are entitled. "And give the women (on marriage) their dower as a gift; but if they, of their good pleasure, remit any part of it to you, Take it and enjoy it with good cheer". (Q4.004)

The Qur'an teaches respect for a woman's body and stresses chastity -- but places the primary burden for chastity on men, not women. While clerics and priests today obliquely declare that women should "get married" or "dress more modestly" to avoid domestic violence, Prophet Muhammad held a different view. While encouraging marriage and modest dress for both genders, the Prophet significantly, and as a foundation, commanded men, "You be chaste yourselves, and women will be chaste." He commanded men to stop obsessing over how women behave and dress and instead demanded men focus on self-reform and self-improvement. While the Qur'an admonishes women to dress modestly in the footsteps of Mary, the Mother of Jesus, it first commands men to "cast down your eyes" and "not stare at women lustfully" -- no matter how a woman chooses to dress. A woman is responsible to herself and God for dressing and acting modestly, while a man is primarily obligated to women, himself, and God to treat women with respect. The real issue is that many vested and unqualified interests have infiltrated the ranks of clerics and are promoting their agendas through flawed and absurd religious edicts.

Detoxification of aberrations in Islam

Something is missing in our current discourse on the role of women in Islam. Namely, when we talk about the pressure on women to conform, we tend to focus only on whether they are physically forced, threatened, or otherwise explicitly told what to do. We overlook that sometimes women make confident choices out of love and the need to be loved.

The religious ideology itself is the whole package of being a Muslim woman, which is as much – if not more – about family loyalty and community cohesion as it is about faith. Although we like to compartmentalize religion and culture – treating them as two distinct entities – they overlap, informing and reflecting each other. Being raised Muslim means you often cannot divorce religious choices from family and community expectations. It is not the fault of Islamic ideology. Islam, in theory, is feminist and progressive. But Islam, in practice, can be challenging for some kinds of women whose concept of liberation and freedom is flawed; it can be impossible to discern where religion ends and cultural pressure begins. It is the problem in trying to find an ideal representative of a group as maligned as Muslims. By sheer virtue of looking at it, the "educated, articulate (and) well-reasoned scholars are still assessing what makes an acceptable Muslim by Western standards,

Unsurprisingly, what makes most women comfortable is someone who isn't too different to them and can soothe their anxieties about the role of women by quoting those Qur'anic verses (and there are many) that elevate the status of women. But this well-meaning desire to strike that perfect balance between Muslim visibility and assimilation is overlooked—the hard choices faced by some Muslim women, which ultimately does Muslim communities no favours. Ultimately, we can't look only to scripture to understand how being Muslim shapes and affects the lives of women – because for many of us, Islam is more than its written word; it is practice, it is culture, and, for better or worse, it is family.

Divorce in Islam

Islam's mandate for modesty has liberated women by rejecting Western sexualisation and the "currency (of) exposed flesh."But – and there has to be a bit – when you live in an environment where "modesty" is itself the most valuable currency in which a woman can trade (both for religious reasons and to preserve her family's good name), it can be a prison from which breaking free may mean losing your family as well as your religion. It was not because the religion itself forbids it or because women did not love their families. Still, because there was no separation between Islam and the context in which the women lived, Islam does not force anyone to stay in a marriage, which does not work even after all possible attempts at reconciliation have failed or a marriage is abusive and cannot provide both men and women with any meaningful and lasting solutions which are at the same time impactful and durable; otherwise, divorce becomes the last and only reasonable resort.

Islam permits divorce under specific circumstances. Traditionally, Islamic law has facilitated the divorce process for men while imposing challenging barriers for women who want to end their marriages. Nevertheless, the Qur'an and *sunnah* emphasize the seriousness of divorce and view it as a last resort. However, Muslim women are now empowered and capable of negotiating these situations. The Prophet Muhammad reportedly said: "Of all the permitted things, divorce is the most abominable with God."(Sunan *Abu-Dawud, Book 6: Book 6, Number 2172,* Narrated by Muharib). A prominent Islamic legal manual characterizes divorce as "a dangerous and disapproved procedure." Because the family is the foundation of Muslim society, the Qur'an encourages husbands and wives to do all they can to resolve their differences and stay together.

The Arabic term for separation by women is *khula*, the Islamic form of divorce when a woman wishes to leave her husband. The word "*Khula*" is derived from the Arabic term "Khal'un," which means extracting one thing from another. The word *Khula* means taking out or taking off. According to Fatwa-I-Qazikhan, *Khula* means to take off your clothes. The spouses are garments to each other, and each takes off their clothes when they make *khula. Sharī'ah* signifies the relinquishment of rights and authority over the wife by her husband, dissolving the marital relationship at the wife's desire in place of compensation paid by her to the husband out of her property.

There is a misconception that Islam does not allow a woman the right to divorce her husband. This lie is spread and made powerful by the halting of the education of girls and women by men, by cultural stigma, and by the mullahs who want to maintain power. In earlier days, husbands wouldn't grant permission, and the *qadi* usually favoured them. But a woman who can read the Qur'an soon learns that her subjugation and oppression are man-made or artificial constructs. A woman doesn't need her husband's permission. The *qadi* (the cleric who solemnizes and dissolves the marriage) will also endorse if he is satisfied with the stand of the women who want separation.

Khula refers to a divorce procedure under Islamic law whereby a woman may obtain a divorce without showing cause by returning her dowry or conceding other financial obligations to her husband. The wife initiates this divorce procedure and is usually not revocable within the waiting period (*iddah*) prescribed for women before remarriage is allowed. Muslim legal sources disagree as to whether the consent of the husband is necessary for this procedure to take effect when a married woman initiates divorce proceedings. It is typically taken recourse for valid reasons such as immoral behaviour, mistreatment from the husband, or if he doesn't provide maintenance. The principle behind *Khula* is to provide women with a way to dissolve marriage in case of an irreconcilable breakdown. It aims to safeguard women's rights and protect them within the framework of Islamic law.

The Fatwi Alamgiri states: "When married parties disagree and are apprehensive that they cannot observe the bounds prescribed by the divine law and that they cannot perform the duties imposed on them by conjugal relationships, the woman can release herself from the tie by giving some property in return, in consideration of which the husband is to give her a *Khula,* and when they have done this, a talaq-ul-bain will take place."

A woman must usually abstain from seeking *khula* for baseless reasons and exert necessary efforts to maintain a harmonious and peaceful relationship with her spouse with mutual respect and love. If the marriage becomes irreconcilable and the husband doesn't issue talaq, she may apply for *khula*. The third caliph of Islam, Umar, once told a man who wanted to divorce his wife as he did not love her: Are all houses built on love? What about loyalty and appreciation? When the continuation of the marriage relationship is impossible for any reason, both men and women are still taught to seek a gracious end as a last resort.

The Qur'an states about such cases:

- "When you divorce women and they reach their prescribed term, then retain them in kindness and retain them not for injury so that you transgress (the limits)." (Q: 2:231. Q: 2:229 and Q33:49).

- "There is no blame upon you if you divorce women you have not touched nor specified for them an obligation. But give them [a gift of] compensation - the wealthy according to his capability and the impoverished according to his capability - a provision according to what is acceptable, a duty upon the doers of good" (Q2:236)

Divorce existed before Islam, but the advent of Islam made the divorce process much more conducive and accessible to women. Women's property was not divisible during a divorce. Whatever a woman earns or is given before and during the marriage remains her property if the marriage ends.[1] It prevents men from taking advantage of women's property or wealth through marriage. On the other hand, the man's property was divisible if a divorce occurred according to the couple's marriage contract.[1] A woman is entitled to support and maintenance from her former husband if required. There are also special instructions on whether divorce occurs before the marriage is consented to or after the dowry. Islam also instituted a three-month waiting period for women called *iddah*. During these three months, women can't re-marry. It can determine whether the woman was pregnant before she remarried. It will ascertain the identity of the natural father correctly.

Moreover, it will also help in correctly establishing the identity and lineage of the child. A husband and wife can also attempt reconciliation during the waiting period. However, men are instructed not to take back their wives to "injure or take undue advantage" of them. When divorce occurs before settling the dowry and consummating the marriage, the Qur'an encourages the man to give the woman money or goods as a goodwill gesture: "O ye who believe! When ye marry believing women and then divorce them before ye have touched them, no period of 'Iddat have ye to count in respect of them: so give them a present. And set them free in a handsome manner" (Q33:49)

The Qur'an seeks a natural solution to human problems that are impactful and durable. It takes into account the embarrassment and humiliation women have to suffer in seeking lifelong maintenance when the relations are estranged: "But if they disagree (and must part), Allah will provide abundance from His all-reaching bounty: for Allah is He that careth for all and is Wise." (Q4:130)

Current awareness of the Islamic position on divorce

Attitudes towards divorce are changing among Muslim women. The earlier generation regarded divorce as immoral, so sustaining a marriage for them was a lifelong project. However, for educated Muslim women, divorce is an entitlement, even within Islamic law. The woe understood that some marriages were not as successful as others, but the notion of her marriage ending in divorce was inconceivable.

Sure, girls who couldn't get along with their in-laws for whatever reason. They bore the injustices because people would say, "That girl isn't worthy. She couldn't conform." There'd be a hint that the girl had some bad habits, or worse, that she was immoral. But that idea of things finishing– well, that was unthinkable. You have never heard about that.

For decades, women maintained that a lifelong separation would have served them better than the dishonour of a divorce. They viewed divorce as the ultimate curse, something the community would use to judge their character.

Although Islam discourages divorce, the faith does acknowledge that situations may arise when marriage no longer fulfils its purpose. She also knew of several examples in Islamic texts and history which emphasise the woman's right to divorce. One oft-quoted *hadith* involves a girl who raised a complaint that her father had given her in marriage against her will. The Prophet told the girl that she could choose or reject her husband. The girl decided to stay in the marriage, explaining that she only wanted to know whether women had any rights.

Many women became victims of how *sharī'ah* law discriminates against gender by making it much easier for a man to end a marriage. A woman can be divorced if her husband pronounces talaq (divorce) three times, although ideally, he should not exercise this right without first seeking counsel or negotiating with his wife. However, the practice can also be misused.

There are ways in which a woman may divorce her husband under Islamic law, although these are cumbersome than the simple pronouncement that men are mandated. At the time of marriage, a woman may ask her husband to delegate the power of pronouncing the divorce to her, thereby giving her the authority to dissolve the marriage contract. Moreover, a husband can no longer reclaim this power once he has transferred it to his wife. Since Islam regards marriage as a contractual relationship, a Muslim woman may also protect herself with the equivalent of a prenuptial agreement. She may seek a divorce if the agreed conditions are not recognized. In practice, however, attaining such entitlements can be difficult. With many unions still arranged by parents, it can be difficult for the bride to make such demands at the time of marriage, mainly if she has not built a rapport with her husband.

Attitudes aren't just changing because Muslim women are becoming more financially independent. Muslim women are also becoming more empowered and ensuring they educate themselves on their religious rights. Although divorce is deeply discouraged in Islam and seen as the last resort, it is nevertheless halal (permissible) for either the husband or the wife to seek the termination of marriage.

Although women still bear the brunt of the burden of shame when it comes to divorce, there is now recognition that the wife isn't automatically at fault if a marriage breaks down. Moreover, with Muslim matrimonial websites now offering specific dating services for Muslim divorcees, there is also a growing appreciation that there is more divorce.

Women's right of inheritance

It is another aspect of a woman's right, which is often held against her by men. The Qur'an says:

- "Men shall have a share in what their parents and kinsmen leave, and women shall have a share in what their parents and kinsmen leave; whether it be little or much, it is legally theirs(Q4:7)

- "O ye who believe! Ye are forbidden to inherit women against their will. Nor should ye treat them with harshness, that ye may take away part of the dower ye have given them except where they have been guilty of open lewdness; on the contrary, live with them on a footing of kindness and equity. If ye take a dislike to them, it may be that ye dislike a thing, and Allah brings about through it a great deal of good" (Q4: 19)

The Qur'an does allocate a woman half the portion of that of her brother in her father's property. We must examine this verse contextually rather than normatively. Women in pre-Islamic society had no right to inherit their father's property. A woman came to the Prophet and complained that when her husband died, since she only had a daughter, her brother-in-law seized all her husband's property, arguing that Arabs do not give any share to daughters in inheritance. On this occasion, the verse on inheritance descended, and the Qur'an created inheritance rights for sisters half that of their brothers. Therefore, the Qur'an created an inheritance right when there was none.

Moreover, like the others, this verse needs to be observed in the context of the existing circumstances. A woman in those days was not an active economic agent; the Qur'an attempted to improve the situation through gradual change. Additionally, the Qur'an tried to compensate her in other ways.

Firstly, she had the right to demand *mehr* (dower) from her fiancé, and unlike in the pre-Islamic period, she had a right to keep the *mehr* amount or property and not her father. No marriage was valid without payment of *mehr* to her, and the Qur'an said she could demand even a heap of gold. Thus, *mehr* tended to be a very substantial amount. There was a proposal to impose a ceiling on the *mehr* amount, but a woman, Fatima, objected. She recited the Qur'anic verse about *mehr* and argued, "O Umar when Allah has allowed us to demand a heap of gold, who are you to put a ceiling over it?" Umar, the second Muslim Caliph, immediately withdrew his proposal.

Additionally, the Qur'an makes it obligatory for a husband to maintain his wife even if she has the means to sustain herself and has substantial property or income. Interestingly, the clergy defined maintenance during Aurangzeb's time (included in *Fatawa Alamgiri*) as serving her cooked food (there not being any obligation on the woman to cook the food), stitched clothes, an independent house to live in and if the husband cannot afford an independent house, an independent room with separate access as well as other necessities for her health and beauty. The idea of maintenance is, therefore, quite comprehensive in Islamic *shari'ah*. If the husband does not pay the wife's maintenance, *shari'ah* entitles her to take out a loan in her husband's name, and the husband will have to pay off the loan. She is also entitled to take the amount due to her from his pocket, without his permission, in case he has not paid her maintenance. Hence, when the verses are observed in totality, even if the sister's share was half that of her brother's, the man accumulated less money because of the many benefits given to the woman.

Umm Salama tells of how two Ansars brought a dispute before the Prophet about a long-standing issue of inheritance for which neither party could produce a witness. "You bring me your disputes," the Prophet told them, "and when no proper evidence is available, I judge them according to my thinking. Based on partial evidence, I might make a settlement in favour of one of the parties, but in so doing, it may be that I take away from the other what his rightful due is. In that case, the one in whose favour I pass judgment should not accept what has been apportioned to him, for that would be like his accepting a firebrand which, on the Day of Resurrection, would stick on his neck." At these words, both the Ansar broke down and wept. "Prophet of God!" they both cried out, "he can have my rightful share!" The Prophet then told them that, given their changed attitude, they should divide the inheritance into two parts, seeking to do what was just and proper. Then, they should draw many figures to show that should have which part. In this way, each would have the other's approval of the share he received (*Kanz al-Umma*)

Contested readings about women's status

There is one verse in the Qur'an which has given rise to debates on the position of women in the Islamic schema. However, most of the misconceptions have veered around the semantics of interpretation and have not tried to analyze the verse in light of the philosophy of the Qur'ān, an organically related text with a textual unity. The Qur'an forbids citation of a verse from the Qur'an—or part of a verse—to derive a ruling without looking at everything that the Qur'an and *hadith* teach. In other words, there are strict subjective and objective prerequisites for *fatwas*, and one cannot 'cherry-pick' Qur'anic verses for legal arguments without considering the entire Qur'an and *hadith*. The Qur'an contains five sentences, which human rights activists say create a cultural climate that excuses violence against women and Islamic scholars say encourages respectful behaviour, not abuse or, cruelty and duplicity.

"Men are the protectors and maintainers of women. Since Allah has given the one more (strength) than the other and because they support them by their means. Therefore, righteous women are devoutly obedient and guard in (the husband's) absence, which is the essence of the injunction. As to those women on whose part you fear disloyalty and ill-conduct, admonish them (first), (next) do not share their beds, (and last) beat (tap) them (lightly); but if they return to obedience, seek not against them means (of annoyance): for Allah is Most High, Great (above you all)." (Q4:34)

This intensely debated verse instructs that a woman should initially be reprimanded, accused, then abandoned in bed and ultimately "beaten" - Nowhere does the Qur'an state that one gender is superior to the other. Some mistakenly translate *"qiwamah"* in Q4:34 as superiority, when in reality, it implies a greater degree of responsibility." At-Tabari, who lived only two centuries after the Prophet, conceptualized the relationship of *"qiwamah"* as being conditional upon the man being able to take care of the socio-economic needs of his wife. This cannot be standardised as any inherent superiority of men over women. In the Qur'an, *"qiwamah"* is used three times and in all three occasions it is conjoined with the idea of justice and fairness. Later in the same verse, Q4:34, another word *"waḍribuhunna"* also has contested meanings.

The term *dharma* is a common Arabic root word with many possible meanings. It can also mean to beat, hit, strike, scourge, chastise, flog, make an example of, spank, go away, strike out on a journey or even seduce. These tools may be used in several ways, as conveyed in the Qur'an. If one were to consult an Arabic dictionary, one would find one of the most extended lists of meanings in the whole Arabic dictionary ascribed to the word *dharma*. In the Qur'an, depending on the context, one can ascribe different meanings to it. For example,

To travel, to get out: 3:156; 4:101; 38:44; 73:20; 1:273

To strike: Q 2:60; 7:160; 8:12; 20:77; 24:31; 26:63; 37:93; 47:04

To beat: Q 8:50; 47:27T

To set up: Q 43:58; 57:13

To give (examples):Q 14:24-45; 16:75,76,112; 18:32,45; 24:35; 30:2858; 36:78; 39:27,29; 43:17; 59:21; 66:10-11

To take away, to ignore: Q 43:5

To condemn: Q 2:61

To seal, to draw over: Q 18:11

To cover: Q 24:31

To explain: Q13:17

The word *waḍribuhunna* originated from the triliteral root *ḍad- ra-ba*, from which 55 verb forms result in the Qur'an. These verbs have wide variations in their meanings - from strike (m*idrib*) to travel or put forth (*darabu*). Literally and parochially translating *waḍribuhunna* as "beating" contradicts the central Qur'anic message of fairness and mercy. In addition, there is no report that Prophet Prophet Muhammad ever struck or beat his wives, even though he, like most mortals, encountered marital challenges.

Classical scholars such as At-Tabari and Ar-Razi both viewed Q4:34 as a staged way to reduce marital conflicts in a culture where violence against women was rampant. At-Tabari went on to note that *waḍribuhunna* means striking without hurting. But Ar-Razi did not even allow that in his explanation. He quoted Prophet Muhammad as proclaiming that men who hit their wives are not among the better men.

They are treating women with the inherent dignity that she was endowed, ensuring that their rights are preserved and advocating that they get equitable opportunities to succeed is necessary to uphold the Qur'anic vision, "O you who have attained to faith! Be ever steadfast in upholding justice," (4:135). If possible, the way forward requires levelling the playing field by changing hearts and minds or instituting affirmative action when antiquated cultural norms prove too intransigent.

When encountering a word with multiple meanings, it is essential to identify the proper meaning according to its context and form the pre-Islamic period, known as *Jahiliyyahh* (the age of Ignorance). It transpires that it was a powerful tool in the hands of men for subjugating and manifested in humiliating women. There were gross practices of physical and emotional abuse of females. If the usual translation of *dharaba* is "a single strike" and is satisfactory in this context, the single strike would restrict the pre-existing practice and is not a recommendation. Later, as Muslim society in Madinah developed towards an ideal state, the final verse in the Qur'an on male-female relationships (Q:9:71) regards women and men as being each other's protecting friends and guardians ('*awliyya*), which emphasizes the cooperation between the two in living together as partners.

Considering the physiological and psychological make-up of men and women, both have equal rights and claims on one another, except for one responsibility, that of leadership. It is a matter that is natural in any collective life and consistent with the nature of man.

The Qur'an thus states:

"And they (women) have rights similar to those (of men) over them, and men are a degree above them" (Q: 2:228). Such a degree is *qawwamun* (maintenance and protection). It refers to that natural difference between the sexes, which entitles the weaker sex to protection. It implies no superiority or advantage before the law. Yet, a man's leadership role concerning his family does not mean the husband's dictatorship over his wife. Islam emphasizes the importance of taking counsel and mutual agreement in family decisions. The Qur'an gives us an example: "…If they (husband and wife) desire to wean the child by mutual consent and (after) consultation, there is no blame on them" (Q: 2: 233).

Reprimanding of women

All human beings are ontologically equal; they are distinct among themselves on their rightful practice or implementation of the fundamental Qur'anic principle of justice. Hence, there is no contradiction between being a feminist and being a Muslim once we perceive feminism as an awareness of constraints placed upon women because of gender. The disputed ideas derive in part from those verses in the Qur'an stating that God has preferred (*faddala*)men to women, given them a degree (*daraja*)over women and made them guardians of women(*qawwamun ala*). The traditions of the Prophet showed that he was opposed to wife-beating.

Fadilah is the Arabic word used in the scriptures to indicate the additional, masculine quality of protectiveness. For a household to run correctly, it should, of necessity, have a guardian. Guardianship is with the family member who is best qualified to undertake this responsibility – namely, the husband- for protectiveness is a virtue nature has granted in more significant measure to men than women. Far from mentioning absolute masculine superiority, the above-quoted verse only implies that man is the master in the home because of the additional attributes. *Faddala ba'dahum'alaba'd* is an Arabic expression meaning 'excelled some on other,' 'which occurs several times in the Qur'an. For instance, various crops and fruits grow from the same soil and water. The Qur'an says: "And in the land, there are adjoining plots: vineyards and com fields and palm groves, the single and the clustered. Yet We make some excel others in taste. Surely in this, there are signs for men of understanding" (Q13:4).

All commentators on the Qur'an have emphasised this difference and variety, rather than some fruits being superior, in an absolute sense, to others. That is to say. Each fruit has some particular quality in terms of colour and taste. Similarly, there are differences between men and women. Just as women have uniquely feminine qualities; men also have uniquely masculine qualities: "For men, it is a share of what they have earned, and for women is a share of what they have earned. And ask Allah for his bounty. Indeed Allah is ever, of all things, knowing" (Q4:32)

Given the general tenor of chapter 4, where women's rights are emphasized with great vigour, and in the same vein, the oppression of women is discouraged and believers are encouraged to be kind to each other, it will be logical sense to interpret and translate Q4:34 in favour of women. Overall, traditions have gone out of their way to emphasise that the term used here for hitting (*dharaba*) has only a symbolic significance and does not amount to physical beating. Literally and parochially translating *dharaba* as "beating" contradicts the central Qur'ānic message of fairness and mercy. In addition, there is no report that Prophet Muhammad struck or beat any of his wives, even though he, like most mortals, encountered marital challenges.

The historians al-Tabari (838–923) and Ibn Kathir emphasized that the beating should not be "severe" or "violent," with interpretations of severity ranging from breaking the bone to breaking the flesh. In the modern period, scholars such as Prophet Muhammad'Abduh (1849–1905) and Rashid Rida (1865–1935) have defended the hitting of women without severe harm. However, Prophet Muammad'Abduh argued that the tradition in which the Prophet said, "the best of you would not beat their wives", amounts to a virtual prohibition. Sayyid Qutb (1906–1966) argued that a man may beat his wife as a preventative measure "in an unhealthy situation to protect the family against collapse." The famous contemporary Islamic scholar Yusuf al-Qaradawi (b. 1926) states that a man is "entitled to the obedience and cooperation of his wife" and that if he does not receive this, as a last resort, he can "beat her lightly with his hands, avoiding her face and other sensitive areas."

Therefore, the mainstream interpretation of the verse is both a literal and de-contextualized reading: men have authority over women, who need to be obedient, and using a weka corporal warning is justifiable in the case of their disobedience. There is also a dispute over the first part of the verse, which focuses on the term *qawwamun*. Like most classical scholars, al-Zamakhshari (1074/5–1144/3) interpreted *qawwamun* to mean that "men are in charge of the affairs of women" because of some inherent superiority. Like many other modernist scholars, Fazlur Rahman agrees that "men are in charge of women" but argues that this is because they must support women. Thus, it is functional rather than an inherent superiority, and this functional authority cannot acquire superiority for men.

Marital harmony

In Q 4:34, as a first step, when there is marital discord, the Qur'an advise the husband to resolve the conflict with his wife through discussions (*fa'izu hunna*). If differences persist, then as a next step, the parties are asked to sexually distance themselves (*wahjuru hunna*) from each other in the hope that temporary physical separation may encourage them to unite. If even this fails, the husband is instructed, as a third step, to once again explain (*wazribu hunna)* to his wife the seriousness of the situation and try r to bring about reconciliation. Prophet Muhammad commented: "The most detestable of the permitted things in the eyes of God is divorce."

Delineating the three-tier measures to deal with a recalcitrant wife, namely admonishing(*wa 'z),* deserting in bed(*hajr),* and beating(*darb),* the jurists expounded their juridical descriptions along with the assigned legal rulings to them- within the frame of five Islamic legal taxonomy of human actions known as mandatory, recommended, prohibited, reprehensible and optional.

(Step 1) *Wa 'z,* which means to encourage, admonish, warn, advise, was delineated to be in the form of reminding the wife about her duty towards the husband and the religious consequences when defying it, coaxing her to be a loving and respectful wife, persuading her to be obedient rather than rebellious and so on. Consultation can be between the parties (as in Q4:34) or between the two parties with the help of judges or *hakim* (4:35, 4:128)

(Step 2) *On the other hand, Hajr* means abandonment, forsaking, and desertion.

(Step 3) *Darb* means to strike, hit, smite, beat, throb, grab, prevent, and voyage.

Modern debates over Q 4:34 inevitably hark back to a still widely used 1930 translation of the Qur'an by Marmaduke Pick hall in British Muslim. Pickthall determined the verse to mean that, as a last resort, men can "scourge" their wives. A 1934 translation of the Qur'an by Indian Muslim scholar A. Yusuf Ali inserted a parenthetical qualifier: Men could "beat them" (lightly).

Several scholars plead that the advice is always broad and relevant to different cultures and times. In our modern context, hitting one's wife is inappropriate, as society deems it hateful, and it will only serve to sow more discord. They feel that medieval traditions have become attached to sacred texts like barnacles and must be filtered. Some Saudi women have been trying to do this by emphasizing the public role played by A'isha. Some analysts hold that the verse cannot be rendered meaningfully into English because it reflects the social and legal practices of the Prophet's time.

Religious scholars outline several main threads in the translation of *dharaba*. Conservative scholars consider that the Qur'an holds that force is an acceptable last resort to preserve essential institutions, including marriages and nations.

The Qur'an itself propounds the philosophy of mutual support between husband and wife. It does not differentiate gender in bestowing benefits directly related to one's piety and good deeds.

- "And the believing men and the believing women are protectors and supporters of one another... " (Q9:17)

- "In God's eyes, the most honoured of you are the ones most mindful of Him: God is All-Knowing, All-Aware." (Q 49:13)

God also says: House the women where you live, according to your means, but do not harass them to reduce them to straitened circumstances. If they are pregnant, then spend on them until they give birth to the child. And if they suckle the child for you, then make the due payment to them and consult each other appropriately. (Q65:6)

There is plenty of material in the Qur'an that is more egalitarian than the Western Christian tradition, which was heavily influenced by the misogyny of Greek thought. Perhaps the most fundamental is that the Islamic God does not have a gender. Arabic may refer to him by use of the male pronoun, but He is never described as "father" or "lord" as He is in the Judaeo-Christian tradition. Indeed, the Islamic God has expressly feminine characteristics; one of his most important "names" is *al-Rahman* (the All-Compassionate) from the Arabic *rahma*, which comes from the *word rahim*, meaning womb. Prophet Muhammad was, by all accounts, a feminist. He gave Muslim women the right to own property and inherit, rights denied to their Jewish and Christian sisters by men until the late 19th century. He ended the Arab practice of female infanticide and worked tirelessly to protect widows and orphans in a brutal desert world.

Polygamy in Islam

The Qur'anic institution of polygamy was a piece of social legislation. It was crafted not to gratify the male sexual appetite but to correct the injustices done to widows, orphans, and other female dependants, who were especially vulnerable. It ensured that unprotected women would be decently married and abolished the old loose, irresponsible liaisons; men could have only four wives and must treat them equitably; it was an unjustifiably wicked act to devour their property.

Polygamy has the usual stereotypes of the Church of Jesus Christ of Latter-day Saints (Mormons) and the harem of the Ottoman Turks. Polygamy has a much richer and fuller history than these images suggest. Key terms such as polygamy, polygyny, polyandry, and marriage need a definition to appreciate this topic thoroughly, as do key themes, including gender, the relations between women and men, and the relations between women and men. Another theme is sex and reproduction. Labor and slavery, especially the role of women in domestic work, as well as rank and status, are also themes that inform this topic. Finally, an essential element to consider is the clash of religion and culture, race, and ideas of progress.

Although polygamy is allowed if the husband treats all his wives equally – something that the very same verse that authorizes multiple marriages says is impossible -- only recently has this been interpreted to mean the prophet preferred monogamy. Islam indeed permits polygamy, but on this point, Muslim law is more elastic and more in harmony with the requirements of society than the other systems of law, which do not permit polygamy in any case. Supposing there is a case in which a woman has young children and falls chronically ill, becoming incapable of doing the household work. The husband cannot employ a maid-servant for the purpose, not to speak of the natural requirements of marital life. She also supposed that the sick woman gives her consent to her husband to take a second wife and that there is a woman who agrees to marry the individual in question. On the contrary, Western law would permit immorality rather than a legal marriage to bring happiness to this afflicted home.

Muslim law is nearer to reason, for it admits polygamy when a woman herself consents to such a kind of life. The law does not impose polygamy but only permits it in some instances. Polygamy is not the rule but an exception. This exception has manifold advantages, social and other - the details would be burdensome here - and Islamic. All Muslims agree that the Qur'an is rich with meaning.

Furthermore, the Qur'anic truth structure is both absolute and dialectical. It is absolute in so far as it is the word of God. It is dialectical because our developing human consciousness comprehends that absolute truth dialectically, which grows as we grow in our understanding. The Qur'an itself recognizes this human limitation in its methodology. The revelation of the verse was gradual, like some of the other prohibitions (such as drinking alcohol), which became applicable gradually. These prohibitions include those relating to women and slavery. They became progressively applicable as they were deeply entrenched and needed gradual abolition to achieve final and stable results.

This part of Qur'anic philosophy is not only based on the principle of gradualism in social change but also on the divine wisdom of fostering human democracy, i.e., the society's collective ability to make its own choices. Otherwise, God would have initially denied us all freedom of choice and imposed all truths upon us. This result, however, would be contrary to the Qur'anic assertion that "there is no compulsion in matters of religion." For example, the Qur'an did not prohibit slavery outright in a world in which slavery was rampant and economically very significant. Instead, it provided rules and principles that, if followed by pious Muslims carefully, would have eliminated slavery in a generation or two. The fact that it took the world in general centuries to achieve the Islamic ideal of eliminating slavery illustrates how deeply rooted that idea was in the world community and how extensive the changes necessary for achieving it were.

Polygamy itself, which Islam allowed under specific circumstances, became a distorted and much-abused practice. Affluent men often practised polygamy to satisfy their physical desires. Yet, in Islam, a man can take another wife only under certain circumstances but carries with it the fulfilment of stringent conditions and terms. The gracious, just, and fair Islam was the first to regulate and restrict polygamy, which several centuries before was accepted by all the existing religions and customs and was exercised with no limitation whatsoever. By way of restriction, Islam put a set of stringent conditions on polygamy, emphasising impartiality among co-wives.

The worst tragedy for a woman is when her husband passes away, and, as a widow, the responsibility of maintaining the children falls upon her. In the Eastern World, where a woman does not always go out to earn her living, the problems of widowhood are indescribable. Prophet Muhammad upheld the cause of widows. Most of his wives were widows.

In an age when widows were rarely permitted to remarry, the Prophet encouraged his followers to marry them. He was always ready to help widows and urged his followers to do the same.

Qur'an's injunction against the exploitation of women

The topic of polygamy engenders a defensive reaction in modern conservative Muslims. It is partially due to Western criticism of that institution. While the conservative defence of polygamy is mainly directed at the West, its real target is those modern Muslims who, in accommodation with Western norms, fail to support polygamy as an intricate part of the moral Islamic social order. In the Arab world, this controversy goes back to the nineteenth century when modernist reformism first decried the post-Muhammadan application of this institution as a social problem in modern Muslim societies. The Egyptian theologian

Muhammad Abduh (d. 1905) wrote in impassioned language about male tyranny and lasciviousness, female exploitation and oppression, and the corruption of the new generation, all features of the nineteenth-century reality of polygamy gone wrong. Indeed, it was this theme that inspired Abduh's most daringly innovative Qur'an interpretations and *fatwas* (legal opinions), in which he called for the abolition of polygamy in Islam. Polygamy, he argued, had been a sound and valuable practice among the righteous early believers (ial-*sala' al-salih)* but had developed into a corrupt practice of unbridled lust, devoid of justice and equity, and thus was no longer conducive to the community's welfare.

Conservative and fundamentalist thinkers reject Abduh's conclusions, although not always his methodology. The vast socioeconomic changes of the past century, expressed in ideological pressures of feminist and other liberal movements and even some government-sponsored legislation (proposed, or in the Tunisian case, enacted have intensified the controversy. It is in reaction to this new world that conservatives rally in solid defence of polygamy. The biographies of the Prophet and his wives speak out in support of the institution through three main arguments. Firstly, polygamy is the more honourable and compassionate system because it protects the older, sick, or barren wife from divorce while ensuring progeny for the man who may take a second young and healthy spouse. Secondly, polygamy is the most equitable and meaningful solution to demographic problems in times of war, when soldiers lose their lives and there are not enough men to ensure marriage and motherhood opportunities for all females. Thirdly, polygamy as a response to situations of necessity is far superior to the type of monogamy practised in the West, where 'favourable laws' leave loopholes (e.g., by tacitly permitting extramarital sexual liaisons) that create grave social inequities and also always lead to social hypocrisy. However, this solution should remain impactful and durable.

9. MUSLIM VEIL – A SYMBOL OF MODESTY

One of the most potent Islamic symbols that has been engaging close attention across feminist, Orientalist, social, religious, and political discourse is the veil - the *hijab* (a scarf wrapped tightly around a woman's head to conceal every wisp of hair). Veiling has become, perhaps more than any other major, even obsessive—topic of public debate over the past two decades.

Few sartorial choices have had such close debates as those of Muslim women. Their clothing is regulated both in countries where Islam is a minority religion and in those where the majority professes it. France bans face coverings, thus outlawing the *niqab*, which leaves just a slit for the eyes. In Iran, a theocracy, and Saudi Arabia, a monarchy reliant on clerical support, women must wear a *hijab* (head covering) and abaya (long cloak), respectively. Only recently did Turkey partially ease a ban, dating from Ataturk's founding of the modern secular state, on female civil servants wearing headscarves.

Veiling, traditionally called in the Islamic lexicon as *hijab*, has become a worldwide phenomenon, expressing a new response to modernity. It also represents a translational form of Islamic feminism marked by the entry of women into all public spheres of Islamic life, including formal religious learning (Qur'anic interpretations, etc). The symbol that had in the past meant public invisibility has become a political expression of Islamic identity, which ensures perfect public respectability and supports the entry of Muslim women fully into contemporary public life.

A veil is understood in most communities as a piece of cloth or netting worn by women over the head, shoulders, and, in some cultures, over the face. Since only women, and often only fertile women, have to conceal their face in this fashion, wearing a veil is a highly gendered practice which is strongly contested in feminist but also in multicultural contexts. Some regard it as a form of female oppression, while others view it as simply a particular cultural practice. Some women who wear the veil argue that they choose to do so, while others regard it as imposed but feel unable to resist the cultural pressure to do so.

The veil has a role that fits different situations. In social meetings in which they mix with non-Muslim friends, work outside the home or interact with strangers, they may wear the veil as a signal to others in their community to show that mixing with others does not compromise their righteousness. It may also strengthen their commitment to their faith and its values in a secular world.

Studies find that, as you might expect, the tendency for veil-wearing decreases among young, highly educated women when they are exposed to modern influences if they are 'averagely religious' Muslim women. However, Muslim women who are 'highly religious' tend to increase their wearing of religious head coverings and use more conservative styles as the level of modernisation, or 'risks' they are exposed to, increase.

Hijab:- veil of controversy

The *hijab* (a scarf wrapped tightly around the heads by Muslim women to conceal every wisp of hair), popularly called the veil, is an ally of empowered modern Muslim women and shouldn't be equated with backwardness. The *hijab* expresses a translational form of Islamic feminism marked by the entry of women into all public spheres of Islamic life, including formal religious learning. The word *ḥijāb* is used in the contemporary Islamic world about a head-covering and a particular style of dress considered modest and Islamic. This style differs from various rural dress traditions and has become much more prevalent in Muslim communities in recent decades.

Hijāb originates from the root h-*j*-*b*; its verbal form, *hajaba*, translates as "to veil, to seclude, to screen, to conceal, or a separation, to mask." *hijāb* translates as "cover, wrap, curtain, veil, screen, partition." The same word refers to amulets carried on one's person (particularly as a child) to protect against harm. Another derivative," h*ijāb* means eyebrow (protector of the eye), was also used during the caliphate period for the official who screened applicants who wished for an audience with the caliph.

The English term "veil" is commonly used to refer to Middle Eastern women's traditional head, face, or body covers. However, in Arabic, different terms refer to diverse articles of women's clothing that vary according to region and era. Some of these Arabic terms are *burquʿ* (*burqa*), *ʿabāyah, ṭarḥah, burnus, jilbāb,* and *milāyah.* Overgarments such as the *ʿabāyah* of Arabia and Iraq and the *burns* of the Maghrib tend to be very similar for both sexes. The word *niqāb* refers to a face veil, which in its contemporary form covers the nose and lower face but not the eyes.

Most Muslim women want to dress modestly in public, as Islam prescribes. But increasing numbers want to be fashionable, too. That is partly because of the Islamic world's relative youth and rising prosperity. A growing sense of religious identity also boosts Islamic style. The Islamic revival of the 1970s, and then a shared understanding of persecution in the aftermath of the September 11th attacks, led many Muslim women to wear their hearts on their sleeves. Many say that Islamic dress is better suited to modern life than their country's traditional garb. The *hijab* helps women by making men look for their minds, not their looks.

The veiling and seclusion of women did not arise with the advent of Islam, nor are these institutions indigenous to Arabs. Strict seclusion and the veiling of matrons were in place in Roman and Byzantine societies. Some evidence indicates that in the southwestern Arab region, only two clans (the Banū Ismāʿīl and Banū Qaḥṭān) may have practiced some form of female veiling in pre-Islamic times. No seclusion or veiling existed in ancient Egypt, either. However, some women may have used a head veil in public later, during the reign of Ramses III (twentieth dynasty).

Though Muslim women may differ in their adherence to tradition, maintaining modesty is the overarching Islamic ethic. Veiling was once an armoury of the impoverished classes. Today, it is the mascot of the most enlightened Muslim girls pursuing prestigious courses in top-class universities. Female education is now a high priority in Muslim societies. The present generation has access to an enormous corpus of primary and highly authentic secondary sources of Islamic knowledge. Many Muslim women are now at the forefront of several pioneering campaigns without compromising their modesty. They are lodestars for their upcoming generations.

The importance of women's decisions to wear the *hijab* leads to a heated discussion about where, how, and why one expresses one's sexuality. It is one of the most significant sources of misunderstanding between Western feminists and Muslim women. Those who use the veil do not wish to express their sexuality in public and believe that its proper place is in the privacy of an intimate relationship. Sexuality is not to be used to assert power but to express love, they add. They hotly deny that veiling and modesty in public is a form of repression.

It is not about the shame of the female body, as Western feminists sometimes insist, but about claiming privacy over their bodies. The Moroccan writer Fatima Mernissi ponders on how, in the West, women reclaiming their bodies have led to the public expression of their sexuality. For Muslim women, wearing the *hijab* is an act of worship as well as a way to practice modesty, a principle expected in the behaviour and dress of all Muslims. Although the visibility of the head coverings has made women targets of Islamophobia, Muslim women who wear them say the decision to wear the cloth covering is a liberating one. By sharing their diverse *hijab* journeys, they say they are proof that Muslim women are not a monolith.

As beautiful as veils are, they are not the best part of being a Muslim woman -- and many Muslim women in Islamic countries don't veil. The central blessing of Islam to women is that it affirms their spiritual equality with men, a principle stated over and over in the Qur'an, on a plane believers hold to be untouched by the social or legalistic "women in Islam" concerns raised by other parts of the Scripture, in verses parsed endlessly by patriarchal interpreters as well as Muslim feminists and used by Islamophobes to "prove" Islam's sexism. It is how most believing Muslim women experience God.

Etymology of *hijab*

The word *hijab* stems from the word *hijab*, meaning "to prevent from seeing In Islamic scholarship, *hijab* refers to broader notions of modesty, privacy, and morality. A history of colonialization Eurocentric and Orientalist discourse depicting non-Western cultures as backward," combined with the Gulf War, the "War on Terror," and the deteriorating situations in Iraq and Afghanistan, have all contributed to the misunderstandings of Islam and, specifically, the *hijab*. The *hijab* has often been misperceived as a symbol of oppression or a sign of extremism, resulting in an idea that Muslim women need to be liberated from it. However both Islamic men and women have done extraordinary things to clear the misunderstood in most cities. We are now at a stage where a veil is a sin of empowerment, and even high women feel that it gives them agency. The entire discourse has now changed the fight against the *hijab* societies whose veil as a threat will not be able to hold back the march towards *hijab*. The *hijab* has now become the most potent symbol of Muslim women's rejection of Western notions of feminism. It articulates a new response to modernity.

The *hijab* also expresses a translational form of Islamic feminism marked by the entry of women into all public spheres of Islamic life, including formal religious learning. Some women wear the *hijab* because it is a national tradition of their country of origin or the norm in their local area, city, or country. Others wear it to demonstrate their commitment to dressing modestly and for religious reasons.

The most fundamental source of Islamic law is the Qur'an, which prescribes the *hijab*. A detailed explanation of the second most essential scripture, the *haditlh* is found in the recorded sayings and actions of the Prophet Muhammad (peace be upon him). Although people usually discuss *hijab* only in the context of women, the Qur'an prescribes for both Muslim men and women to be modest in both character and dress. Any differences between the Islamic dress of men and women are concerned with the differences between men and women in nature, temperament, and social life. A *hijab* is a way of ensuring that the moral boundaries between unrelated men and women are respected. In this sense, the term *hijab* encompasses more than a scarf and more than a dress code. It is an instrument for engendering morality and uprightness. But at the same time, the *hijab* cannot be used as a marker or benchmark to judge the morality of a Muslim woman and her "Muslimness". The purity of her spiritualism and the virtue of her character are more important than the moral value of her *hijab*. For instance, if a Muslim woman were wearing a scarf but at the same time using foul language, she would not be fulfilling the requirements of the *hijab*.

The serene spirit sent from God is called by a feminine name, "sakinah," in the Qur'an, and some Muslim women prefer to wear their prayer clothes for more than prayer, to take that *Sakinah* into the world with them. They wore a (smaller) version of the veil when they went out. What a loss not to have this alternating structure covering outdoors and uncovering indoors in life. It signifies the presence or peace of God. As mentioned in the Qur'an (Q48:4) and elsewhere, God sent it into the hearts of believers and upon His messenger, Prophet Muhammad, as support and reassurance. Associated with purity and moments of divine inspiration, *Sakinah* in Islamic mysticism signifies an interior spiritual illumination.

The origin of seclusion

The veiling and seclusion of women did not arise with the advent of Islam, nor are these institutions indigenous to Arabs. Strict seclusion and the veiling of matrons were in place in Roman and Byzantine society. Some evidence indicates that in the southwestern Arab region, only two clans (the Banū Ismāʿīl and Banū Qaḥṭān) may have practised some form of female veiling in pre-Islamic times. No seclusion or veiling existed in ancient Egypt, either. However, some women may have used a head veil in public later, during the reign of Ramses III (twentieth dynasty).

Veiling and seclusion were prevalent in Mesopotamian cultures and among the Tasmanians of Persia before Islam adopted it. In ancient Mesopotamia, the veil for women was a sign of respectability and high status; decent married women wore it to distinguish themselves from enslaved women and unchaste women—indeed, the latter could not cover their heads or hair. In Assyrian law, harlots and enslaved people did not veil, and those caught illegally veiling were liable to severe penalties. Thus, veiling was not simply to mark aristocracy but to distinguish "respectable" women from disreputable ones.

Successive invasions led to some synthesis in the cultural practices of the Greek, Persian, and Mesopotamian empires and the Semitic peoples of the regions. Veiling and seclusion of women appear subsequently to have become established in Judaic and Christian systems. Gradually, these spread to Arabs of the urban upper classes and eventually to the general urban public. Covering the head (but not the face) was widespread in rural areas. In medieval Egypt, public segregation of the sexes existed among Jewish Egyptians; women and men entered their temples through separate doors. Evidence also suggests that Jewish women of that period veiled their faces, as did Muslim women, who were encouraged to behave modestly.

Veiling of Arab Muslim urban women became more pervasive under Ottoman rule as a marker of rank and exclusive lifestyle, and the geographic and occupational differences in dress existed in seventeenth-century Istanbul. By the nineteenth century, upper-class urban Muslim and Christian women in Egypt wore the *habarah*, which consisted of a long skirt, a head cover, and a *burqa*, a long rectangular cloth of white transparent muslin placed below the eyes, covering the lower nose and the mouth and falling to the chest. A Black Muslim veil known as the bisha became a practice in mourning. Perhaps related to the origins of the practice among Jews and Christians, the word *habarah* itself derives from early Christian and Judaic religious vocabulary.

There are important implications for policymakers, such as if the option of wearing a veil has come from Muslim women. They fall on costlier ways of proving their morality and righteousness. A veil is a genuine expression of a woman's religiosity. Paradoxically, the women engaging with the modern world appear to rely on the veil to signal to others that they will not succumb to the temptations of contemporary urban life.' Highly religious women who have more native friends and live in areas dominated by natives use the veil to keep their pious reputation while being integrated. Banning or shunning veiling would deprive them of a means that allows them more opportunity for integration rather than marking their differences.'

The debasing power of gaze

Recognizing the potentially intrusive and debasing power of the gaze, God instructs men and women alike in the Qur'an to lower their eyes and dress modestly in public. "Say to the believing men that they restrain their eyes and guard their private parts. That is purer for them. Surely, God is well aware of what they do." (Q24:31)

The Qur'an further proclaims:-"And say to the believing women that they restrain their eyes and guard their private parts and that they disclose not their natural and artificial beauty except that which is apparent thereof, that they draw their head-coverings over their bosoms, and that they disclose not their beauty save to their husbands, or their fathers... (a list of exceptions)." (Q24:32)

It recorded that the wives of the Prophet went veiled, and in this way, we're able to recognize one another and be honoured by other women for their distinction. The conflicts in Iraq and Afghanistan resulted in several misunderstandings of Islam, and the *hijab* was the most prominent symbol of revolt. The previous and current misunderstandings of Islam have fostered several state restrictions placed on the *hijab*. Courts have avoided a decision on the merits and ruled against the *hijab* wearer. Agencies have courts which have formulated arbitrary or inconsistent standards permitting *hijab* only with several restrictions.

The debates around *hijab* soon spread, and several countries began reinterpreting them. It is according to their contexts. The traditions relating to *hijab* were further analysed, scrutinized, and critiqued. The *hijab* is an Islamic concept of modesty and privacy, usually expressed through women's clothes. It is often a cultural, not a religious, construct which has now acquired a new s; symbolism with Muslim women. The *hijab* soon became a controversial concept as modern societies took a view that depicts the *hijab*-wearing woman as a traumatised, weakened woman, stripped of her 'equal rights', forced to 'veil' her sexuality, and mandated as inferior by the tenets of Islamic principle. Even though this view is severely flawed and distorted the Islamic tenets, the *hijab* became an easy target *hijab* an easy target and. Several countries and cultures use it to advance political agendas and facilitate and justify discrimination.

Several faiths practice the *hijab*

The *hijab* is not unique to Islam, but it has also been part of other religions, such as Judaism (where the idea of modesty is called *Tzuniut*) and Christianity. The *hijab*'s purpose is simply modesty: modesty of clothing, modesty of thoughts, and modesty of actions. It was once an armoury of the impoverished classes. Today, it is the mascot of the most enlightened Muslim girls. They often describe how it liberates them from the toxic consumerist culture, from men's predatory gaze, sexism, and impure moral thoughts. Women wearing *hijab* have been very candidly and publicly emphasizing that dressing modestly and covering their hair minimizes sexual harassment in the workplace. It is a path that aids self-purification and coming nearer to their Creator. Paradoxically, it is the women who rely on the veil to signal to others that the argument that the veil is indicative of oppression has no logic. A woman can wear it as an instrument of modesty yet still embrace all the rights and opportunities given to other modern women.

People in France have come to regard the veil as a political lens in a territory where Islam appears to be a threat on account of the French embracing Islam in large numbers. However, this surge finds no hindrance in integrating with their co-students or from encouraging their co-religionists to integrate as long as Islam is no longer a threat. In Islam, there is no threat for the French school children who can look forward to feminism as a comment and as a warning against several social hazards.

They see both feminism and Islam as inherently at odds, not because of their ideology but because the people of France are embracing Islam. Islam provides more structure and discipline than other religions. It is a way to "refuse modernism" and return to a society with more family values and a more apparent distinction between men and women.

The administrative authorities of organizations see the veil as more about social exclusion than this revival of 'communities. It is labelled maliciously as a social disrupter, which precludes integration alibi for several discriminatory policies and arbitrary rules of Muslim women into secular society. The *hijab* expresses a translational form of Islamic feminism that has been nuanced by the entry of Muslim women into all public spheres, including formal religious learning. It is a vehicle for distinguishing between women and men and a means of controlling male sexual desire.

Tool for confidence and courage

The *hijab* is not a piece of cloth but a mascot, an ex to enjoy a woman's personality transformation and something which makes her upbeat and enhances her confidence and courage in addressing her concerns. Muslim women are seeking to reclaim their right to speak to re-appropriate their destinies. Indeed, today, many female Muslim intellectuals living in Muslim societies and the West are questioning several negative preconceptions surrounding these issues. In particular, they contest the classical analysis, which stipulates inequality between men and women, by asserting that it is the biased readings endorsed by patriarchal customs which have legitimised these distorted perceptions.

The Muslim women argue that Western women must understand the necessity of recognising and consciously accepting the broad cultural differences between Western and non-Western conceptions of autonomy and respecting social standards that reflect non-Western values. Muslim women must work in full partnership with Muslim men, rejecting Western models of liberation but also, and more importantly, negotiate their issues within the Qur'anic paradigm.

The Arabic word for modesty is *haya*. The exciting thing about this word is that it is linguistically related to the Arabic word for life (*hayat*). Muslim scholars and sages have taken from this that there is an intimate connection between the two terms. Modesty is the virtue that gives spiritual life to the soul. This connection between spiritual life and modesty exists because the virtue is not just about outward appearances; instead, it is tolerance first and foremost about the inward state of having modesty before God - meaning an awareness of divine presence everywhere and at all times that leads to propriety within oneself and in one's most private moments.

Outward modesty means behaving in a way that maintains one's self-respect and the respect of others, whether in dress, speech or behaviour. Inward modesty means shying away from any character or quality offensive to God. The outward is a reminder of the inward, and the inward is essential to the outward. The natural modesty lies not in dress but in inner innocence and purity of character.

The defining emblem of Islam

Modesty, of which *hijab* is an outward expression, is the defining emblem of Islamic values. The Arabic word for modesty is *haya*. The exciting thing about this word is that it is linguistically related to the Arabic word for life (*Hayat*). Modesty is the virtue that gives spiritual life to the soul. This connection between spiritual life and modesty exists because the virtue is not just about outward appearances; instead, it is tolerance first and foremost about the inward state of having modesty before God – meaning an awareness of divine presence everywhere and at all times that leads to propriety within oneself and in one's most private moments.

Outward modesty means behaving in a way that maintains one's self-respect and the respect of others, whether in dress, speech or behaviour. Inward modesty means shying away from any character or quality offensive to God. The outward is a reminder of the inward, and the inward is essential to the outward.

Once the erroneous understanding and flawed logic behind the *hijab* gets cleared, the world will acknowledge that *hijab* is a woman's cultural armour. There's nothing veiled about the *hijab*. There's nothing veiled about the *hijab*. We must get rid of an imaginary Islamic culture, referring to the clichés and misapprehensions connected to Islam in France. We must show that French culture and Islam can live together peacefully.

The Western discourse has consistently argued that the *hijab* is not a symbol of freedom but one of oppression. It believes that women in Islam are second-class citizens and that this status is encoded in both sacred text and tradition, enforced by culture and law.

However, research suggests that contrary to Western notions, Muslim women choose to wear the *hijab* as a way of showing self-control, power, and agency. For example, many well-educated women working in hospitals and libraries wear it.

For many Muslim women, wearing a *hijab* offers a way to control their bodies and challenges how men marginalize women. They justify wearing the *hijab* as a public statement of their spiritual quest. Veiling was once the armour for the impoverished classes. Today, it is the mascot of the most enlightened Muslim girls pursuing prestigious courses at top-class universities.

Prophet Muhammad said, "Every religion has a chief characteristic, and the chief characteristic of Islam is modesty." In Islam, modesty is a virtue for both men and women. The Prophet was the epitome of modesty in his behaviour with people. When the Qur'an tells believers to lower their lustful gazes and guard their chastity - a critical aspect of the modesty tradition - it begins by commanding this to men before women (Q24:30-31).

A woman's attire has never been about perception. It is solely a matter of interpretation. What got lost amid such interpretive crossfire is the core message that was objectified. Historically, modesty in dress got contaminated by local customs that sometimes even predate Islam.

Chastity has little to do with garments and symbolises the purity of heart and character.

For women who observe *hijab*, it is not merely a piece of cloth or a symbol of defiance. Instead, it is a path that aids in self-purification and brings them nearer to their creator. It is a means to teach modesty. A veil is a genuine expression of a woman's religiosity. It's a badge of womanhood, representing their resilience as females in a world determined to control every aspect of their being. Paradoxically, women engaging with the modern world rely on the veil to signal to others that this is their way of expressing their freedom.

The notion of policing women's dressing

The shift in focus of religion from an ethical guide to policing of appearances (dress codes, rituals) is a curious phenomenon. This virus seems to have seeped its way into mainstream Muslim consciousness. Our religious priorities have shifted from spiritual transformation to quotidian concerns about rituals and dress codes. This fixation reflects the very cursory manner in which we approach religion.

Education, as always, is the key here. Let's start getting offended by expressions like "men will be men" because men are not monolithic sexual beasts who have no autonomy over their desires. Let's not tie down a woman's morality to her dress. And let's stop objectifying women and seeing them primarily as avenues for consumerism.

One of the Islamic symbols that has attracted enormous attention in the Western world is the veil - the *hijab* (a scarf wrapped tightly around a woman's head to conceal every wisp of hair). Veiling has become, perhaps more than any other single issue, the defining "women's question".

The *hijab* is the most potent symbol of Muslim women's rejection of Western notions of feminism. For these empowered and educated women, the *hijab* has articulated a revolutionary response to modernity. The *hijab* expresses a translational form of Islamic feminism. It has catapulted women into all public spheres of Islamic life, including formal religious learning and several entrepreneurial enterprises, though they are empowering their fellow women.

The Western discourse has consistently argued that the *hijab* is not a symbol of freedom but a sign of oppression. It believes that women in Islam are second-class citizens and that this status is encoded in both sacred text and tradition, enforced by culture and law. Have we forgotten that less than 100 years ago, American women did not have the freedoms and access that we now take for granted and promote as universal human rights?

Contrary to Western notions, Muslim women choose to wear the *hijab* as a way of showing self-control, power and agency. For example, many well-educated women working in hospitals and libraries wear it confidently and as a symbol of self-assertion. For many Muslim women, wearing a *hijab* offers a way for them to take control of their bodies and challenge those men who marginalise women. They justify wearing the *hijab* as a public statement of their spiritual quest and their belief in its spiritual facet and virtues.

Veiling was once armouring for the impoverished classes. Today, it is the mascot of the most enlightened Muslim girls pursuing prestigious courses in top-class universities. Attempts to force Muslim women to stop wearing the veil might, therefore, be counterproductive by depriving them of the choice and opportunity to integrate into mainstream society.

Modesty applies to both men and women

The Arabic word for modesty is *haya*. The exciting thing about this word is that it is linguistically related to the Arabic word for life (*hayat*). Muslim scholars and sages believe that the two terms have an intimate connection. Modesty is the virtue that gives spiritual life to the soul. This connection between spiritual life and modesty exists because the virtue is not just about outward appearances; instead, it is tolerance first and foremost about the inward state of having modesty before God - meaning an awareness of divine presence everywhere and at all times that leads to propriety within oneself and in one's most private moments. Outward modesty means behaving in a way that maintains one's self-respect and the respect of others, whether in dress, speech or behaviour. Inward modesty means shying away from any character or quality offensive to God. The outward is a reminder of the inward, and the inward is essential to the outward.

From Morocco to Iran to Indonesia, as well as in Europe and North America, the veil has come to signify the unreachable difference between the West and Islam. The black *burqa* (in Syria, women who wear them are sometimes called 'walking tents') tries to prevent looking altogether. It makes a face and other body parts invisible and indivisible, as making any part of the woman distinct would provoke a threat from vandalism of men. The many different sorts of the veil – headscarf, *tagelmust, parandja, niqaab, muhapatti*, bridal veil, sari, *hijab, chadri, batula, abaya, kufiyya* – make it possible to see and be observed. A woman can see out from inside a *burqa*, though with darkened vision. In this respect, the *burqa* functions like sunglasses. By contrast, most veils highlight and minimally reveal the eyes while covering other parts of the face and body. Most women who wear the veil do so to enter the public sphere on particular terms, though these terms may be difficult to discern. They remove the veil in private, in the company of intimates, where there is no possibility of baring their vulnerable parts to strangers.

The Qur'anic view of the ideal society is that Muslim men and women must uphold social and moral values and ensure justice for all, i.e., between man and man and between man and woman. The Qur'an asks women to behave with dignity and decorum, befitting a secure, self-respecting and self-aware female rather than an insecure female who feels that her survival depends on her ability to attract or entice those men who are interested not in her personality but only in her sexuality.

The under-noted verse sums up quintessentially the Qur'anic injunctions on modesty:" And say to the believing women that they should lower their gaze and guard their modesty; that they should not display their beauty and ornaments except what (must ordinarily) appear thereof; that they should draw their veils over their bosoms and not display their beauty except to their husbands, their fathers, their husband's fathers, their sons, their husbands' sons, their brothers or their brothers' sons, or their sister's sons, or their women, or the enslaved people whom their right hands possess, or male servants free of physical needs, or small children who have no sense of the shame of sex; and that they should not strike their feet to draw attention to their hidden ornaments. And O ye Believers! Turn ye all together towards Allah, that ye may attain Bliss "(Q24:31)

The second verse concerning veiling is: "O Prophet! Tell thy wives and daughters, and the believing women, that they should cast their outer garments over their persons (when abroad): that is most convenient and should be known (as such) and not molested. And Allah is Oft-Forgiving, Most Merciful." (Q33:59)

Although this verse is in the first place to the Prophet's "wives and daughters", there is a reference also to "the believing women". Hence, Muslim societies understand that this injunction applies to all Muslim women. According to the Qur'an, the reason why Muslim women should wear an outer garment when they leave their houses is that the "believing" Muslim women are discerned and protected from the streetwalkers, and sexual harassment is an occupational hazard. The purpose of this verse was not to confine women to their houses but to make it safe for them to go about their everyday lives without attracting unwholesome attention. A "believing" Muslim woman could be discerned and protected from the others when she wears the outer garment. The older Muslim women who are "past the prospect of marriage" are not required to wear "the outer garment". The Qur'an proclaims: "And women of post-menstrual age who have no desire for marriage - there is no blame upon them for putting aside their outer garments [but] not displaying adornment. But too modestly refrain [from that] is better for them. And Allah is Hearing and Knowing." (Q 24:60)

The fundamental rules of *hijab*

An important aspect of the *hijab* is that women should not make it a fashion statement. The Qur'an defines it as *taqbarruj* :" And stay quietly in your houses, and make not a dazzling display, like that of the former Times of Ignorance; establish regular Prayer, and give regular Charity; and obey Allah and His Messenger. And Allah only wishes to remove all abomination from you, ye members of the Family, and to make you pure and spotless." (Q33:33)

The newer generations of Muslim women firmly believe in the idea that feminism should not be about collectivized standardization but rather a freedom of individual expression. Women shouldn't feel cowed by the tyranny of a perceived majority into letting other women dictate how they should set their standards.

The *hijab* is not unique to Islam but also a part of the dress of other religions, such as Judaism (where the idea of modesty is called Tzuniut) and Christianity. The Islamic concept of *hijab* ranges from simple head scarves (khimaar or *hijab*) to head-to-toe cloaks such as abayas and *burqas*. The English term "veil" is commonly used to refer to Middle Eastern women's traditional head, face, or body covers. However, in Arabic, different terms refer to diverse articles of women's clothing that vary according to region and era. Some of these Arabic terms are burqa(*burqa*), 'abāyah, ṭarḥah, burnus, jilbāb, and milāyah. Overgarments such as the 'abāyah of Arabia and Iraq and the burns of the Maghrib tend to be very similar for both sexes. The word niqāb refers to a face veil, which in its contemporary form covers the nose and lower face but not the eyes.

The veiling and seclusion of women did not arise with the advent of Islam, nor are these.

Institutions indigenous to Arabs. Strict seclusion and the veiling of matrons were in place in Roman and Byzantine societies. There is evidence that in the Western Arab region, only two clans (the Banū Ismāʿīl and Banū Qaḥṭān) may have practised some form of female veiling in pre-Islamic times. No seclusion or veiling existed in ancient Egypt, either. However, some women may have used a head veil in public later, during the reign of Ramses III (twentieth dynasty).

In ancient Mesopotamia, the veil was a sign of respectability and high status; decent married women wore it to distinguish themselves from enslaved and unchaste women—who veiled, and when caught illegally, they suffered severe penalties. Thus, veiling was a mark of aristocracy and a symbol for distinguishing "respectable" women from "disreputable ones".

The assimilation of cultural practices in Islam

In medieval Egypt, public segregation of the sexes existed among Jewish Egyptians; women and men entered their temples through separate doors. Evidence also suggests that Jewish women of that period veiled their faces, as did Muslim women, who were urged in prescriptive literature to behave more modestly.

Veiling of Arab Muslim urban women became more pervasive under Ottoman rule as a marker of rank and exclusive lifestyle. By the nineteenth century, upper-class urban Muslim and Christian women in Egypt wore the *ḥabarah*, which consisted of a long skirt, a head cover, and a long rectangular cloth of white transparent muslin placed below the eyes, covering the lower nose and the mouth and falling to the chest.

Perhaps related to the origins of the practice among Jews and Christians, the word *ḥabarah* itself derives from early Christian and Judaic religious vocabulary.

Modesty in Islam is for both sexes, "Tell the believing men to lower their gaze and guard their modesty, and say to the believing women to lower their gaze and guard their modesty" (Q 24:30–31). *Hijab* means 'veil', 'covering' or, barrier', while the Arabic word *khimar* refers to the head scarf. However, the *hijab* has come to take on the meaning of a Muslim woman's head-dress. *The hijab* symbolizes many things: religious devotion, discipline, respect, identity and modesty. Many Muslim women view it as a part of the worship of God.

Evidence from its usage in the Qur'an and early Islamic feminist discourse supports the notion of *hijāb* in Islam as referring to a sacred divide or separation between two worlds or two spaces: deity and mortals, men and women, good and evil, light and dark, believers and nonbelievers, or aristocracy and commoners. The phrase *min warā ʿ al-ḥijāb* (from behind the *hijāb*) emphasizes the element of separation or partition.

Revelation of the verses of veiling

The Qur'ānic verses clearly emphasise modesty in women, which the Muslim society considers a fundamental norm of civilized society. The Qur'ān strictly abjures the modern feminist notions of near obscenity in female garments, and Muslims have always taken strong objection to Western societies for associating the *hijab* with backwardness.

Many Muslims claim that the Qur'an and *sunnah* (the practice of the Prophet) mandate veiling and seclusion. However, some scholars believe such arguments are tendentious. Of the seven Qur'anic verses using the word "veil" (*hijāb*). The following verses descended on veiling in Mecca: (Q7:46, 17:45, 19:17, 38:32, 41:5, 42:51), and none of them refers to veiling Muslim women. The seventh verse (Q33:53), revealed at Medina, requests male guests to address the Prophet's wives "from behind a *hijāb*" when they ask them something. At the time of its founding, as Islam gradually established itself in the Medina community, "seclusion" for Muhammad's wives is in a Qur'anic verse: "O ye who believe enter not the dwellings of the Prophet unless invited… And when you ask of his wives anything, ask from behind *hijāb*. That is purer for your hearts and their hearts" (Q33:53).

Although the verse does not pertain to Muslim women in general, some Muslims argue that what applies to the Prophet's wives, exemplars of virtue, inheres all the more for Muslim women on the assumption that they are less chaste. The *hijāb* in the verse is intended to be a curtain rather than a head-covering and may have led to the seclusion of the Prophet's wives. However, medieval Islamic commentators coupled this verse with verses specifying general Muslim women's clothing (Q24:30–31), in which women have to draw their scarves (*khumūr*) over their bosoms (*juyūb*) to enable Muslim women in Abbāsid times to emulate the cultural tradition of veiling and seclusion observed by Byzantine and Persian upper-class women. Qur'anic scholars such as al-Wāhidī, in his *Asbāb al-nuzūl*, and others maintain that the reference in Q 24:31 to *khumūr* should cover both head and bosom lies in the need to differentiate between free women and enslaved people.

A *muhajjabah* (woman wearing *hijāb*) wore *al-jilbāb*—an unfitted, long-sleeved, ankle-length gown in austere solid colours and thick opaque fabric—and *al-khimār*, a head cover resembling a nun's wimple that covers the hair low to the forehead, comes under the chin to conceal the neck, and falls over the chest and back. Whereas the nun's wimple is an aspect of her seclusion and a sign of her state of celibacy and asexuality, the Muslim woman wears *al-khimār* to desexualize public social space when she is part of it. Modesty extends beyond her clothing to her subdued, severe behaviour and austere manner and is ideal for both sexes. A *munaqqabah* (woman wearing the *niqāb*, or face veil) more conservatively adds *al-niqāb*, which covers the entire face except for eye slits; at the most extreme, she would also wear gloves and socks to cover her hands and feet.

Other references further stress the separating aspect of *hijāb*. For example, *al-hijāb* is

Alluded to in non-gendered contexts separating deity from mortals (Q42:51), wrongdoers from the righteous (Q7:46, Q41:5), believers from unbelievers (Q17:45), and light from darkness and day from night (Q38:32). Concerning the sexes, one verse tells men and women to be

Another Qur'anic verse is an exordium for all women:" Stay quietly in your houses, and do not make a dazzling display like the former times of Ignorance; establish regular prayer, give regular charity, and obey Allah and His Messenger. And Allah only wishes to remove all abomination from you, ye members of the Family, and to make you pure and spotless "(Q33:33)

In contemporary times, the veil has made a comeback as Muslim women are encouraged to take it on as a sign of their holiness and to use their garments to display their proud identity as Muslims in a postcolonial era. Such calls for the pious display of faith could be acceptable in part as a struggle for cultural nativism in the face of an ever-globalizing American culture preceded by Western colonization. The colonial British identification of Muslim backwardness with the seclusion and veiling of women has, in a reverse move, made veiling (and not necessarily seclusion) the signifier of all that is forward in Islamic culture, where the woman has respect for her mind and her morals rather than showing her skin. Veiling has allowed women to enter the public sphere without fear of retribution for entering previously male-dominated spaces, whether in the street or the boardroom. With steady increases in women's education and employment, as more women enter the legal and public professions, they face societal pressures.

According to this *hadith*, the second caliph (Umar ibn al-Khattab) commanded the Prophet's wives to veil their faces. Narrated 'A'isha: "The wives of the Prophet used to go to Al-Manasi, a vast open place (near Baqia at Medina), to answer the call of nature at night. 'Umar used to say to the Prophet, "Let your wives be veiled," but the Prophet did not say so. One night Sauda bint Zam'a the wife of the Prophet, went out at 'Isha' time, and she was a tall lady. 'Umar addressed her and said, "I have recognized you, O Sauda." He said so, as he eagerly desired that the verses of Al-*Hijab* (the observing of veils by Muslim women) descended on the Prophet. This logic appears again in "Al-*Hijab*. (Sahih Bukhari, Volume 1, Book 4, and Number 148)

Niqab

The niqab is different from the *hijab—the hijab* refers to covering everything except the hands and face. *Niqab* is the term used to refer to the piece of cloth covering the face; women who wear it also usually cover their hands. Many Muslim women across Saudi Arabia and the Indian subcontinent, as well as those in the West, use It in the West.

Historically, the veiling of the face was part of many cultures before Islam, and scholars say the adoption of its practice by Muslims was part of fitting into society. Although the majority of scholars agree that *hijab* is obligatory, only a minority of them say that the *niqab* is obligatory. There are further divisions of opinions. Some say the eyes may be left unconcealed, while others emphasise covering the entire body. However, those scholars who rule that the *niqab* is not an obligation do not necessarily oppose those who choose to wear it. According to most scholars, the most authentic ruling is that it is unnecessary and, unlike a *hijab*, there is no sin if not used. Some scholars state that wearing the *niqab* as an act of extra piety, provided they do not believe it is an obligation, will receive divine blessings.

There are few references to veiling in the *hadith,* most of which refer to the *khimar,* which is restricted linguistically to head covering. The covering of the face is only alluded to in three *hadiths.* In fact, in one *hadith,* the companions of the Prophet Prophet Muhammad are even surprised at one woman's wearing the *neap* during her time of grief.

Scholars, such as Abul A'la Mawdudi from the Indian subcontinent, suggest that these verses cover the entire body, including the face and hands. The order instructing 'cast their outer garments' in Arabic is similar to 'draw together'. Scholars say that following this verse, women in the Prophet's era drew together their garments over their entire bodies, including the face.

Several scholars have argued that the faces were unrecognisable because they were dark and not covered up. Interestingly, A'isha says it applies to 'some' women and not all. She also refers to the early Morning Prayer, not any other one. It would make it difficult to ascertain who the individuals are if they use cloaks before sunrise. In addition, the scholars argue that the order to 'cast their outer garments over their persons' has been misunderstood. They say that the word 'face' has not been indicated in Arabic, and it would be wrong to extrapolate the meaning. The proponents of the *niqab* use this Qur'anic verse as evidence for the *niqab."* And when ye ask (the Prophet's wives) for anything ye want, ask them from before a screen: that makes for greater purity for your hearts and theirs. (Q33:53)

The wives of the Prophet were indeed required to wear the *niqab* by this Qur'anic verse. Their special status meant they had to be clear of all gossip and slander. Scholars say that the wives of the Prophet were the best feminine examples and were required to wear the *niqab.* However, earlier in the same chapter, the Qur'an clearly states that the Prophet's wives were not similar to other women. Most scholars agree that the verse about the screen, or concealing of the face, is only obligatory on the wives of the Prophet. They say the verses are a clear indication that the wives of the Prophet have limited mobility due to their political position and that their code of conduct does not constitute a code of conduct for women in general.

The case against the *neap*

Most scholars, including those from four leading schools of Islamic jurisprudence, believe that the *niqab* is not an obligation. They cite several references for this opinion: "Say to the believing men that they should lower their gaze and guard their modesty, which will make for greater purity for them. And Allah is well acquainted with all that they do. And say to the believing women that they should lower their gaze and guard their modesty; they should not display their beauty and ornaments except what (must ordinarily) appear thereof." (Q24:30-31)

According to most contemporary scholars, 'what is apparent of it' refers to the hands and face. Scholars holding this view also state that all scholars will accept that the Prophet categorically forbade people from covering their faces or hands during the *hajj*, the pilgrimage to Mecca. If the hands and face needed covering at all times, he would not have stated its impermissibility during one of the most sacred points of a person's life. It is also generally held by the majority of scholars, including those who believe the *niqab* is obligatory, that covering the face during the five daily prayers is discouraged.

More frequently, the younger and the more vocal young women insist that far from familial pressure, it is their choice that they have now started exercising while veiling themselves. Some of the new practices reflect informed individual decisions regarding career, dress mode and lifestyle. The only caveat is that the egalitarian spirit and lifestyle modesty must be true Qur'ānic. Arguments in some circles insist that the *hijab* and *niqab* are tools of oppression and inequality. It misses the point entirely - governments getting involved in prescribing and proscribing dress sense ascribes sinister notions to an innocuous custom of civilized value dressing. Freedom of religious and individual expressions holds the state to keep out of moralizing about either. The idea that equality should be defined by and wedded to a single set of ideas is obtuse in the extreme.

We need to work against the reductive interpretation of veiling as the quintessential sign of women's restrictions, even if we object to state imposition of this form, as in Iran or with the Taliban (the modernizing states of Turkey and Iran had earlier in the century banned veiling and required men, except religious clerics, to adopt Western dress.) What does freedom mean if we accept the fundamental logic that humans are social beings, always raised in specific social and historical contexts and belonging to particular communities that shape their desires and understandings of the world?

In the Islamic paradigm, women have equal rights– educational accessibility, employment opportunities, equal pay and political representation. The crucial component is the population's mindset, which should genuinely honour equal rights for all sexes. A significant cultural change undeniably takes time and enormous patience from all sectors. The women are upbeat with their newfound enthusiasm. They are addressing and negotiating their concerns ably. Taking extreme measures violates the primary goal of gender equality, which aims at harmonious social relationships. What Muslim women genuinely aspire for is gender equality and not gender neutrality, which men obliquely believe to be a trampling of their freedom and liberty.

The most sobering words came from Michelle Obama when she addressed *hijab*-wearing students as the First Lady of the United States:

"Maybe you read the news and hear what folks are saying about your religion, And you wonder if anyone ever sees beyond your headscarf to see who you are instead of being blinded by the fears and misperceptions in their minds. And I know how painful and how frustrating all of that can be. But here's the thing -- you all have everything, everything. You must rise above all the noise and fulfil every last one of your dreams."

10. TWENTY-FIVE FEMALE MUSLIM ICONS

This woman, who is your beloved, is, in fact, a ray of His light,
She is not a mere creature. She is like a creator.
– Jalaluddin Rumi

Rumi was the greatest Sufi poet, and several women Sufis followed his path. Filled with platitudes of love, understanding, and acceptance, the writings of Rumi, as translated into English, have sparked a renaissance of interest in 18th-century Persian poets around the world. However, the Islamic current is missing in several of his admirers' devotion to Islam, which is crucial in his writing. There have been several Sufi saints. The Sufi ascetic Rabia Al-Adawiyya insisted that women were the spiritual equals of men. Women behaved relatively autonomously in early Islam. In Sufi circles, they were teachers, "spiritual mothers," and even inheritors of the spiritual secrets of their fathers. Here's a Rumi sample :

"Love comes sailing through, and I scream.
Love sits beside me like a private supply of itself.
Love puts away the instruments
and takes off the silk robes. Our nakedness
together changes me completely."

Rumi based his life and poetry on the Islamic religious s system. The son of an Islamic preacher, he prayed five times a day, made pilgrimages to Mecca, and memorized the Koran. Under the influence of an older dervish, Shams of Tabriz, he devoted his life to Sufism, an ancient, mystical branch of Islam. Sufis are less concerned with the codes and rituals of Islam than with making direct contact with God. Still, the traditional Islamic texts are central to the faith. "I am the slave of the Qur'an and dust under the feet of Muhammad," Rumi writes. "Anyone who claims otherwise is no friend of mine."Movements for Muslim women to seek roles in national leadership have increased rapidly. More significant opportunities for women in education have encouraged their involvement in different fields. The Qur'an contains verses that appear to support the role of women in politics, such as its mention of the Queen of Sheba, who represented a ruler who consulted with and made important decisions on behalf of her people. The *hadith* provides numerous examples of women having public leadership roles.

Though leadership opportunities for Muslim women are cemented in religious text and continue to expand today, earlier generations had different understandings of women's roles.[Despite modern developments and greater inclusion of Muslim women in political life, there are Muslims in certain countries who maintain that the ideal Muslim woman should confine herself to the role of mother and wife.

A closer look at and evaluation of the roles Muslim women have played in diverse fields including literature, law, art, Islamic studies, the humanities, social sciences and administration — reveals that women, past and present, have contributed a great deal to the intellectual and cultural life in the Islamic world, despite their encounter at the problematic intersections of thought and patriarchal politics. From the first centuries of Islam, women enjoyed – and held authority – as religious scholars, teachers and leaders, such as narrators and teachers of *hadith*. Few became rulers. Some received the reins of power by inheritance; others had to fight the heirs to take control. Many themselves led battles, inflicted defeats, and concluded armistices. Some had confidence in competent viziers, while others counted only on themselves. Each had her way of treating people, rendering justice, and administering the policies they formulated. Some managed to stay on the throne long, while others scarcely had time to settle down.

For hundreds of years, women left their mark on their societies, changing the course of history by influencing significant spheres of life. In Muslim civilisation, extraordinary women from different backgrounds worked alongside men to advance their agendas. Several of them courageously encountered scary events in their societies. These women participated in all fields of life at the time. Some women championed educational and cultural efforts, like Fatima al-Fihri, and others excelled in mathematics, such as Sutayta al-Mahamili. The others researched in the fields of medicine, administration and management, philosophy, and the arts. Others played critical political roles and ruled essential territories in the Muslim civilisation. Some of those included Lubana of Cordoba of the 10th century (Spain), Sitt al-Mulk of the 11th century (Egypt), Melike Mama Hatun of the 12th century (Turkey), Razia (or Raziyya) Sultana of Delhi of 13th century (India) and many more.

The first wife of the Prophet, Khadijah, saw the ethical values and commercial acumen in an orphaned young man. She was the first to accept Islam. Later on came the Yemeni queen Arwa, who ruled for seven decades and even issued coinage in her name, and also Noor Inayat Khan, the Sufi-Muslim British spy who went into Nazi-occupied France to radio enemy movements back to Britain.

God proclaims:" Indeed, the Muslim men and Muslim women, the believing men and believing women, the obedient men and obedient women, the truthful men and truthful women, the patient men and patient women, the humble men and humble women, the charitable men and charitable women, the fasting men and fast women, the men who guard their private parts and the women who do so, and the men who remember Allāh often and the women who do so - for them, Allāh has prepared forgiveness and a great reward. (Q33: 35)

Most women rulers acquired religious stature because their names preceded the *khutbah* (religious sermon). *Khutbah,* in Islam, is the sermon delivered primarily at a Friday service (*ṣalāt al-jumʿah*), at the two major Islamic festivals (*ʿīds*), at celebrations of saintly birthdays (*mawlids*), and on extraordinary occasions. The *khutbah* probably derived, though without a religious context, from the pronouncements of the *khaṭīb*, a prominent tribal spokesman of pre-Islamic Arabia. The *khaṭīb* expressed himself in beautiful prose that extolled the nobility and accomplishments of his tribe members and denigrated the weakness of the tribe's enemies. Even Prophet Muhammad presented himself as a *khaṭīb* after taking Mecca in 630. The first four caliphs, the Umayyad caliphs, and the Umayyad provincial governors delivered *khutbah*s in their respective areas. However, the content of the speeches was no longer strictly exhortatory; they dealt with practical questions of government and political problems and, on occasion, even included direct orders. Under the Abbasids, the caliphs no longer preached but assigned the function of *khaṭīb* to the religious judges (qadis). The pointed insistence of the Abbasids on clearing Islam of the secularism of the Umayyads helped strengthen the spiritual aspect of the *khutbah*.

The defining women in Islamic history

1. Khadījah b. Khuwaylid (555-619). Even before her famous marriage to the Prophet Muhammad, Khadijah was an essential figure in her own right, being a successful merchant and one of the elite figures of Mecca. She played a central role in supporting and propagating the new faith of Islam and was the first Muslim. She saw Prophet Muhammad through the roughest years of his becoming, leading to his prophethood. The Prophet brought his fears of madness and his tears of wonder to her. She began to balance everyday life with divine wonder as part of ordinary reality. Known for her business acumen, she gave up everything -- her wealth, prestige, everything -- to believe in and support her husband as her prophet.

As the Prophet Muhammad said in a *hadith* preserved in *Sahih Muslim*: "God Almighty never granted me anyone better in this life than her. She accepted me when people rejected me; she believed in me when people doubted me; she shared her wealth with me when people deprived me; and God granted me children only through her." While she lived, Prophet Muḥammad took no other wives. Indeed, another of the most influential women of early Islam, Fāṭima al-Zahrā', was the daughter of the Prophet by Khadīja, and it is only through Fāṭima (primarily through her two sons, al-Hasan and al-Husayn), that the lineage of the Prophet finds continuity. These facts make Fāṭima and her mother Khadīja among Islamic history's most revered female personages.

Khadijah was undoubtedly a pious woman with a visionary and business acumen. More importantly, she had a steely determination and trusted her instincts, which never let her down because they were grounded in righteousness. The absence of primary male support following the death of her husband did not appear to weaken her resolve. She did not sell off her business or compromise her feminine morality grace and continued her vocation. She relied on her mental agility and human relations skills to manage her small but trusted team, whose members equalled up to her trust.

Khadijah combined commerce with compassion, social conscience, and financial finesse. Having been deprived of the protective umbrella of parents in her youth, she summoned the deeper emotional springs to the last dregs to nourish her soul and spirit. Islam is solidly rooted in traditions of mercantilism and private enterprise. Khadijah made sure that neither femalehood nor widowhood came in the way of her pursuit of Islamic ideals.

Prophet Muhammad) faced ridicule, oppression, financial boycotts, and even physical abuse when he started preaching a novel faith – Islam – in the heartland of Arabia, Mecca, from 610 onwards. Prophet Muhammad and Khadijah had six children: two boys, Abdullah and Qasim (both of whom died in infancy), and four daughters, Zainab (l. 599-629), Ruqayyah (601-624), Umm e Kulthum (603-630), and Fatima (born between 605 and 615).

2. Ghazālah al-Shaybāniyyah (d.696). Born into the Arab Banū Shaybān tribe that had migrated to Iraq during the Islamic conquests in the early seventh century, she rose to become a leading member of the infamous Ḥarūrī sect of early Kharijism, a group notorious for its puritanical interpretation of the Qur'an, rejection of non-Kharijite rule and use of violence against their opponents, combatants and non-combatants alike. Her husband was the renowned Ḥarūrī military commander Shabīb b. Yazīd al-Shaybānī (d.696) elected the leader of the sect with the title *Amīr al-Mu'minīn*. The Ḥarūrīyyah, for all their violence, advocated a staunchly egalitarian worldview for the members of their sect—the only "true Muslims" as far as they were concerned—which enabled Ghazālah to rise as an essential leader in her own right and command armies, a rare feat for an Arab woman in the 7th century. According to several narrations,

Ghazālah once defeated an army commanded by the Umayyad general al-Ḥajjāj b. Yūsuf, compelling the latter to flee the battlefield. Following this victory, she composed a short poem taunting al-Ḥajjāj as "an ostrich posing as a lion." Around 695, she and her warriors briefly occupied the town of Kufa. At this point, Ghazālah ascended the pulpit in the Great Mosque of Kufa and delivered a rousing sermon to her troops before praying two rak'as (units of prayer), allegedly reciting Surah al-Baqarah (Chapter 2) of the Qur'an during the first rak'a and Surah Al-'Imran (Chapter 3) of the Qur'an in the second, both chapters being the longest in the Qur'an. Ghazālah was responsible for defeating several Umayyad armies sent against her but eventually died in battle against an Umayyad force outside Kufa around 696.

3. Khawla b. al-Azwar (d. 639). She was also a contemporary of the Prophet Muhammad. She is best known for participating in the Battle of Yarmuk (636) against the Byzantines. According to the later narratives of the Islamic conquests, the penetrative authors describe her as having the skill and fighting ability of the famed Muslim general Khālid ibn al-

Walīd. It is notable that scholars such as al-Azdi, writing in the eighth and ninth centuries, in his "Futuh al-Sham" (a work often incorrectly credited to al-Waqidi) and later chroniclers such as Ibn Kathir and al-Zirkali ascribed such importance to a female warrior in the conquests.

Khawlah was the daughter of one of the chiefs of the Bani Asad tribe, and her family embraced Islam in its early days. Her father's name is either Malik or Tariq Bin Aws. Al-Azwar was his nickname. Her brother, Dirar, was the knight and poet of his tribe and was well known for his wisdom. His love for his sister and confidence in her capabilities were legendary. The brother and sister were so close that she was his companion wherever he went. He trained her in swordsmanship, and she became a perfect knight" In a battle in Bayt Lahyah near Ajnadin, Khalid watched a knight in black attire, with a large green shawl wrapped around his waist and covering his chest. That knight broke through the Roman ranks as an arrow. Wondering about the identity of the unknown knight Khalid, the others followed him and joined the battle,

Her name remained vastly unknown until the battle of Ajnadin, not far from Jerusalem, where Dirar lost his spear, fell from his horse, and was taken prisoner. She donned a male knight's attire, took her arms and rode her mare through the Roman ranks, using her sword skillfully against those who tried to stop her. The Muslim soldiers and their leader, Khalid, watched her with great admiration, presuming she was a man.

She was astonished to see that the Romans attacked the women's camp and captured several of them. Their leader gave the prisoners to his commanders and ordered Khawlah to spend her time in his tent. She was furious and decided that to die was more honourable than living in disgrace. She stood among the other women and called them to fight for their freedom and honour or die. The others were enthusiastic about her plan. They took the tents' poles and pegs and attacked the Roman guards, keeping a formation of a tight circle, as she had instructed them.

Khawlah led the attack and killed the first guard with her pole, with the other women following her. According to Al Waqidi, they managed to kill 30 Roman knights while Khawlah was goading them with slogans: 'I swear that I'll be the one to cut off your head for your insolence.' In the ensuing battle, the women proved their mettle, keeping their ground for some time, encouraging each other and driving off the attackers with their long poles. Suddenly, Khalid and the army reached the battlefield. In the ensuing fight in which over 3000 Romans were killed, Khawlah killed five nights, including the leader who insulted her.

In another battle, the Muslims were overwhelmed by a much bigger Roman army. Many soldiers fled away, but not for long. Khawlah and the other women met the fleeing soldiers, questioning their bravery claims and forcing them to return to the battle. The men were stunned when they saw Khawlah drawing her sword and leading a counter-offensive. They turned their horses and joined the fight, which they eventually won.

4. Nusayba b. Kaʻb al-Anṣārīyya (d. 634). Known also as Umm ʻAmmara, she was a member of the Banū Najjār tribe and one of the earliest converts to Islam in Medina. She was a companion of the Prophet and a highly virtuous women. She was celebrated for her military skills and took part in many battles. She is remembered for participating in the Battle of Uhud (625), carrying a sword and shield and fighting against the Meccans. She shielded the Prophet from enemies and even sustained several lance wounds as she cast herself in front to protect him. When she sustained her twelfth wound, she fell unconscious, but her willpower, attachment and devotion to the new faith made her overcome her wounds.

Praising her courage, the Prophet said her position on the battlefield that day was unsurpassed by anyone else, man or woman. She was one of the first advocates of the rights of Muslim women. She asked the Prophet, "Why does God address only men (in the Qur'an.)?". Following this interaction, the Prophet received a revelation that alluded to the fact that women can attain every status to which men are entitled. The verse also conclusively settled that women can stand on the same spiritual plane as men.

Nusayba fought in the Battles of Uhud, Hunain, Yamama and Hudaibiyah. Initially, she accompanied the Prophet Muhammad to assist A'ishah and Ramlah. Prophet Muhammad said that when he turned to his left, he saw Nusayb. When he turned to his right, he saw Nusayba. She sustained a deep wound in her shoulder during combat.

5. Ā'isha b. Abī Bakr (died 678). Ā'isha, nicknamed the "ruddy-cheeked one," was married to Prophet Muhammad and has sparked many controversies. Scholars believe. Ā'isha may have been young, but she was not younger than was the norm at the time. Other Muslims doubt the very idea that Ā'isha was six at the time of marriage, referring to historians who have questioned the reliability of Ā'isha's age as given in the saying. In a society without a birth registry and where people did not celebrate birthdays, most people estimated their age, and that of others would have been no different. What's more, Ā'isha had already been engaged to someone else before she married Muhammad, suggesting she had already been mature enough by the standards of her society to consider marriage for a while. It doesn't seem easy to reconcile this with her being six.

Ā'isha was instrumental in questioning the patriarchal sayings credited to the Prophet. Ā'isha's rising power prompted Abu Bakr to recount that he had heard the Prophet say, "Those who entrust power to a woman will never know prosperity."Ā'isha played a crucial role in the emergence of Islam and an active role in the social reform of Islamic culture. Not only was she supportive of Muhammad, but she also contributed scholarly intellect to the development of Islam. She was named al-Siddiqah, meaning 'the one who affirms the truth'. A'ishah was known for her expertise in the eclectic field encompassing the Qur'an, inheritance rules, jurisprudence, poetry, Arabic literature, Arab history, genealogy, and general medicine. In time, her intellectual contribution to the verbal texts of Islam was transcribed into written form, becoming the official history of Islam.

Aiisha was instrumental in questioning patriarchal sayings attributed to the Prophet. In later life, A'isha 's rising power prompted Abu Bark to recount that he had heard the Prophet say, "Those who entrust power to a woman will never know prosperity." she was a central figure in spreading Islam after his death and even led an army to battle. 'Ā'isha was also a well-known authority in medicine, history, and rhetoric and also noted for the number of *hadīths* that cite her as a source.

A'isha's scholarship and courage matched Khadijah's munificence and steadiness. She was a highly respected authority in Islamic jurisprudence. A'ishah was the daughter of Abu Bakr, one of Prophet Muhammad's closest companions, one of the first converts to Islam, and the first to assume leadership as part of the close circle of the caliphate over the Muslim community.

Ā'isha had a proverbial memory and could accurately recall the Prophet's answers and responses to clarifications sought from him by visitors. Ā'isha was known for her expertise in the Qur'an, Arabic literature, history, general medicine, and juridical matters in Islam. A top Islamic scholar, a military commander riding on camelback, and a fatwa-issuing jurist. Ā'isha's religious authority and intellectual standing were astonishing by the standards of our own time and hers. She was a primary source of authentic *hadith*, or traditions of the Prophet, which form part of the foundation of Sunni Islam.

Prophet Muhammad fostered Ā'isha's education and nurtured her intellectual pursuits. A'ishah also issued legal edicts (*fatwa*) and was a powerful and eloquent public orator. As the woman closest to Prophet Muhammad), A'isha had access to most intimate issues handled by the Prophet and was well positioned to sensitise Ā'isha to intimate conversations with her husband. Her services to popularise and promote the knowledge of traditions and *fiqh* (Islamic jurisprudence) have few parallels in the annals of Islamic history. Her decision was final whenever there was a complex problem relating to Islamic jurisprudence. The historian Ibn Khaldun describes *fiqh* as "knowledge of the rules of God which concern the actions of persons who own themselves bound to obey the law respecting what is required (*wajib*), forbidden (*haraam*), recommended (*mandūb*), disapproved (*makrūh*) or merely permitted (*mubah*)".

Ā'isha served at various times as a judge, a political activist and a warrior. An eminent traditionalist, she transmitted *Hadith* to several of the foremost early Muslim traditionalists. Some 2,210 *habits* have their origin in her lineage through her. Women's contribution to this critical literature indicates that at least the first generation of Muslims—the generation closest to *jahilia* days and *jahilia* attitudes had no difficulty in accepting women as authorities. Among Muhammad's eleven other wives were a leatherworker, an imam and an advocate of the impoverished. Because the prophet's wives assumed such distinguished positions in society, it, therefore, follows that any emphasis on Muslim women's domestic confinement did not emerge from Prophetic teachings.

6. Fatima al-Fihri (d.880). The University established by this Tunisian lady was established in 859 and is the world's oldest academic degree-granting university. All sources agree that she was born around 605. Fatima al-Fihri migrated with her father, Mohamed al-Fihri, from Kiroan in Tunisia to Fez. She grew up in an educated family with her sister and learnt *fiqh* and *hadith*. Fatima inherited considerable wealth from her father and used it to build a mosque and university. The University of Qarawiyyin in Fez, Morocco, is still operating today. It is the world's oldest institution of education to operate continually, and after its construction in 859, it quickly became one of the leading education centres in the world. It is appropriately located within the compounds of a mosque that would, in the coming centuries, expand to become the largest enclosed mosque in the continent of Africa—a capacity of 22,000—the university attracted scholars from all over the world.

The university led the cultural and academic relations between the Islamic world and Europe in the Middle Ages. One of the most fabulous non-Muslim alums of the university was the Jewish philosopher and theologian Maimonides (1135-1204), who studied under Abdul Arab Ibn Muwashah. The cartographer Mohammed al-Idrisi (d. 1166), whose maps aided European exploration in the Renaissance, lived in Fes for some time, suggesting that he may have worked or studied at the university. The university has produced numerous scholars who have strongly influenced the intellectual and academic history of the Muslim world. Among these are Ibn Rushayd al-Sabti (d. 1321), Mohammed Ibn al-Hajj al-Abdari al-Fasi (d. 1336), Abu Imran al-Fasi (d. 1015), a leading theorist of the Maliki School of Islamic jurisprudence, and Leo Africanus, a renowned traveller and writer.

Fatima was undoubtedly a pious woman with a visionary insight guided by a generous heart and a wise mind. She had a fortune bequeathed by her father. Far from revelling in wealthy pursuits, Fatima used the resources very frugally to set up a mosque, university and library, the highest trinity of Islamic piety. She supervised the entire gigantic enterprise, from building the foundation to functionalising these institutions. When she embarked on her mission, she had lost her father, husband and brother. With all primary sources of support and protection for a woman dried, any other Muslim woman would have retreated to the backwaters of domestic life. But Fatima appears to have been an extraordinarily inspired and determined woman with steely grooves. All her outstanding accomplishments came during periods of loneliness when women typically shun the world and seek company with the home.

The most glorious period for the institution was between the 12th and 15th centuries when her institutions were lavishly patronized by Almohades and Merinids. The university quickly became one of the leading education centres in the world. The university was pivotal in the cultural and intellectual interactions between the Middle East and Europe. Various subjects formed part of the syllabus at the university, including Islamic law, medicine, mathematics, astronomy, chemistry, history, and" music.

7. Zaynab b. 'Alī (d. 681). She was the grand-daughter of the Prophet Muhammad through his daughter Fāṭima (d. 633) and her husband 'Alī ibn Abī Ṭālib (d.661). She was a leading figure of the Ahl al-Bayt (family of the Prophet) during the late seventh century. She played a central role both during and after the massacre at Karbala (680), where her brother al-Ḥusayn ibn 'Alī and 72 of her nephews and other brothers died at the hands of the Umayyads. She was the effective leader of the Ahl al-Bayt for a time and served as the primary defender of her brother's cause, al-Ḥusayn. At Kufa, she defended her nephew—'Alī ibn al-Ḥusayn (d. 712)—from certain death by the governor of the city and, when presented to the Yazīd ibn Mu'āwiya at Damascus, gave such a passionate and forceful speech in the royal court that the advisers convinced the caliph to release her and the prisoners taken at Karbala. Her strength, patience, and wisdom make her one of early Islam's most influential women. Her shrine at Damascus remains a significant place of visit by both Sunnis and Shi'is, a fact that emphasises the universality of her legacy among Muslims.

Zaynab condemned the oppression of her clan and scorned Yazeed in his court. With a heart filled with the fire of truth, she spoke her eternal words: "So scheme whatever you may scheme, and strive for whatever you may strive, and put forth your best efforts – but, by Allah, you will never erase our mention (the family of the Prophet). And are your days not numbered? And is your gang not dispersed – on that day when the caller shall call: Is not the damnation of God upon the oppressors"

8. Fatima bint Muhammad (605-632) is commonly known as Fatima al-Zahra Fatima (born between 605 and 615 CE, died sometime in 632. She was the youngest daughter of the Prophet Muhammad and his first wife, Khadijah. Fatima became highly spiritual and devoted to Islam. Fatima was married to Ali ibn Abi Talib (l. 601-661), a cousin of Prophet Muhammad, in 624 CE, and the marriage lasted until the end of her days. Her sons Hassan (624-669/670 CE) and Hussayn (626-680) were the only surviving grandchildren of the Prophet. Like their fathers, the Shia Muslim community revered them as imams (spiritual leaders). Fatima is termed the mother of Imams and is held in high esteem by both Sunni and Shia Muslims. Fatima chastised the Prophet's feuding followers after his death: "You have left the body of the Apostle of God with us, and you have decided among yourselves, without consulting us, without respecting our rights".

Later in life, Fatima grew up in a difficult time for the Prophet. He had just started to receive revelations, and the Meccans were very hostile to the new faith. Fatima was known to be an empathetic child and was deeply affected by the persecution that her father had to endure. There are several stories in which Fatima, even though a young child, would defend her father. One example occurred when the Prophet went to the Ka'bah to pray. While he was praying, some of the Meccans threw the entrails of a slaughtered animal on him. Fatima ran to her father, wiped off the dirt, and yelled at the Meccans.

Shia Muslims consider only Fatima to be the biological daughter of the Prophet and the rest to be Khadijah's children from her previous husbands (she had been married and widowed twice before). At the same time, Sunni Muslims maintain that all four daughters were Prophet Muhammad's. It turned out to be a consequential sidelining; the schism between those who believed the Prophet's male heirs should inherit leadership of the faith (Shia) and those who thought that the successor should be from the Prophet's associates (Sunni) remains pivotal.

When Prophet Muhammad died in 632, Fatima and her husband Ali refused to acknowledge the authority of the first caliph, Abu Bakr. The couple and their supporters held that Ali was the rightful successor of the Prophet. Controversy surrounds Fatima's death within six months of Muhammad's. Sunni Islam holds that Fatima died from grief. Shia Islam, however, Fatima's (miscarriage and) death are a result direct result of her injuries during a raid on her house to subdue Ali, ordered by Abu Bakr. Fatima's dying wish was that the caliph should not attend her funeral. She was interred secretly at night, and her exact burial place remains uncertain.

Abu Bakr and Umar proposed Ali's marriage to Fatima. Still, the Prophet evaded their requests both times, awaiting the suitor God had intended for his youngest and most beloved daughter. Abu Talib knocked at the Prophet's door the second year after migration. Ali had his upbringing in the same household as Fatima. They knew each other well. The Prophet believed Ali to be the suitor God had intended for Fatima. Unlike her three sisters, Fatima had to bear the brunt of financial difficulty. Her sisters married wealthy men. They lived considerably different lives than Fatima. Yet she had the great honour of living near her father; ultimately, her lifestyle was similar to his.

Fatima spent most of her time nursing him when the Prophet fell gravely ill. She left his side during the night to rest her eyes and would return immediately to be with him. The Prophet knew that his passing would be difficult for all those who loved him, but Fatima would grieve the most. Once, as he lay ill, he began whispering in her ear, so she leaned in close to hear him better, but what he said made her weep. He then whispered something else, and it made her laugh. Before she left that day. Ā'isha asked Fatima what the Prophet had said, but Fatima did not divulge the secret. When the Prophet passed. Ā'isha asked again, and Fatima said, "He first told me that he was going to pass soon, so I wept. But then he said I would be his family's first to join him, so I laughed.

9. Rābi'a al-'Adawiyya of Basra (717-801). Born in 715, Julian in Basra, Rabia al-Adawiyya, also known as Rabi'a Basra, was the first Islamic Sufi saint. A teacher of both women and men, she significantly contributed to the development of Sufism. After being freed from slavery, Rabia came to live a free, independent life, beholden to no man or master. As such, she was way ahead of her time. Rabi'a was not born into slavery. Her parents were impoverished people from Basra in Iraq. Her name means fourth, and she was child number four. It was only after her parents' deaths that she became a victim of slavery. By day, she did her master's household chores. But night, she prayed. Legend has it that one night, this master saw a light surrounding her.

Rabi'a was a Female mystic of slave origin from Basra, often called the first Islamic saint, who introduced the doctrine of selfless love into Sufism. She demonstrated the importance of attitude and spiritual motivation for actions rather than mere ritual correctness. She emphasised ascetic detachment, renunciation of the world, meditation, and love of God. She taught that people should worship God out of love rather than the fear of hell or the promise of paradise. She wrote passionate poems about the desire to be joined to God, permanently influencing the development and nature of Sufism. She symbolizes the importance of spiritual excellence over gender and is a historical example of female autonomy and freedom from male authority.

Since her youth, her father believed in his daughter's spirituality and conveyed it to the ruler, who joined her in his beliefs and cared for the family. On her father's death, Rabia's life changed as famine hit her city, and the dacoits captured her and sold her into slavery. Despite her misfortune, Rabia's love for God grew intensely. It reached such an extent the very master she worked with released her after hearing her prayers and being touched by her passion and dedication to the divine. Rabia then spent the rest of her life in the deserts of Arabia, loving God not out of fear of hell or desire for paradise but out of absolute and unconditional love for the divine.

Rabia is remembered for her prayer: " O God! If I worship You for fear of Hell, burn me in Hell, and if I worship You in the hope of Paradise, exclude me from Paradise. But if I worship You for Your Own sake, grudge me, not Your everlasting Beauty."

Rābi'a placed herself immediately in the service of God, in other words, without an intermediary, without mediation, without someone who as an intermediary, but also, now and forever, in a time that her contemporaries also considered her a teacher of character. There are vital elements of a philosophy of religion in her collection of poems, and she was one of the earliest to set forth a doctrine of divine love. The concepts she propounded include a daring taxonomy of love and the notion that this self-effacement does not erase one's gender. She thus emphasized that women's righteousness is superior to men's (which suggests a feminist consciousness). Her poems reveal a refined mastery of Arab meters and an intricate reflection of Arabic letters and language. Her writing is part of early Sufi philosophy and has inspired Muslim mystics for centuries. These include luminaries like al-Ghazzālī (d. 1111) and Farīd al-Dīn al-'Aṭṭār (d. 1221). Some of her verses are present in all genres of Arab songs, even today.

Rabia's reputation excels that of many Muslim men within the early days of Sufism. She belongs to that elect company of Sufi women who have surpassed most of the contemporary masters of their time in wayfaring to God. She is a symbol of saintliness among women Sufis. Her love of mysticism, which she is widely credited as pioneering, triumphed over other expressions that feared God rather than adored the divine. She was a teacher of men and women, a woman who called no man her master, indeed whose surrender to God was so complete that she placed all her trust in God to ensure she was fed and clothed. Her devotion to God was so intense that relatively few solid facts about her life survived, except that it was lived in complete and loving surrender to God, which is the Islamic path.

10. Sit al-Mulch (970-1023). Sitt al-Mulk, born in a Fatimid palace, did not need to add a title to her name, which means 'lady of power'. Nor did she have to struggle to gain first place in the eyes of the caliphs. They were always pressing around her, fascinated by that mixture, so irresistible to Arabs, of great beauty allied to great intelligence. Sitt al-Mulk was one of the most beautiful Fatimid princesses who took power in 1020 after the mysterious disappearance of her brother, Imam al-Hakim Ibn 'Arnri Allah, who one fine morning declared to his people in delirium that he was God in person and that they should worship him as such. The first to succumb to the charm of Sitt al-Mulk was her father, Caliph al-'Aziz, the fifth Fatimid caliph (365 -411).

Sitt al-Mulk's involvement in politics began during her father's reign when he recognised her intelligence and wisdom. He brought her closer to the upper echelons of his government and was always keen to consult her on matters of state. After the death of her father and the succession of her younger brother, Al-Hakim bi-Amr Allah, Sitt al-Mulk took over the reins of government and exercised an upper hand when it came to decision-making. She shared power with Minister Barjuwan, the caliphate's de facto ruler at the time.

Sitt al-Mulk was encouraged by her father, Fatimid caliph Nizar al-Aziz Billah, to become involved in politics to handle several power-hungry opponents, including her brother. She retained control of the Fatimid Empire until she died in 1023. The caliph al-'Aziz, her father, idolized her, but her brother al-Hakim tormented her out of jealousy. Finally, in the name of a third caliph, her nephew al-Dhahir, she exercised power for four years. She administered the empire between 411 and 415 in the name of a child on whom she bestowed the title of al-dhahir, 'the eminently visible', because her power, as the holy law demanded, was circumscribed by invisibility. Her name preceded the *khutbah* (sermon). It was in the name of the child-imam that the faithful chanted the ritual Friday prayers. And yet it was undoubtedly she who administered the empire and 'showed exceptional ability, especially in legal matters, and made herself loved by the people. The story of Sitt al-Mulch is as fascinating as it is exemplary. It is the story of a woman forced by circumstances to take on the unimaginable: to assume the place of a caliph to save millions of the faithful from the madness of the imam.

Sitt al Mulk was the product of a mixed marriage as her parent's only child, and she was not ashamed. There is ample evidence that clearly shows she was "proud of her double identity and defended it as an ideal". There was also a significant age gap (15 years) between Sitt al Mulk and her brother, and that's a pretty long time between pregnancies; obviously, there's a possibility her mother had miscarriages/stillbirths, etc., in the years after Sitt al Mulk's birth but the age gap does make it seem unlikely the same woman gave birth to them both. The religious beliefs of Sitt al Mulk's mother had an undeniable effect on Al-Aziz and the way he ran the caliphate; it's a well-known fact that "under his rule non-Muslims – Christian and Jews had the rights to privileges they had never had before. They had access to the highest offices of the empire; they participated in all political activities, made decisions and acquired a pre-eminence that aroused jealousy.

Sitt al-Mulk was not friendly with her brother, who effectively excluded her, limiting her political involvement. Most historians, however, indicate that she regained control of state affairs by 1021 AD. As she grew older, Sitt al-Mulk's political participation and the extent to which her father listened to her intensified. Likely, she was frequently approached by those wanting to curry favour with

On the 14th of October, 996, Sitt al Mulk's world changed forever when her very tolerant and famous father died suddenly and unexpectedly, leaving Sitt al Mulk's younger brother Al-Hakim, then just 11 years old. The exciting thing about the Fatimids is that they didn't follow the practice followed by European monarchies, which automatically designated the eldest son as the heir.

Sitt al Mulk was in the political shenanigans; however, considering her status as the highest-ranking woman in the dynasty, she likely had some involvement. Al-Hakim's tutor, Barjawan, seized the reins of government for himself in 997 and remained de facto regent for three years, demonstrating a talent for balancing power between the various factions and encouraging the rise of men of diverse backgrounds. In 1000, however, Al-Hakim decided he was ready to take control himself. Suffice it to say it did not end well.

After the disappearance of Al-Hakim, the caliphate swore allegiance to his son, Az-Zahir li A'zaz li Din-illah, who was still only 16 years old. Because of his tender age, Sitt al-Mulk again assumed the responsibility of ruling the caliphate, and her decisions were the final word. She managed all state affairs firmly and remained on the throne until she died in 1023 AD. Sitt al Mulk proved to be a competent leader, and contemporary medieval chroniclers praised her leadership skills. She remained in control of the state until she died, likely in 1023.

11. Asma Bint Shihab al-Sulayhiyya (d. 1087). Born into a high-ranking family, Asma's husband was an Isma'ili Shiite. Hence, the Yemeni sovereigns were vassals of the Fatimids of Cairo and opponents of the Sunni caliphate of Baghdad. Asma directed the crucial matters of the state alongside her husband, Ali. Her name was included in the *khutbah* (the Friday prayer), which proclaimed the name(s) of the sovereign(s), and chroniclers report that she attended the councils of state with "her face uncovered" (unveiled), thus breaking tradition.

Her full name was Arwa b. Ahmad b. Muhammad al-Sulayhī. From 1067 to 1138, she ruled independently as the queen of Yemen. She was well-versed in various religious sciences such as the Qur'an, *hadith*, poetry, and history. Chroniclers describe her as being incredibly prodigious. She ruled as a queen with selfless courage because her name was alluded to in the *khutbah* (Friday sermon) directly after the name of the Fatimid caliph, al-Mustanṣir-billah. Arwa was given the highest rank in the Yemeni Fatimid religious hierarchy (that of *ḥujja*) by the Fatimid caliph al-Mustanṣir. She was the first woman in the history of Islam to be given such an illustrious title and to have such authority in the religious hierarchy. She governed Yemen with her husband, 'Ali Ibn Prophet Muammmadal-Sulayhi, founder of the dynasty that bears his name. Alongside her husband and with him, she directed all the important affairs of the kingdom until he died in 458.

During her reign, Asma deputed a contingent of Ismaili missionaries to Gujarat, where she also established a major Ismaili centre (Gujarat)) continues to be a stronghold of the Ismā'īlī Bohra faith. She played a significant role in the Fatimid schism, supporting al-Musta'li (and later al-Tayyib), and the lands under her rule—Yemen and parts of India— would follow her in this. Indeed, Yemen became the stronghold of the Tayyibī Ismā'Ili movement. Various construction projects marked her reign. She improved Yemen's infrastructure and increased integration with the rest of the Muslim world. She was perhaps the most important example of an independent queen in Muslim history.

Later, she went on a pilgrimage to Mecca, escorted by Ali and thousands of soldiers. Their convoy suffered an attack on the road by Sa'id Ibn Najah, the prince of nearby Zubayd, which resulted in Ali's murder. Spared by Sa'id, Asma then spent about a year in captivity. Her son al-Mukarram launched a rescue mission to free his mother from her captors with the support of many notables of the Yemeni capital to save the honour of their imprisoned queen. Whilst the operation was a success, al-Mukarram faced emotional trauma on site, which left him permanently paralysed. Back at the court, Asma took over the country's management until she died.

The chroniclers report that she attended the state councils with her face uncovered. When 'Ali was officially authorized to declare himself the sovereign, he presented her with the most royal gift that can be offered to a woman - to associate her publicly with his life, to acknowledge her as an equal and a partner. The *khutbah* would be in her name. The mosques of Yemen would proclaim her name after the names of the Fatimid sovereign and her husband. Asma created a veritable tradition of a couple of sharing power, raising her son, al-Mukarram, in the idea that a wife is a force that would be absurd to leave to stagnate in the shadow of the harem.

12. Padishah Khatun (1256–1295). Padishah was born in 1256 as the youngest daughter of Qutb al-Din (d. 1257) and Kutlugh Turkan of Kirman. She already had her fiefdom in Sirjan thanks to her mother Kutlugh Turkan's visit to the coronation ceremony of Abaqa in 1265. Padishah was not content with her beauty was content and wanted to display her accomplished poetry. as a poet. No one was surprised when, after being widowed, she married Gaykhatu, the fifth ruler of the Ilkhan dynasty, who succeeded in power in 690 and was one of the sons of her former husband. This marriage was not in conformity with the Muslim *shari'a and* Mongol customs. Padishah Khatun lost no time and demanded that her new husband, Gaykhatu, give her the throne of Kirman as proof of his love for her

Gaykhatu acceded to her demand, and Padishah Khatun came to Kirman as head of state. One of her first acts was to arrest her half-brother Suyurghatamish and imprison him. When he tried to escape, she got him strangled. After this act, Padishah Khatun took the title Safwat al-dunya wa al-din (The purity of the earthly world and the faith). She became the sixth sovereign of the Kutlugh-Khanid dynasty - not only officially but also unchallenged. She had money coined in gold and silver in her name. Some coins still exist in a museum in Berlin and bear the following inscription: *KikhanPadishah Jihan Khadawand 'Alam*

Padishah Khatun. Khadawand'Alam means 'Sovereign of the world' and comprises a first word in Turkish meaning 'sovereign' and a second in Arabic meaning 'world'.

Interestingly, at least in the inscription on the coins, she only claimed the world below and did not refer to the faith (*al-diri*). She reigned over Kirman until the death of her husband in 694 and the accession to power of his successor Baydu. He was more inclined to listen to her enemies and to support the clan that still sought to avenge the killing of Suyurghatamish. This clan was under the leadership of a woman, Khurdudjin, the widow of Suyurghatamish, who didn't enjoy any power - she was a Mongol princess of royal blood, a descendant of Hulagu. The grieving, vengeful widow demanded of Baydu, the new ruler, that he put to death Padishah Khatun.

When Gaykhatu, her husband, was murdered on 21 March 1295, Padishah was detained and imprisoned on the orders of Kurdujin Keaton and Shah Alam -- Suyurghatmish›s widow and daughter. She was tortured to death on her way to Baydu›s court in Kushk-e Zar. She was buried in Gubba-i Sabzm as her mother during the reign of Muzaffar al-Din Mohammad.

13. Al-Malika al-Ḥurra Arwa al-Sulayhi (1048-1138). al-Ḥurra's full name was Arwa b. Ahmad B. Prophet Muammadal-Sulayḥī. From 1067 to 1138, she ruled as the queen of Yemen. She was an Ismāʿīlī Shi'i and was well-versed in various religious sciences, Qur'an, *hadith*, poetry, and history. Chroniclers describe her as being incredibly prodigious. Her name preceded the *khutbah*. She was the daughter-in-law of Asma, the wife of her son al-Mukarram, who married in his father's tradition and shared power with his wife.'Arwa held power for almost half a century (from 485 till her death in 532. The two queens bore the same royal title: *alsayyidaal-hurra,* the noble, free, independent woman sovereign who bows to no superior authority. We know the precise wording used by the believers all over Yemen when the *khutbah* was said in 'Arwa's name: 'May Allah prolong the days of al-Hurra the perfect, the sovereign who carefully manages the affairs of the faithful.' Women frequently took over political power from the men with whom they shared their lives. However, it is exceptional in the Arab part of the Muslim Empire that a tribute to her preceded the sermon (*khutbah*).

al-Mustanṣir-billah. Arwa was given the highest rank in the Yemeni Fatimid religious hierarchy (that of *ḥujja*) by the Fatimid caliph al-Mustanṣir. She was the first woman in the history of Islam to be given such an illustrious title and to have such authority in the religious hierarchy.

14. Turkan Khatun (1053 –1094). Turkan Khatun led the social and political changes through her husband's participation in making critical decisions in state affairs. Turkan Khatun's influence had a clear impact on the political life of the state, as well as her interest in scholars and jurists - and her frequent standing before some of the unwise decisions of her son Sultan Alaeddin Muhammad, especially his unjust orders to kill every Samarkandi in Khwarazm unjustly.

Turkan Khatun was the wife of Malikshah, the Seljuk sultan who made Baghdad and its caliph tremble. Of Turkish origin, Malikshah demanded grandiose titles from his caliph in exchange for protection, for the caliph was incapable of defending even his capital. After the death of Malikshah, Turkan Khatun tried to take power since her son Mahmud, the crown prince, was only four years old. As a matter of principle, Islam forbids power to a child. Hence, the stakes were enormous: The Friday *khutbah, which was* in the mosques in the name of Malikshah, was heard throughout the empire that extended from the borders of China in the east as far as Syria in the west and from the Muslim countries of the north to Yemen in the south.

Malikshah was the solid sword of Islam, defending the Sunnism incarnated by Baghdad and its caliph from the attacks of the Shi'ites, who had become a formidable force. To ensure the succession as she understood it and to defend herself against the other pretenders to the throne, Turkan Khatun needed the collaboration of the Abbasid caliph of the period, al-Muqtadi, the twenty-seventh of the line, who ruled between 467 and 487. She kept the death of her husband secret and tried to reach an agreement with Baghdad. The caliph began by saying that Mahmud was a child. Turkan got a *fatwa* (decree) saying that Mahmud could reign despite the 'detail' of his age. But the caliph was not ready to let a woman install herself on a throne, however powerful she might be.

What was important to him was that the *khutbah,* the privilege that went with sovereignty, could not be delivered in a woman's name. The *khutbah* was officially preached at Friday prayers and was of religious and political significance, affirming the caliph's right to rule. Al-Muqtadi insisted that the sermon (*khutbah)) be in* her son's name. But that was not enough; he imposed a vizier of his choice on Turkan. At first, she baulked, considering the caliph's conditions too humiliating. Finally, she accepted all his conditions, for without the blessing of Baghdad, she had no chance to challenge t her rivals.

15. Razia Sultan (d. 1240). The story of Razia, the 13th-century ruler from the Mamluk dynasty, who wore male clothes, exuded strength and fearlessness, and, alongside her father, Emperor Iltutmish, fought in numerous battles is a fascinating saga. She was the first female Muslim ruler of the subcontinent. While Emperor Iltutmish's final resting place lies in the city's famous Mehrauli Qutub Minar complex, our revered queer icon, Razia Sultan, rests in this forgotten neighbourhood of Old Delhi.

Razia was the ruler of the Sultanate of Delhi between 1236 and 1240. Her father, the fourth emperor of the Vassal Dynasty, who reigned from 1236 to 1240, has the unique distinction of being the only woman to occupy the throne of Delhi. As a ruler, she refused to be addressed as sultana because it meant "wife or consort of a sultan" and insisted on being addressed as sultan. Razia was born to Iltumish (1210-1236) — a doting father. Razia was an accomplished archer and horse rider who frequently accompanied her father on military expeditions.

Shams al-Dīn Iltutmish (1210-1236) had Razia as his heir before his death, making her the sultanate's official ruler. She was a significant patron of learning, establishing schools and libraries across northern India. She behaved like a sultan, leading armies, sitting on the throne, and even adopting her father's royal dress. To the outrage of many, she also insisted on appearing unveiled in public. In 1240, she was overthrown in a rebellion by the nobles of the kingdom, who—among other things— were vehemently opposed to being led by a woman and killed.

The religious authorities, whom he liked to surround himself with and very influential in the country, tried to dissuade him. While the decree naming Razia as heir apparent was ready, many nobles expressed their reservations. That did not keep Razia from acceding to power. Iltumish ruled out all objections, saying, "My sons are engrossed in the pleasure of youth, and none of them can administer the country's affairs. After my death, people will realise that none among my children is more worthy to succeed me than my daughter Razia."

Iltumish often said, "This daughter of mine is better than many sons." Once, when he was leading the forces in the siege of the Gwalior fort, he assigned the government in Delhi to Razia. On his return, he was greatly impressed by her management and decided to appoint her as his successor. In contrast, the decree naming Razia as heir apparent was ready and assented. Many nobles expressed their reservations. Bur Razia defied their apprehensions.

But the opposition was latent and was brandished by her rivals. After Iltutmish's death, the princes and viziers tried to push Razia aside in favour of her half-brother Rukn al-Din, who first attempted to seize power by killing Razia's other half-brother, believing it would intimidate her and send her back to the oblivion of the harem. But he got a big surprise. Not only did Razia not hide behind her veils, but she also recaptured power by appealing directly to the people of Delhi. Ibn Battuta writes that her speech stirred the emotions of the people who seized the royal palace, deposed the king and installed Razia as the new emperor.

16. Shajar al-Durr (d. 1257). Shajar was the widow of the Ayyubid sultan al-Sālih Ayyūb (1240-1249) and played an important role in Egyptian politics following her husband's death. She was most likely of Turkic origin, beginning her life as a vassal girl in the Ayyubid court. By 1250, she had become Egypt's ruler (or sultana); her reign marked the beginning of the Mamluk sultanate of Egypt. She defended northern Egypt against the Seventh Crusade, defeating the Crusaders (although she was not present) at the Battle of Fariskur (1250) and took King Louis IX of France captive. She was the effective head-of-state, and her name preceded the *khutbah* and coins minted with the title "Malikat al-Muslimīn" (Queen of the Muslims).

It was difficult for people to accept being ruled solely by a woman. In August 1250, due to various pressures, she married her commander-in-chief ʿIzz al-Dīn Aybak, who became the first Mamluk sultan. Despite the marriage, Shajar al-Durr retained her authority and even ensured that state documents bore the names of both sovereigns rather than only those of Aybak. However, in 1257, she decided to eliminate her husband (for political reasons in addition to discovering that he was engaged in an affair with another woman or sought to marry an additional Wife). The Syrian emirs refused to pay her homage. The caliph took the side of the Syrians and asked the Egyptian emirs to choose a man in her place. To elude this command, the emirs of Egypt appointed Aybak as commander-in-chief, and he married Shajar al-Durr.

From modest beginnings, which she spent as a life vassal of probable Turkic origin in the royal household, "Tree of Pearls" became Egypt's only queen in the Islamic period. Although she ruled the country directly for only 80 days, her proxy reign continued through her husband. She not only repelled the Seventh Crusade, but she also instigated the unique Mamluk era during which elite vassal warriors ruled Egypt.

To alleviate the Syrian Ayyūbids, who were still dangerous, the emirs elected Musa, one of the Syrian branches of the family, as a consultant, and his name appeared on documents and coins. Aybak, however, was an effective ruler. His administration had rough vigour, but he lacked the higher qualifications for leadership in Mamlūk Egypt. He tormented the emirs; on September 18, 1254, he killed a commander who had successfully suppressed an Arab rebellion in middle Egypt. Many Mamlūks, among them the future sultan Baybars I, fled to Syria out of the tyrant's way. Aybak met his death in a palace intrigue when his consort, Shajar al-Durr, in a fit of jealousy, got him murdered. After that, a few days later, the vassal woman of Aybak's first wife battered her to death. Aybak was succeeded as sultan by his son ʿAlī.

Shajar was the first woman in Islamic history to assume independence. Her husband, King Sala al-Din, died during the Crusaders' invasion of Egypt. She continued to issue military and operational orders, keeping the news of his death secret for over two months to avoid undermining the morale of the troops. She found Swab al-Suhayla, who forged her husband's handwriting so well that no one doubted the king issuing the orders himself. She drew up plans, encouraged soldiers and instructed officers to lead the battle against the Crusaders, during which King Louis IX of France (Saint Louis) was vanquished, making Shajarat al-Dur's victory final. Once the battle was over and victory secured, Shajarat al-Dur announced her husband's death, gave him a royal funeral, and openly assumed the throne. At that time, Egypt was within the control of the caliphate of Baghdad, and Shajarat al-Durr had just won a great military victory against the Crusaders.

She deserved at least one of the many titles of her husband, who held, among others, the most rhetorical title that a general could dream of claiming: 'Sultan of the Arabs and the non-Arabs, King of the Lands and the Seas, King of India and China, of Yemen, of Zabid, San'a, and Aden, Master of the Kings of the Arabs and the non-Arabs, and Sultan of the Countries of the Rising and the Setting of the Sun'. Shajarat al-Durr probably did not demand such a grand title but asked for a simple recognition by al-Musta'sim of her power as Egyptian head of state. The caliph then sent the Egyptian amirs the famous message, which was so humiliating to her, in which he proclaimed that he was ready to provide them with some capable men if they no longer existed in Egypt since they had to choose a woman. Shajarat al-Durr tried to operate without his authorization, believing that she had the support of the army under her leadership and had just beaten the Crusaders at Damietta. She gave herself a title that was less long than her husband's but which was a gesture of defiance to the caliph because it challenged his prerogatives. The title was *Malikat al-Muslimin,* Queen of the Muslims. But she did not last long because the caliph's rejection proved fatal to her and brought on her tragic end, despite all the talent she displayed to hold on to her position and her desperate struggle to overturn the rules of the power game.

17. Sayyida al-Hurrah (d. 1542). Sayyida al-Hurra, originally from the Nasrid Kingdom of Granada, had to flee following its conquest by Christian Spain in 1492. Like many Andalusi Muslims, she settled in Morocco and, along with her husband, fortified and ruled the town of Tetouan on the northern coast. Following the death of her husband in 1515, she became the sole ruler of the city, which grew in strength and population as more Andalusi Muslims had to flee from Iberia in the early sixteenth century. For various reasons, including the desire to avenge the destruction of al-Andalus and the forcible conversion to Christianity of Muslims there, she turned to piracy. She morphed Tetouan into a significant base of naval operations against Spain and Portugal. She allied with the famous Ottoman corsair-turned-admiral Hayreddin Barbarossa in Algiers and dealt a severe blow to Spanish imperial power in North Africa and the Western Mediterranean. It is crucial to record that Muslim sources are generally relatively silent about

Sayyida al-Hurra, and most of the information about her originates from Spanish and Portuguese documents, which emphasize her effectiveness as a pirate queen and the destructiveness of the raids that she wrought against the southern shores of the Iberian Peninsula.

She married the Moroccan Wattasid Sultan, Abūl Abbās Muhammad (r. 1526-1545, Sayyida al-Hurra was one of the most interesting Muslim figures of the sixteenth century. She was originally from the Nasrid kingdom of Granada but had to flee following its conquest by Christian Spain in 1492. Like many Andalusi Muslims, she settled in Morocco and, along with her husband, fortified and ruled the town of Tetouan on the northern coast. Following the death of her husband in 1515, she became the sole ruler of the city,

We don't even know her real name. The name by which she attained the title of Sayyida al-Hurra is most likely her title, although there were several titles. Morocco, ruled by the Wattasid dynasty, was also significantly weakened. The colonial expansion of the Spaniards and the Portuguese across the Straits of Gibraltar had already begun during the early 15th century. The Portuguese occupied Cueta in 1415, and then, after breaking the truce with the Wattasids in 1471, they conquered Asila and Tangier, not only occupying those two cities but also taking thousands of enslaved Muslims in the process. The Spaniards also took Melilla in 1494. By 1500, the Christian Iberian powers had occupied almost all of Morocco's coastal towns and cities along the Atlantic and Mediterranean coasts, giving them nearly complete control over the maritime trade.

Tétouan, a major Mediterranean seaport and naval base in Northern Morocco, was central to the events of al-Sayyida al-Hurra's life and career. The Castilians destroyed it in 1399 and also enslaved its population. The Portuguese destroyed it again in 1437; after its rebuilding, Tétouan remained in ruins until the late 15th century when it was, once again, rebuilt by Andalusi Muslims fleeing from the advancing forces of Ferdinand and Isabella.

18. Amina of Zaria (1533-1610). Amina was a warrior and ruler of Zaria, a Hausa city-state in Northern Nigeria. Amina was born as Aminatu, a royal family member. Her grandfather was King Sarkin of Nohir, and her grandmother's name was Marka. Her father was King Nikatau of Zazzau, and her mother was Queen Bakwa Turunku. Amina was the eldest of three children. She had a brother named Karama and a sister named Zaria.

Amina was born around 1533 in Zaria, a province of today's Nigeria. She was the daughter of Bakwa of Turunku. Their family's wealth came from the trade of leather goods, cloth, kola, salt, horses and imported metals. When Bakwa died in 1566, the crown of Zazzua passed to Amina's younger brother, Karama. Although Bakwa's reign was known for peace and prosperity, Amina chose to hone her military skills with the warriors of the Zazzau military. As a result, she emerged as the leader of the Zazzua cavalry. When her brother Karama died after a ten-year rule, Amina matured into a fierce warrior and earned the respect of the Zazzau military, and she assumed the kingdom's reign.

Amina was crowned Queen of Zaria after her brother's death. In her efforts to provide safe passage for Hausu traders, Amina expanded the kingdom's borders through a series of successful strategic battles within three months of her rule. Her military innovations included introducing protective armour to the Zazzau Army. Queen Amina personally led her army of 20,000 soldiers, conquering towns to the north and south in the Nupe and Jukun kingdoms and through Kasashen Bauchi, a region in what is now known as the middle belt of Nigeria. During her reign, Zaria dominated trade routes connecting western Sudan with Egypt to the northeast and Mali to the north.

Amina attended an official state business meeting while sitting on her grandfather's lap. She was wielding a dagger by her grandmother as a child, which indicated her natural abilities as a warrior. Although she was required to participate in daily activities with her mother as a young woman, Amina also trained vigorously with the royal guard. Amina was 16 when her mother became queen and named her Magajiya, heir apparent to the throne. Suitors lined up daily, bringing gifts, including offers of 10 Makama enslaved people. It is a fact that the Emir of Kano offered her 50 bags of white and blue cloth, 50 enslaved women, and 50 enslaved men, but Amina refused to marry or have children. Amina's parents died in 1566, and her brother, Karama, was named the King of Zazzau through tradition. During Karama's reign, Amina became the lead warrior of the kingdom's army. For ten years, her successes across the region gained her a fierce reputation and personal wealth outside of her royal family connection.

Amina collected tributes from conquered cities and regions, including kola nuts and enslaved men, according to the era's and region's customs. Although she did not begin the practice, Amina built walls around conquered cities and her military camps in conquered areas. Many of those walls still stand in contemporary northern Nigeria. They are known locally as the 'granular of Amina,' which in the Hausa language means Amina's walls. Amina reigned for 34 years. She died in battle in Altagara, near Bida, in 1610 at the age of 77. In contemporary Nigeria, she is known as 'Amina, rana de Yar Bakwa ta San,' meaning Amina, daughter of Nikatau, a woman as capable as a man. She ruled for 34 years from 1576 until she died in 1610. Around 1533

19. Kösem Sultan (1589-1651). Her name was Anastasia, but it was changed after her conversion and her admission to the palace to Mâh-Peyker (moon-shaped), later by Sultan Ahmet to Kosem. Kösem Sultan's legendary beauty was why the sultan fell in love with her. She wielded immense influence and was perhaps the most powerful woman in Ottoman history. Originally a Greek named Anastasia, she was enslaved at a young age and brought to the Ottoman palace, where she became the concubine of Sultan Ahmed

In 1616, Kösem was the most powerful of the sultan's associates: "She can do what she wishes with the Sultan and possesses his heart absolutely, nor is anything ever denied to her." Between 1623 and 1632, she served as regent for her son Murad IV, who took the throne as a minor. Due to court intrigue, she significantly influenced Ottoman politics until her assassination in 1651. Like many royal brides, Kösem entered palace influence through her marriage to Sultan Ahmed I. She was said to have been of Greek origin and beautiful when young. Her particular beauty helped gain her favouritism from Ahmed and, combined with her intelligence, earned her considerable authority and influence in the palace among his wives.

On Ahmed's death in 1617, she used her influence to support the claim of his brother, Mustafa I, to the throne. He was considered mentally ill, and Kösem was able to exercise power through him, but he was declared incompetent and deposed after only three months. Osman II, Ahmed's son through another wife, replaced Mustafa, and Kösem lost the throne. But Osman's reign was cut short after a revolt of the Janissary Corps in 1622 ended his life. Mustafa was later temporarily reinstalled.

Kösem's son Murad IV became sultan in 1623, giving Kösem the prestigious position of *valid sultan* ("mother of the sultan"). This influential position—complete with pomp and circumstance—had gained considerably more authority in recent generations, significantly as the authority of the grand vizier had waned. Kösem's position was all the more potent as she enjoyed full regency for the first five years of Murad's reign when he was still a minor. When he came of age, he ruled with a heavy hand but was occasionally known to consider input from his mother. He continued to rule until he died in 1640, thought to be related to chronic alcohol consumption.

The throne then went to İbrahim, Kösem's only remaining son. His rule was marked by neglect and mismanagement as Kösem left the palace. Though absent from the palace, her relationships and influence in court remained intact. In 1648, with the empire in a sad state, she and other court officials conspired against İbrahim, and the Janissaries overthrew him.

Kösem governed the empire successfully for ten years. She was the most powerful individual in the Ottoman Empire. It was difficult for Murat IV to take control when he grew older. Several charitable projects marked her reign. She sent people to Istanbul to find orphan girls, provided for their education and got them married. She paid the debts of those who were kept in dungeons because of their debts and had them released. All of Istanbul's hungry people ate in soup kitchens that she opened. She was known as the 'hand of deus ex machina' among people. When she died of the wounds inflicted on her, the people of Istanbul mourned for 40 days. She used to say, 'I show my anger to the palace, my milk to the public'.

20. Nana Asma'u bint Uthman (1793-1864). Nana Asma'u was born in 1792 in Degel, which is 25 miles northwest of Sokoto in what is now Northern Nigeria. She was the daughter of Uthman don Fodio, the founder of the Sokoto Caliphate. Nana Asma'u had a robust Islamic upbringing. She memorized the Qur'an at a young age and learned *fiqh* and jurisprudence. She was also fluent in four languages: Arabic, Fulfulde, Hausa and Tamachek.

Nana Asma'u was a prolific poet from the West African Sahel. She was the daughter of Shaykh Uthman ibn Muhammad ibn Uthman ibn Salih (d. 1817), known as Uthman dan Fodio, the founder of the powerful Sokoto caliphate and one of the most esteemed scholars in the traditions of law, Sufism, and governance in the early modern period. Raised in a poetry-loving culture, Nana Asma'u used poetry to teach the Qur'an and transmit Islamic values, memorialize great people, and preserve her people's history. Asma'u's brother Muhammad Bello, who succeeded their father as caliph, also wrote many poetic and prose treatises in the Islamic sciences and avidly recorded the history of the Fulani people, especially the monumental changes made under the leadership of his father.

She was among the most esteemed scholars in law, Sufism, and governance traditions in the early modern period. Raised in a poetry-loving culture, Nana Asma'u used poetry to teach the Qur'an, transmit Islamic values, and preserve her people's history. Asma'u's brother Muhammad Bello, who succeeded their father as caliph, also wrote many poetic and prose treatises in the Islamic sciences and avidly recorded the history of the Fulani people, especially the monumental changes made under the leadership of his father.

In 1840, Asma'u initiated a cadre of women teachers called the Yan Taru and devoted her to teaching them the Qur'an and Islamic morality so they could teach the female masses. State leadership recognized that ordinary people had got caught in the crosshairs of toxic superstitions, and hierarchical tradition dominated the family structures. *Da'wa* efforts, like those of Asma'u's itinerant women teachers, sought to bring women the purity of *tawḥīd* and all the social benefits of adopting a Muslim way of life. These teachers—equipped with numerous rhyming stories of the *awliyā'*, companions, and messengers—were charged with teaching the basics of Islam. While women in the Fodio clan certainly had access to higher levels of learning than others,

Asma'u's initiation of the Yan Taru indicates that she perceived significant gaps in women's access to knowledge and teachers. Asma'u lived ruefully through revolutionary times and the period in which Sokoto consolidated its authority. She outlived her father and brother. Her proximity to political leadership certainly influenced her desire to record her community's history—their worldly and spiritual successes. But Asma'u's vision and leadership were accomplishments in their own right; they were instrumental in spreading Islam in the region, assimilating new subjects into the empire, and championing education and literacy.

Nana Asma'u's writings and educational advocacy illustrate Islam's embeddedness in Nigeria and West Africa. They are expressions of her profound faithfulness and depth of knowledge. With her life as a lens, we come to learn of the Islamic textual resources available in West Africa and the commitment of the West African scholarly class to reproducing knowledge that was relevant and intelligible to the laity both in language and style. Asma'u's contributions to Muslim thought in the region preceded significant political and social shifts like British colonialism and the eclipse of the Islamic educational system by Europeanized schooling models.

Asma'u is also a reminder of poetry's educational potential. She was a devotee of poetry and its capacity to communicate knowledge in a lasting way. As far as we can deduce from her philosophical commitment to poetry and belles-lettres, she believed them to be a unique and beautifully defining aspect of our humanity. We can imagine that she found great comfort and inspiration in Prophet Muhammad's unparalleled eloquence, concurrent with his passionate and productive use of language.

21. Lubna of Cardoba (927-984). Initially, a vassal girl of Spanish origin, Lubna became one of the most influential figures in the Umayyad palace in Cordoba. She was the palace secretary of the caliph 'Abd al-Rahmān III (d. 961) and his son al-Hakam b. 'Abd al-Rahmān (d. 976). She was also a skilled mathematician and presided over the royal library, which comprised over 500,000 books.

Lubna translated books written in different languages under the authorship of famous philosophers and scientists like Archimedes and Euclid. She would spend hours teaching children about the ratio between circumferences and their diameter and arrive home late at night satisfied that students of Cordoba are learning mathematics.

Lubna was also in charge of the Library of Cordoba, where she transcribed, translated, and annotated many texts, including the manuscripts of Archimedes and Euclid. Lubana worked with Jewish scholar and patron Hasdai Shaprut to found the influential Madinat al-Zahra Library in Cordoba, which has over 400,000 books and specializes in books on Astronomy and Mathematics. Lubna also worked as a math tutor outside the palace, teaching mathematics to the public. Lubna tutored children in math. As she returned to the palace, the children would follow, reciting multiplication tables—the Medina Azahara library, home to more than 500,000 books.

Interestingly, this was uncommon, with Moorish Iberia being an egalitarian society where education was the privilege and right of all. During Caliph Al-Hakam II (915–976), as al-Andalus continued to flourish culturally, there were more than 170 female scribes in different regions of Cordoba alone, as per reliable sources. Perhaps so little is known about her because, despite her uniqueness, women of her stature were rare. Thus, not finding anything extraordinary about them, historians and biographers may have chosen to omit these women from their accounts.

22. Melike Mama Hatun, or simply Mama Hatun or Mamakhatun, was a female ruler of the Saltukids, with its capital in Erzurum, for an estimated nine years between 1191 and 1200. During her reign, she had a caravanserai, a mosque, a bridge, and a hammam built in Tercan, located midway between Erzincan and Erzurum, still standing and bearing her name. She was a wealthy 14th-century lady. According to Professor Hüseyin Çınar of the Yıldırım Beyazıt University, she was probably the daughter of Kayqubad III, the Anatolian Seljuks sultan (1298–1302). *The Khatuns, 1206–1335*, the linguistic origins of the term "khatun" are unknown, though possibly of Old Turkic or Sogdian origin

Mama's tomb, built by masters from Ahlat, is also in Tercan. Mama's architecture stands in Tercan Village, 20 km from Erzincan, and the Tomb and Complex of Melike Mama Hatun is a Saltukid dynasty monument from the 13th century. The portal inscription credits the construction to a master builder from Ahlat, Abu'n-Nema, son of Mufaddal al-Ahwal, but the date of construction is unknown.

The complex includes a monumental tomb, caravanserai, and bath in the town centre, surrounded by a circular enclosure with unique architectural features. The door's exterior has Arabic calligraphy; on the inside are Qur'anic verses in Kufic script and shapes representing Prophet Muhammad and four caliphs at the bottom centre. She inscribed the artist's name and decorated the surroundings with aesthetic calligraphy.

The two-story tomb has a square base with rounded corners on a raised centre area, topped by an eight-lobe roof. Access to both floors is through doorways in the south, with a few steps leading to the upper floor and an arch doorway with an empty plaque. Geometric bands adorn the tomb with vegetal decorations and Kufic calligraphy, including a striking ornament of a bunch of grapes above the left window niche.

23. Zaynab b. Ahmad (d. 1339). She was perhaps one of the most eminent Islamic scholars of the fourteenth century. Zane belonged to the Ḥanbalī School of Jurisprudence and resided in Damascus. She had acquired several *ijazas* (diplomas or certifications) in various fields, most notably *hadith*.

Zaynab was perhaps one of the most eminent Islamic scholars of the fourteenth century. She belonged to the Hanbalī School of Jurisprudence and resided in Damascus. She had acquired several *ijazas* (diplomas or certifications) in various fields, most notably *hadith*. In the early fourteenth century, she taught such books as Sahīh Bukhāri, Sahīh Muslim, and the Muwatta' of Mālik b. Anas, the Shamā'il of al-Tirmidhī, and al-Tahāwī's Sharḥ Ma'ānī al-Athār. Among her students were the North African traveller Ibn Battūta (d. 1369), Tāj al-Dīn al-Subkī (d. 1355), and al-Dhahabī.

She taught such books as *Sahīh Bukhāri*, *Sahīh Muslim*, and the *Muwatta'* of Mālik b. Anas, the *Shamā'il* of al-Tirmidhī, and al-Tahāwī's *Sharḥ Ma'ānī al-Athār*. Among her students were the North African traveller Bin Battūta (d. 1369), Tāj al-Dīn al-Subkī (d. 1355), al-Dhahabī (d. 1348), and her name appears in several dozen of certifications of Ibn Ḥajar al-Asqalānī (d. 1448). It is essential to point out that Zaynab was only one of hundreds of female scholars of *hadith* during the medieval period in the Muslim world.

24. Parī Khan Khānum (d.1578). A Safavid princess and daughter of Shah TahmaspI (1524-1576) by a Circassian mother, she was one of the most influential Iranian women in the sixteenth century. Pari Khan Khanum was born in 1548 to Shah Tahmasp and his consort, Sultan-Agha Khanum. She was raised uniquely for women at the time in what is now modern-day Iran—being well-educated in the Islamic sciences, law, jurisprudence, and poetry. She was renowned as an educated woman and was well-versed in traditional Islamic sciences, such as jurisprudence. She was also known to be an excellent poet. Parī Khan Khānum was instrumental in securing the succession of her brother IsmāʻIli to the Safavid throne. However, during IsmāʻIL's short reign, her influence waned. During the reign of IsmāʻIi's successor, Mohammad Khodabanda, she was slained because she wielded enormous influence and power.

Contemporary chronicles praised her intelligence and sharp insights, both of which, along with her birth and lineage helped her to achieve a higher social status and political power. At a young age, she got engaged to Prince Badi'al-Zaman, whom she appointed governor of Sistan, but the pair never married. Instead, Pari Khan Khanum took on a political role during her father's reign, helping him to rule during his last years of illness. She persuaded him to undertake charitable acts and was known as a benefactor for low-income people.

25. Noor Jehan (b. 1577). Noor Jehan was born Mehr un Nissa on 31 May 1577 to Persian nobility. Jehan was born Mehr-un-Nisa to noble but refugee parents, Asmat and Ghias, who fled Iran following Ghias's fall in the court's favour. It was a hurried exit; the two and their entourage had to join a commercial caravan despite Asmat being visibly pregnant. The baby, the intrepid empress-to-be, was born by the side of the road, near the town of Kandahar, her birth "a moment of pleasure to the caravan community amid the hardships of the road".

When she was 17, she married Ali Quli Istajlu, who died of wound injuries after a decade of their marriage. On the death of her first husband in 1607, she was summoned to court along with her daughter Ladli Begum to serve as the dowager empress in the court of Jahangir, the son of Emperor Akbar. Here, the intimacy between Jahangir and Mehr-un-Nissa began, culminating in a proposal in the bazaar in 1611. They were married that same year, and she was titled Noor Mahal (light of the palace), later changed to Noor Jehan (light of the world).

An ingenious architect, she innovated using marble in her parents' mausoleum on the banks of the Yamuna, which inspired her stepson's Taj Mahal. She was celebrated and reviled for her political acumen and diplomatic skill, which rivalled those of her female counterparts in Europe and beyond. In 1611, thirty-four-year-old Noor Jehan, daughter of a Persian noble and widow of a subversive official, became Emperor Jahangir's twentieth and most cherished wife. While other wives were secluded and died following Muslim traditions behind walls, Noor ruled the vast Mughal Empire alongside her husband and governed in his stead when his health failed and his attention wandered from matters of state. An astute politician and devoted partner, *Noor* led troops into battle to free Jahangir when one of his officers sent him to the gallows. She signed and issued imperial orders, and coins of the realm bore her name.

Although Noor Jehan was the Emperor's twentieth wife, his intimacy for her gave her significant power, and she effectively ran the empire. She was considered the real force behind the Mughal throne during this period. Noor Jahan was popularly known as a tiger slayer. After Jahangir's death, a crisis broke out as the emperor had not yet named an heir. The war broke out between Shah Jahan and Shahryar, Jahangir's two (and competent) sons. Thinking she could manipulate Shahryar more easily than Shah Jehan, Noor Jehan sided with Prince Shahryar. In 1628, they lost the battle and were ruefully dejected. Shah Jehan became the new Mughal emperor.

During her life, Noor Jehan underwent both pain and pleasure through her respect for her refined art tastes and military mind as Empress of the Mughal Empire. She did this beside the emperor Jahangir, the same man who killed her previous husband and brother and whose legacy she saved. Noor Jehan was unbreakable. She spent the remainder of her days in a mansion in Lahore with her daughter, building a mausoleum for her father and designing her tomb, where she would rest after her death on 16 December 1675. Noor Jehan was an imperfect character, though an exceptionally courageous one. In a world and time in which a woman's power depended on the men she could manipulate, Noor Johan deployed charm, wit, and threat to bolster her influence.

GLOSSARY OF ISLAMIC TERMINOLOGY

Adab	manners, proper behaviour
azwaja	mates
al-adl	equilibrium
al-ahsan	compassion
bida	innovation
caliph	from Khalifat, successor. Ruler of Islam
deen	religion, the life of righteousness
dunyadunya	world, the life of the world; the here and now—see
din	annihilation, Sufi idea, merger with God
Fiqh'ItIt	is an Arabic term meaning "deep understanding" or "full comprehension"
ghairah	male sexual honour and jealousy
hadith	sayings—and doings—of the Prophet, his traditions
hajj	is the annual pilgrimage; it is obligatory for every Muslim once in a lifetime
haya	female sexual modesty and shyness
hijra	departure, emigration; from the Prophet 'shijra to Madinah
ijtihad	independent judgment
ilm	knowledge. Hence

alim	scholar
iitihad	religious activity of interpretation
ijma	means consensus of the people
ulema	scholars
Jahiliyya	age of ignorance; time before the coming of Islam
jihad	striving spiritually or physically against evil; colloquial: religious war
khula	female Initiated divorce. It isn't easy to obtain and requires the husband's consent. Technically, a woman can appeal to an Islamic court to force the husband into a divorce, but in practice, this rarely ever happens
mashwara	advice
mehr	bride-price paid by the groom's family to the bride. This money becomes legally her property
muṣḥaf	
mehr	dower
min anfusikum	part of us
nasab	ancestry, lineage
nafaqa	maintenance, the woman's right to be financially supported by her husband *qiyas* analogical reasoning
nafsin wahida	soul
nushuz	A legal state of disobedience if a wife does not obey her husband
Rahman, Rahim	Beneficent, Merciful—names of Allah
salaam	peace, colloquial: greetings. Hence, Islam, the religion of peace

salat	prayer
shari'a	commonly translated as 'Islamic law' al-Shura consultation; colloquial: consultative body
sulh-i-kul	peace with all; Sufi saying and motto
sunnah	a collection of Prohet's prescriptions
talaq	'Repudiation of the wife.' Male-initiated divorce. It is straightforward to obtain. The husband's declaration of talaq causes the divorce to come into effect
taqlid	the following of predecessors tauhid unity of God
ummah	the global spiritual community of Muslims

BIBLIOGRAPHY

Abbas, Shemeem Burney. *The Female Voice in Sufi Ritual: Devotional Practices of Pakistan and India.* Austin, Tex., 2002.

ʿAṭṭār, Farīd al-Dīn. *Muslim Saints and Mystics.* Translated from the Persian by A. J. Arberry. Oxford, 1966.

Azari, Farah, ed. *Women of Iran: The Conflict with Fundamentalist Islam.* London, 1983. Provocative set of articles by Iranian Muslims critical of the Islamic regime as oppressive to women.

Bellhassen, Souhayr. "Femmes tunisiennes islamistes." *Annuaire de l'Afrique du Nord, 1979,* pp. 77–94. Paris, 1980. One of the few studies includes interviews with ordinary women participating in an Islamic movement.

Berkey, Jonathan P. "Women and Islamic Education in the Mamlūk Period." In *Women in Middle Eastern History: Shifting Boundaries in Sex and Gender,* edited by Nikki R. Keddie and Beth Baron, pp. 143–157. New Haven, Conn., and London, 1991.

Betteridge, Anne H. "The Controversial Vows of Urban Muslim Women in Iran." In *Unspoken Worlds: Women's Religious Lives in Non-Western Cultures,* edited by Nancy E. Auer Falk and Rita M. Gross, pp. 141–155. San Francisco, 1980.

Clancy-Smith, Julia. "The House of Zainab: Female Authority and Saintly Succession." In *Women in Middle Eastern History: Shifting Boundaries in Sex and Gender,* edited by Nikki R. Keddie and Beth Baron, pp. 254–274. New Haven, Conn., and London, 1991. On a woman who became a Ṣūfī *shaykh* in colonial Algeria.

Dwyer, Daisy Hilse. "Women, Sufism, and Decision-Making in Moroccan Islam." In *Women in the Muslim World*, edited by Lois Beck and Nikki R. Keddie, pp. 585–598. Cambridge, Mass., 1978. Information on women's auxiliaries in the Ṣūfī orders and the influence wives have on the affiliation of their husbands with particular orders.

El Guindi, Fadwa. "*The Emerging Islamic Order: The Case of Egypt's Contemporary Islamic Movement.*"Journal of Arab Affairs1 (1981): 245–261. Reprinted in Political Behavior in the Arab States, edited by Tawfic E. Farah, pp. 55–66. Boulder, Colo., 1983.

Elias, Jamal. "Female and Feminine in Islamic Mysticism." Muslim World78 (1988): 210–211.

Farah, Madelain. *Marriage and Sexuality in Islam: A Translation of al-Ghazālī's Book on the Etiquette of Marriage from the Iḥyā ʿ.* Salt Lake City, Utah, 1984.

Fernea, Elizabeth W, and Robert A. Fernea. "Variation in Religious Observance among Islamic Women." In *Scholars, Saints, and Sufis: Muslim Religious Institutions since 1500*, edited by Nikki R. Keddie, pp. 385–401. Berkeley, 1972.

Friedl, Erika. "Islam and Tribal Women in a Village in Iran." In *Unspoken Worlds: Women's Religious Lives in Non-Western Cultures*, edited by Nancy E. Auer Falk and Rita M. Gross, pp. 159–173. San Francisco, 1980.

Haddad, Yvonne Yazbeck, Jane I. Smith, and Kathleen M. Moore, eds. *Muslim Women in America: The Challenge of Islamic Identity Today.* New York, 2006.

Haeri, Shahla. "Obedience vs. Autonomy: Women and Fundamentalism in Iran and Pakistan." In *Fundamentalisms and Society: Reclaiming the Sciences, the Family, and Education*, edited by Martin E. Marty and R. Scott Appleby, pp. 181–213. Chicago, 1993. This rare comparative essay on the presentation of women by Islamic activists in two different countries, one Shī'ī and one Sunnī. Particularly good regarding using important early female figures as models of courage and heroism in Iran.

Hoffman-Ladd, Valerie J. "Mysticism and Sexuality in Sufi Thought and Life." Mystics Quarterly18 (1992): 82–93. Women and sexuality in early and medieval Sufism, highlighting the writings of Ibn 'Arabī.

Hoffman-Ladd, Valerie J."Polemics on the Modesty and Segregation of Women in Contemporary Egypt."International Journal of Middle East Studies19, no. 1 (February 1987): 23–50. Discussion of Islamist perspectives on women's participation in public life.

Hoffman-Ladd, Valerie J. *Sufism, Mystics, and Saints in Modern Egypt.* Columbia, S.C., forthcomingIt has a chapter on women and sexuality in the Ṣūfī orders of Egypt.

Hujwīrī, 'Alī ibn 'Usmān. The *Kashf al-Maḥjūb: The Oldest Persian Treatise on Sufiism.* Translated by R. A. Nicholson. 2d ed. London, 1976.

Ibn al-'Arabī. *The "Rūh al-quds" and "al-Durrat al-fākhirah."*Translated by R. W. J. Austin. London, 1971.

Jaschok, Maria, and Jingjun Shui. *The History of Women's Mosques in Chinese Islam: A Mosque of Their Own.* Richmond, U.K., 2000.

Lane, Edward. *An Account of the Manners and Customs of the Modern Egyptians.* London, 1836.

Lewis, I. M."The Past and Present in Islam: The Case of African 'Survivals.'" Temenos19 (1983): 55–67. Study of the *zār* and *bori* spirit possession cults, making a good case for their compatibility with Islam.

Macleod, Arlene Elowe. *Accommodating Protest: Working Women, the New Veiling, and Change in Cairo*. New York, 1991. An excellent study of the social milieu of the lower middle class in Cairo that leads ordinary women to don Islamic dress.

Mahmood, Saba. *Politics of Piety: The Islamic Revival and the Feminist Subject*. Princeton, N.J., 2005.

Mernissi, Fatima. "Women, Saints, and Sanctuaries."Signs: Journal of Women in Society and Culture," 3 (1977): 101–112.

Nelson, Cynthia. "Self, Spirit Possession, and World View: An Illustration from Egypt. International Journal of Social Psychiatry, 17 (1971): 194–209. On the *zār*in Egypt.

Nūrbakhsh, Javād. *Sufi Women*. New York, 1983. Biographies of some 124 Ṣūfī women, translated into English.

Rosen, Lawrence. "The Negotiation of Reality: Male-Female Relations in Sefrou, Morocco." In *Women in the Muslim World*, edited by Lois Beck and Nikki R. Keddie, pp. 561–584. Cambridge, Mass., 1978.

Saunders, Lucie Wood. "Variants in Zār Experience in an Egyptian Village." In*Case Studies in Spirit Possession*, edited by Vincent Crapanzano and Vivian Garrison, pp. 177–193. New York, 1977.

Schimmel, Annemarie. *Mystical Dimensions of Islam*. Chapel Hill, N.C., 1975. See Appendix II, "The Feminine Element in Sufism."

Schimmel, Annemarie. "Women in Mystical Islam." Women's Studies International Forum, 5 (1982): 148.

Sharī'atī, 'Alī. *Fatima Is Fatima*. Translated by Laleh Bakhtiar. Tehran, 1981. Critical and revisionist interpretation of women's role in society by men who inspired many young Iranian intellectuals to seek an Islamically-oriented culture in the decade before the revolution.

Smith, Jane I, and Yvonne Yazbeck Haddad."Women in the Afterlife: The Islamic View as Observed from Qur'an and Tradition." Journal of the American Academy of Religion, 43 (1975): 39–50.

Tabari, Azar, and Nahid Yeganeh, eds. *In the Shadow of Islam: The Women's Movement in Iran*. London, 1982. Collection of translations from various primary sources relevant to the status of women and feminism in the Islamic Republic of Iran.

Winter, Michael. *Society and Religion in Early Ottoman Egypt: Studies in the Writings of 'Abd al-Wahhāb al-Sha'rānī*. New Brunswick, N.J., 1982. Exciting information on the participation of women in the Ṣūfī orders in Mamlūk and Ottoman Egypt.

Zuhur, Sherifa. *Revealing Reveiling: Islamist Gender Ideology in Contemporary Egypt*. Albany, N.Y., 1992. Comparison of the opinions of women inside and outside the Islamic movement on the meaning of veiling and being religious within the context of both Islamic paradigms and Egyptian feminism.

www.ingramcontent.com/pod-product-compliance
Lightning Source LLC
Chambersburg PA
CBHW032011150726
47990CB00005B/1928